# Cry *from the* Cotton

# Cry *from the* Cotton

THE SOUTHERN
TENANT FARMERS' UNION
AND THE NEW DEAL

## *by Donald H. Grubbs*

*The University of North Carolina Press* • *Chapel Hill*

*For Bobbie and Donnie*

# Foreword

The agrarian myth that celebrated a rural America of sturdy and independent yeomen reached the limits of credibility when it came to the southern sharecropper. Victimized by chronic poverty, cultural backwardness, and the semifeudal structure of the southern plantation system, hundreds of thousands of "croppers" in the 1930's found themselves further imperiled by the depression, the mechanization of agriculture, and the New Deal's crop-reduction program. "I have traveled over most of Europe and part of Africa," the English novelist Naomi Mitchison declared in 1935, "but I have never seen such terrible sights as I saw yesterday among the sharecroppers of Arkansas." It was in Arkansas—in the rich cotton land of the Mississippi Delta —that the desperation and hope of the early New Deal years led thousands of tenant farmers to do the unimaginable, to rebel and to organize in their own defense. Their struggle, in the face of determined and often violent resistance from their landlords, proved in the long run to be unavailing. But it made an impression upon the landscape of the thirties. Among other things, it dramatized the plight of the sharecropper and, for a moment at least, stirred the national conscience.

Professor Donald H. Grubbs has sought in this book to write a scholarly history of the sharecroppers' movement. He begins, appropriately, with the origin of farm tenancy in the South, the

evolution of the institution, and the crisis that eventually overtook the plantation system. He describes the damaging impact
of the Agricultural Adjustment Administration upon the region's
sharecroppers and the efforts of liberals in the AAA to protect
the landless farmers from discriminatory and oppressive treatment by landowners in the allocation of New Deal benefits and
in the implementation of the new acreage-restriction policies.
Mr. Grubbs then discusses the organization of the Southern
Tenant Farmers' Union and traces its painful progress during
the half-dozen years of its greatest influence. He pictures the
reign of terror that sporadically swept the Arkansas Delta in the
wake of the STFU's organizing activities, follows the work of
outside supporters like Norman Thomas and Gardner Jackson,
and analyzes the internal problems of leadership and organization that culminated in the union's rapid decline after 1939. He
also deals with the relationship between the experiences of the
STFU and the New Deal's broadening attack on rural poverty
through the Farm Security Administration. Finally, he shows
how the wretched condition of the sharecropper became the
subject of national controversy and indignation in the 1930's.

The story of the Southern Tenant Farmers' Union is a remarkable one, and Professor Grubbs tells it well. Indeed, he has given
us the first complete account of the organization. His monograph
is based on extensive research in all available sources, including
the records of the STFU, interviews and correspondence with
its leaders, and valuable materials in the National Archives. The
narrative is tightly written but comprehensive in its coverage,
providing the broad context necessary for an authoritative evaluation of the union. The author develops some important
themes, and he advances them with a refreshing vigor and forth-
rightness. While some readers may disagree with his interpretation at certain points, they will, I think, applaud his attempt to
examine all of the evidence and to present a scholarly appraisal
of the embattled sharecroppers and their adversaries.

Professor Grubbs's book makes several contributions to the
historical literature on our recent past. In addition to giving us
a reliable account of the STFU's activities, this work throws a
good deal of light on the structure of society in the Delta, on the
way in which the institutions and population groups of that

subregion interacted, on the extent to which the social order reflected economic conditions and political realities. The analysis helps us understand the landlord-tenant relationship, the importance of economic and social class, and the role of race in the plantation system. At one level, then, Mr. Grubbs has written a useful study of the Arkansas Delta.

The book also contributes to our understanding of southern history. Despite the unique characteristics of life in the Delta, the basic institutions and attitudes that determined the fate of the Southern Tenant Farmers' Union were regional rather than local. The most typical scene in the South, wrote Arthur F. Raper and Ira De A. Reid in 1941, was "a cotton field with a solitary man—a sharecropper—plowing in it." The collapse of cotton tenancy was most vividly dramatized perhaps in the Mississippi Delta, but the crisis that threatened the cropper and the cotton economy was an important aspect of life throughout the South in the 1930's. Thus what Mr. Grubbs says about the plantation system in Arkansas and the plight of the tenant farmer in the Delta also reveals much about the cotton belt and rural life in the region as a whole.

At still another level Professor Grubbs has added to the growing list of scholarly works devoted to the Great Depression and the New Deal. His book throws new light on the New Deal's halting attack upon agricultural poverty in the United States. It takes its place with several other studies of agrarian insurgency and agricultural democracy during the New Deal, including David Eugene Conrad's *The Forgotten Farmers: The Story of Sharecroppers in the New Deal* (1965); Louis Cantor's *A Prologue to the Protest Movement: The Missouri Sharecropper Roadside Demonstration of 1939* (1969); Sidney Baldwin's *Poverty and Politics: The Rise and Decline of the Farm Security Administration* (1968); and Paul K. Conkin's *Tomorrow a New World: The New Deal Community Program* (1959). The history of the Southern Tenant Farmers' Union reveals the difficulties that hampered the New Deal's search for social reform on the rural scene. Although the STFU failed as a labor union, it was important as a critic, not only of the discrimination against poor farmers in the South but also of the inadequacy of Franklin D. Roosevelt's agricultural reforms.

The sharecroppers' movement is also significant because it was a manifestation of American radicalism, an expression of a radical impulse that revealed itself in such disparate groups as the Farmers' Holiday Association, Upton Sinclair's EPIC plan in California, Huey P. Long's Share Our Wealth program, and a variety of Marxist and fascist-like organizations. Despite its traditional hostility toward social radicalism, the South produced a few small bands of radical reformers, including the Highlander Folk School and the Southern Tenant Farmers' Union. Some Socialists asserted that the organized sharecroppers were "the true proletariat" moving "irresistibly towards revolution." This was wishful thinking; the sharecroppers were militant but not revolutionary. The STFU was "an indigenous movement," as Howard Kester pointed out in 1936, "springing up out of the very soil which bore the sharecroppers' bitter grievances." All of this is made clear in Mr. Grubbs's book, which helps to explain the varied character of American radicalism in the 1930's.

In reading this instructive volume, one returns again and again to the man in the center, the sharecropper himself. His lot was one of persistent poverty, human suffering, and social injustice. It is significant that he was finally driven to revolt and to organize during the New Deal period. That movement is a part of our history that Professor Grubbs has done well to reclaim.

*Vanderbilt University*      DEWEY W. GRANTHAM
*November 1, 1970*

# Preface

*T*his book is about a tortured cry from the cotton belt, a cry that was never understood and only partially heard.

Through the Agricultural Adjustment Administration, Franklin Roosevelt gave Southern planters the means and the incentive to substitute machines and underemployed casual labor for their tenants. Later, through the Farm Security Administration, he attempted to help displaced tenants, but he allowed the basic pattern of subsidy for landlords and poverty for rural workers to become permanent.

Particularly for black people in this country, the cry from the cotton was a shriek against white ignorance or callousness. Driven off the land as planters happily replaced them with tractors, attracted north by the hope for freedom and employment, they found that their life in America was undergoing a second major change. Hideously inhuman as slavery was, they at least had employment and security; with the switch to share-cropping, they kept employment but lost security; and today on welfare they are allowed neither employment nor security.

Yesterday, through ignorance or greed, the propertied drove the propertyless off the land; tomorrow, Harlem and Watts and the South Side will be burning.

White America could not understand the cry from the cotton; can it understand the cry for black power?

# Introduction
# and Acknowledgments

*W*hy another treatment of the Southern Tenant Farmers'
Union?

After all, several pages of a comprehensive study, two scholarly articles, and a book[1] have been largely devoted to a union
which most authors of works on the New Deal dismiss with a
line or a paragraph. Is this not enough coverage?

The answer must be no, for only one previous author has ex-
tensively mined the available manuscript collections; two have
used the records of the Agricultural Adjustment Administration,
but, inexplicably, none has thoroughly examined the Depart-

1. The works mentioned are Stuart Jamieson (ed.), *Labor Unionism in
American Agriculture*, Bureau of Labor Statistics Bulletin 836 (Washington: Government Printing Office, 1945); M.S. Venkataramani, "Norman
Thomas, Arkansas Sharecroppers, and the Roosevelt Agricultural Policies,
1933–1937," *Mississippi Valley Historical Review*, XLVII (September,
1960), 225: David E. Conrad, *The Forgotten Farmers: The Story of
Sharecroppers in the New Deal* (Urbana: University of Illinois Press,
1965); and Jerold Auerbach, "Southern Tenant Farmers: Socialist Critics
of the New Deal," *Labor History*, VII (Winter, 1966), 3. All four of these
works have value. Jamieson, however, omits any mention of the STFU's
later years or its impact on the New Deal; Conrad is primarily concerned
with the AAA; Venkataramani's article and that of Auerbach—by far the
best researched—take Norman Thomas, the Socialists, and civil liberties as
their points of departure, resulting in several interpretations with which
the author of this book disagrees. The most important of these concern the
degree to which the STFU was controlled by the Socialist party and, with
Auerbach, the extent of its racial integration.

ment of Agriculture papers. Since the most assiduous previous researcher has contributed, on this subject, only a fifteen page article, this book is the first to reveal the central role of Gardner Jackson in the union[2] and its direct causal connection with the purge of the "radicals" from the AAA; also, the following pages go considerably farther than previous publications in showing Franklin Roosevelt's AAA cotton program as a device for landlord subsidy and worker unemployment. Moreover, the STFU's exposure of peonage as a new form of slavery, the union's instigation of the President's Committee on Farm Tenancy—which resulted in the Bankhead-Jones Farm Tenancy Act and the establishment of the Farm Security Administration—and the union's premature battle against what it saw as "Communist rule or ruin tactics" in the CIO are revealed here in book form for the first time. In addition, while Jerold Auerbach has previously shown the STFU's connection with the LaFollette Civil Liberties Committee, emphasizing the latter body and the total milieu, this book examines the relationship with emphasis on the STFU.

While the author is indebted to the staff of all libraries used, particular thanks must go to Archivists Kathleen Cheape of the Southern History Collection at the University of North Carolina, Helen Finneran of the National Archives, and Jerome Deyo of the Franklin Delano Roosevelt Library, whose help was outstanding beyond the call of duty. Warm thanks also go to Claude Williams, A. E. Cox, and Clay East for making valuable private papers available. Entirely frank and thoroughly cooperative were the following persons, identified in the bibliography of this book, who furnished much information through correspondence, interviews, or both: Sam Bledsoe, J. R. Butler, Leif Dahl, Chester Davis, Clay East, Lee Hays, R. W. Hudgens, Gardner Jackson, Howard Kester, Edwin and H. L. Mitchell, Reinhold Niebuhr, Milo Perkins, Pete Seeger, Norman Thomas, and Claude Williams. Of these persons, four—and their wives—have been notably kind. Mr. and Mrs. "Pat" Jackson, after meeting the author once, took him into their

2. At full book length. The author, however, did make this point earlier in his "Gardner Jackson, That 'Socialist' Tenant Farmers' Union, and the New Deal," *Agricultural History*, XLII (April, 1968), 125.

home for over a month so that he could combine their rem-
iniscenses with work in the National Archives; the Rev. and
Mrs. Williams also harbored this wandering scholar while allowing him to examine their large collection of personal papers;
and the H. L. Mitchells and Clay Easts have repeatedly offered
their hospitality and that of friends. Parts of the manuscript
have been read, or related help extended, by Mitchell, East,
Jackson, and Professors Rembert W. Patrick, Arthur W. Thompson, Dewey Grantham, George Tindall, Walter Brown, William
H. Cobb, Van Perkins, Sidney Baldwin, and Jerold Auerbach.
The absolution from error which I afford them, in keeping
with custom, is firmly based upon their wisdom and my stub-
bornness. Finally, the author wishes to extend appreciation to
the Southern Fellowships Fund, the University of Florida, the
University of the Pacific, and Uncle Sam's NDEA program for
the *sine qua non*: time with money.

In the pages that follow, all footnote references to manuscript
collections are abbreviated from the beginning. These abbrevia-
tions, and the collections to which they refer, are as follows:

*STFU Papers*: Southern Tenant Farmers' Union Papers, including scrapbooks, account books, letters, pamphlets, reports,
etc.; Southern Historical Collection, University of North Carolina Library, Chapel Hill.

*S P Arch, Duke*: Socialist Party Archives, chiefly letters;
Manuscripts Division, Duke University Library, Durham, North
Carolina.

*RG 16, N Arch*; *RG 145, N Arch*: and *L-TS, RG 145, N Arch*:
respectively indicate Record Group 16 (Correspondence of the
Department of Agriculture), Record Group 145 (General Correspondence of the Agricultural Adjustment Administration),
and the Landlord-Tenant Section of Record Group 145, all in
the Agricultural Records Section, Social and Economic Branch,
National Archives, Washington, D. C.

*OF 407–B, FDR Library* and *OF 1650, FDR Library*: Official
File 407–B and Official File 1650, official letters and memoranda
relating in part to tenancy; Franklin Delano Roosevelt Library,
Hyde Park, New York.

*CCP, Reels 1–3*: Commonwealth College Papers, an almost
complete file of the student newspaper, with press releases, cor-

respondence, and other papers collected by E. W. St. John, publisher of the Mena (Ark.) *Star*; Microfilm No. 356, three reels, University of Arkansas Library, Fayetteville.

Illustrative material has been provided courtesy of H. L. Mitchell and the Rev. Claude Williams.

In addition to these manuscript collections, future researchers may wish, among other chores, to consult the author's doctoral dissertation: a compendium of additional evidence, associated discoveries, and parenthetical observations from which most of this book has been distilled. The final chapter and parts of others, however, appear here for the first time.

DONALD H. GRUBBS

*Stockton, California*
*May 1, 1970*

# Contents

# List of Illustrations

# Cry *from the* Cotton

# 1.

## The Crisis
## of the Plantation System

*D*own through the heart of North America the Mississippi River rolls, thick with soil from half the states of the Union. Shortly after it meanders into the cotton country it sweeps in a half-mile-wide arc past the unofficial capital of the Mid-South: Memphis, the home of the Cotton Carnival, Beale Street, and the blues. Behind the city the red clay hills undulate back into Mississippi and Tennessee, but across the river in Arkansas lies a different country, flat, relatively treeless, and almost completely devoted to cotton production. East of Memphis nearly every farm has a vegetable garden and a cornfield; over the river, gardens are rare.

In the dull gray years of the Great Depression a motorist who could still afford to buy gasoline might have driven his boxy black automobile over the old Harahan Bridge from Memphis into Arkansas to see if the newspaper stories were really true. The traveler could be no ordinary tourist, for the sights he might see would hardly be pleasant, and they would seem painfully incongruous to him.

For the land across the big river is rich, consisting of thousands of square miles of floor-flat sedimentary soil from forty to a hundred feet deep laid down over the millennia by the Mississippi; yet the vast majority of the people living here in the 1930's were incomparably more impoverished than other

Americans. The contrast struck Jonathan Daniels sharply. "The land runs in flat loveliness to the lines of trees left standing for windbreaks or for fuel," he wrote. ". . .Certainly it ought to give men plenty: but it betrays. Everywhere in the South, the poorest men are on the richest land."[1]

Some of these people owned their own farms, under heavy mortgages, to be sure, but at least the land was theirs. Most of these small farmers lived up in Crowley's Ridge, that strange long strip of hills that runs down from Missouri through the Delta country, looking as out of place as a cypress tree in a desert. The Ridge dwellers grew little cotton; they might raise mules or horses, grow peaches or apples, or work in the Delta county seats which, from Jonesboro to Helena, nestle comfortably in the narrow range of hills.

But from the foot of the Ridge across the miles to the big river, scattered among the flat black fields of the cotton country, there lived thousands of human beings whose land was held at another man's pleasure and whose daily battle was with starvation. Most of them had been drawn into the area in the prosperous 1920's. The whites came down from the hills and the Negroes crossed the river from Mississippi to make a better living on the huge Delta plantations or in the humming sawmills. As the nation plunged into depression the sawmills shut down, the price of cotton plummeted, and, adding the final ingredient to the witches' brew of misery, many workers who had left for the cities were forced back into the cotton country. Often, if they were Negroes, they displaced white workers on the plantations because the whites, for one thing, were not as docile as the Negroes had learned to be.[2] There was no place for the

1. Jonathan Daniels, *A Southerner Discovers the South* (New York: Macmillan, 1938), pp. 135–37; for a factual geography of the area see J. W. Reid, "Geographic Distribution of Arkansas Crops and Livestock," Arkansas Agricultural Experiment Station Bulletin No. 367 (Fayetteville, Ark., November, 1938), *passim*.

2. Howard R. Jackson, "An Economic and Social Analysis of Three Cotton Plantations in Arkansas in 1934" (Master's thesis, University of Arkansas, 1937), pp. 81–82; Henry Irving Richards, *Cotton and the AAA* (Washington: The Brookings Institution, 1936), pp. 148–49; C. B. Baldwin to Darwin J. Meserole, April 18, 1935, in "Tenancy (1935)" folder, Record Group 16, National Archives (referred to hereinafter as RG 16, N Arch); William H. Metzler, "Population Trends and Adjustments in

displaced persons to go. They crowded into vacant shacks or lived along the river bottoms with the rats and mosquitoes, existing in the only way they could.

The resulting scenes of human deprivation were horrifying. Local conservatives apologized for the embarrassing situation, while visitors with any degree of social empathy returned home in a state of shock. Norman Thomas, the Socialist leader, called Arkansas conditions "worse than they are in China,"[3] and so graphically elaborated upon his charges that curious and often skeptical newspapermen traveled to the area to judge for themselves. They never left unconvinced. "Tenant houses," said one, are "incomparably the worst I have ever seen being used for human habitation."[4] Added another, "There are certain conditions in America so bad it is almost impossible to get anyone to pay attention to them. The condition of the sharecroppers in our cotton country [is] just such a subject. . . . We have conditions in America that are not being tolerated today anywhere in Europe, unless the Russians tolerate them as a form of Asiatic punishment to be inflicted on the enemies of the State."[5] A young Arkansas attorney named Brooks Hays, later a nationally known Congressman, commented on one case he found: "I had seen many dilapidated tenant houses, but I could hardly believe that people lived in the one that I found on this country road. . . . This home was about ten feet by twenty, and was made of corrugated tin and scraps of lumber. It was flat upon the ground, and had only one or two small openings." And yet this hovel belonged to a man who was a good enough farmer to own two mules, a wagon, two cows, and a number of farm implements.[6]

Such living conditions made their most spectacular impact upon religious behavior—with Methodist-Baptist orthodoxy en-

Arkansas," Arkansas Agricultural Experiment Station Bulletin No. 388 (Fayetteville, Ark., May, 1940), *passim*.

3. Memphis *Press-Scimitar*, March 14, 1935; Memphis *Commercial Appeal*, March 15, 1935.
4. "Sharing Poverty," *Today*, March 30, 1935, p. 20.
5. Herbert Agar, "Time and Tide: How to Make Communists," *Louisville Courier-Journal*, March 30, 1936, clipping in STFU Papers.
6. Brooks Hays, "Memorandum for Mr. [Paul] Porter," n.d. [1935], in Landlord-Tenant Section, Record Group 145, National Archives (referred to hereinafter as L-TS, RG 145, N Arch).

livened periodically by orgiastic revivals and such esoterica as religious eggs[7]—and upon sex: "a hypocritical Bible-belt denial of its existence, like the hard crust over a carbuncle," wrote the artist Thomas Hart Benton, "makes it fester and ferment into a stinking poison."[8] Less astonishing, and consequently less noted in the literature of the period, was the impact of dire poverty on the sharecropper's health. Cold air and malaria mosquitoes poured through the chinks in his shack, while bacteria swam in his drinking water. When illness struck, the cropper had to rely on patent medicines or home remedies. Vervain or hog-hoof tea, turpentine, lard, and a mixture of egg and rubbing alcohol were among the concoctions ill sharecroppers tried to swallow. A great many of their offspring, naturally, never survived past childhood.[9]

If thousands of children were ephemeral spirits who drifted into life and out of it again, the plantation system which destroyed them was very permanent indeed. It had come to America with the first colonizers, who instituted in the Carolinas and Virginia a combination of ancient manorialism and contemporary capitalism: vast holdings, no longer the badge of rank for a nobility, but a means of enrichment for an agrarian bourgeoisie who kept earnings above debts by exploiting black people, by opening virgin lands to the west, and, in 1776 and 1861, by declaring independence from the debt holders. (There is no implication here that either the war for colonial independence or the war for Southern independence was caused *solely* by the planters' need to keep earnings ahead of debt, but there can be little doubt that this economic imperative played an important role in bringing both wars about.) During the second of the Southern-

7. In "Hen Near Keiser Lays Freak Egg," The *Osceola* (*Ark.*) *Times*, May 1, 1936, the alleged appearance of an egg with a religious message imprinted, direct from the chicken, was reported as straight news. For other religious oddities see any Delta area newspapers on microfilm at the University of Arkansas; see also Norman Thomas, *The Plight of the Share-Cropper* (New York: League for Industrial Democracy, 1934), p. 10.

8. Thomas Hart Benton, *An Artist in America* (New York: Halcyon House, 1939), pp. 151, 194, 196.

9. Isabella C. Wilson, "Sickness and Medical Care Among the Negro Population in a Delta Area of Arkansas," Arkansas Agricultural Experiment Station Bulletin No. 372 (Fayetteville, Ark., March, 1939), *passim.*: U. S. Department of Agriculture, Bureau of Agricultural Economics, *Farm Tenancy in Arkansas* (Washington: G. P. O., 1941), p. 12.

ers' wars against their creditors, the Civil War, passage of Federal confiscation acts and the demands of such men as Thaddeus Stevens gave the planters reason to fear that defeat might bring the destruction of their entire system. But the threat passed, and slavery was transformed into sharecropping after a few crop seasons during which wage payment was adopted, then rejected largely because cash wages gave the former slaves too much independence. What freedom of action they had left faded away during the last three decades of the century as the crop-lien replaced the overseer's whip: the merchant or planter-merchant, in exchange for the credit he alone could furnish, took a lien on the "freed" slaves' crop which, carried over from year to year, bound the cheap labor supply to the plantation almost as effectively as slavery had.[10]

During the same period, the constantly falling price of cotton drove thousands of poor whites, bankrupt ex-farmers from the hills, into the plantation system alongside the former slaves. After the opening of the twentieth century, however, the plunge in the price of cotton was arrested; for landlords, the period of distress was over. Demand increased, marketing improved, and numerous uses for cottonseed were discovered. But the farm tenancy rate, a rough index of the prevalence of sharecropping, continued to rise. There were many reasons: mortgage foreclosure in poor seasons, the purchase of land by absentee owners or prosperous planters, or, particularly in Arkansas, the bringing of croppers onto land owned by lumber companies, now shorn of timber and being planted to cotton for the first time. After about 1910 the entire Delta was brought under cultivation, and by the 1930's tenancy dominated the area more completely than ever. Six out of ten Arkansas farms were tenant-

10. This summary account of the development of the plantation system to the end of the nineteenth century is based largely on such standard sources as Kenneth M. Stampp, *The Era of Reconstruction, 1865–1877* (New York: Alfred A. Knopf, 1965), pp. 122–31; Comer Vann Woodward, *Origins of the New South* (Baton Rouge: Louisiana State University Press, 1951), pp. 172–208; Fred A. Shannon, *The Farmer's Last Frontier* (New York: Farrar and Rinehart, 1945), pp. 83–84; see especially Maude Carmichael, "The Plantation System in Arkansas, 1850–1876" (Ph.D. dissertation, Radcliffe College, 1935), pp. 71–79, 463–65, 471–506; and James Harry Street, *The New Revolution in the Cotton Economy* (Chapel Hill: The University of North Carolina Press, 1957), pp. 19–30.

operated in 1935, but the tenancy rate in the Delta was 80 per cent. Within the Delta, tenancy correlated almost perfectly with the incidence of three characteristics of the plantation system: high farm land value, high cotton acreage per farm, and high percentage of Negro population. Crittenden and Mississippi counties, with the highest tenancy rates in Arkansas, also rated highest with respect to the three characteristics mentioned.[11]

The customary types of tenancy were known as sharecropping, share renting, and fixed or cash renting. Sharecropping was often called farming "on halves," for half of the proceeds of the croppers' cotton went to the landlord who had furnished the cropper with everything he needed to make the crop, from shack to seed. Contributing only the labor of himself and his family, the cropper was actually more a hired laborer than a tenant. One-fourth of all farmers in Arkansas were in this category in 1935; two-thirds of these croppers were Negroes. Rare was the cropper who rose to the status of a share tenant: to do so he had to save enough money to buy a team of horses or mules and some farm implements, fertilizer and seed. With this stock of equipment he need ask a landlord only for a tract of land with a cabin on it. Then his rental would customarily be a third of the grain grown—usually corn—and a fourth of the cotton: he was now a "third and fourth" renter. Fixed renting, often called fixed share renting, in which the tenant paid a smaller stipulated amount of the crop and enjoyed great freedom of management, was not often found in the Delta. Neither was cash renting. Much more prevalent than these two higher types of tenure was the operation of a plantation with wage laborers, who had not even the slim security of sharecroppers. Their use signified an oversupply of labor so great that the planter no longer needed to fix his laborers to the soil; he was assured of having plenty whenever he needed them.[12]

11. STFU, "Statement to Governor's Commission on Farm Tenancy," n.d. [August, 1936], STFU Papers; M. C. Blackman, "Farm Tenancy in Arkansas," *Arkansas Gazette Magazine*, April 11, 1937, p. 2; J. A. Baker and J. G. McNeely, "Land Tenure in Arkansas: I, The Farm Tenancy Situation," Arkansas Agricultural Experiment Station Bulletin No 384 (Fayetteville, Ark., 1940), pp. 3–13; T. C. McCormick, "Recent Increases of Farm Tenancy in Arkansas," *Southwestern Social Science Quarterly*, XV (June, 1934), pp. 64–66.
12. Charles Spurgeon Johnson, Edwin R. Embree, and W. W. Alex-

Only once a year, during the last weeks of December, did the heavily supervised sharecropper or share tenant have a chance to make a decision on his own. If he were out of debt, if his former landlord agreed to release him, and if he felt that he could earn more by farming elsewhere, he could pack his goods in a wagon and greet the new year by searching for those fertile acres that were always just over the horizon. Seldom did the cropper who moved sign a contract; his new landlord told him what would be expected of him, perhaps included a garden and some chickens along with the cabin, might agree to break new land with gang-plows if necessary, and then introduced him to his new "riding boss," an overseer on horseback, whose words would be law as long as the cropper remained on the plantation. The sharecropper's previous harvest earnings were supposed to last him until March, when he could begin receiving supplies on credit, "furnish." The "furnish" system gave the worker another master, the storekeeper, who could disallow any purchase he felt unwise and could figure interest on supplies at any rate he felt proper. On a yearly basis, interest generally ran about 33 to 40 per cent, with many instances of almost unbelievably usurious rates. Planters claimed that they had to play Shylock because of the high interest charges they themselves faced, but there was little basis for this claim; they paid a standardized 7 or 8 per cent for credit, with only isolated instances of higher charges.[13] Tenant farmers who tried to see wry

ander, *The Collapse of Cotton Tenancy* (Chapel Hill: The University of North Carolina Press, 1935), pp. 6–7; Blackman, "Tenancy," *Arkansas Gazette Magazine*, April 4, 1937, p. 7; Arthur Franklin Raper, *Preface to Peasantry* (Chapel Hill: The University of North Carolina Press, 1936), pp. 146–47; Henry William Blalock, "Plantation Operations of Landlords and Tenants in Arkansas," Arkansas Agricultural Experiment Station Bulletin No. 339 (Fayetteville, Ark., 1937), pp. 4–5; Karl Brandt, "Farm Tenancy in the United States," *Social Research*, IV (May, 1937), pp. 142–45.

13. Raper, *Preface to Peasantry*, pp. 173, 248–49; Donald Crichton Alexander, *The Arkansas Plantation, 1920–1942* (New Haven: Yale University Press, 1943), pp. 55–56, 64–65, 68–69; Bueford Monroe Gile and A. N. Moore, "Farm Credit in a Plantation . . . District in Arkansas," Arkansas Agricultural Experiment Station Bulletin No. 228 (Fayetteville, Ark., 1928), pp. 34, 40–43, and *passim.*; Blalock, "Plantation Operations," pp. 6–7, 33–34, 36–37; Blackman, "Tenancy," April 11, 1937, p. 2; Baker and McNeely, "Farm Tenancy," pp. 39–40.

humor in the situation told of the teacher who asked her bright-est pupil, "If the landlord lends you twenty dollars, and you pay him back five dollars a month, how much will you owe him after three months?" "Twenty dollars," was the reply. "You don't understand arithmetic," chided the teacher. And then came the pupil's rejoinder, "You don't understand our landlord!"[14]

Through the spring and summer, as the cotton plants and the "furnish" bill grew according to God's inexplicable will, the cropper labored in the fields. In midsummer the work was easy, but during spring chopping time, when weeds had to be chopped out from the cotton rows, and during the late summer harvest, hard labor lasted seven days a week from "can to can't" —from the time one first can see before sunrise until visibility fades after sunset. Finally, in the mellow light of a September afternoon, having brought his cotton to be ginned and baled, the cropper would stand patiently outside the plantation book-keeper's office waiting to hear what, if anything, his year's net earnings might be. "When the last bit is Picke," wrote a sharecropper, "you may have something are you may not. then you are force to go back to Working for your Land Lord, at a low wages. If you ask him for help, his answer is What did you do with your money, then he will offer you Work at his price."[15] Most tenants got some cash at "settling time," though many re-ceived nothing at all. If one considers the cash value of the rent-free shack and garden produce, the sharecropper's yearly income was about $240 to $300. Share tenants made $100 or $200 more than that figure, wage hands quite a bit less—the latter actually earned less cash than their grandparents had during Reconstruction.[16]

When critics of the plantation system cited examples of such coolie wages, planters often defended themselves, as slavehold-

14. Retold in *The S.T.F.U. News*, May, 1938.
15. Hattie Walls to Claude Williams, September 6, 1940, in Claude Williams Papers (Helena, Ala.).
16. Carmichael, "Plantation System," pp. 485–87; Benson Y. Landis and G. E. Haynes, *Cotton Growing Communities . . . in Arkansas* (New York: Federal Council of Churches of Christ in America, 1935), pp. 9–14; Blalock, "Plantation Operations," pp. 21–33; Howard R. Jackson, "An Economic and Social Analysis of Three Cotton Plantations in Arkansas in 1934" (Master's thesis, University of Arkansas, 1937), pp. 48, 60.

ers had done a century before, by painting themselves as sponsors of an agrarian welfare state. Religion, recreation, health
and education all were alleged products of planter paternal-
ism. The actual situation in the Arkansas Delta was somewhat
different. The planters' major contribution to education was the
payment of taxes; a study of nearly one hundred plantations
disclosed that in addition to taxes each planter paid an average
of less than a dollar a year to support schools for the children of
his sharecroppers. Landlords paid about five times more for
recreation than education. Recreation usually meant big all-
day holiday picnics for the tenants. For the support of tenant
churches, landlords paid ten times more than they paid for education, and church attendance was much more encouraged than
school attendance. (Churches contributed to "a constructive
social relationship between the landlord and his workers," a
student of the plantation system noted.)[17] Health was generally
poor because the rent-free cabins were also screen-free and
sanitary privy-free, but it is true that landlords paid quite a few
medical bills. One study found eighty-nine landlords who paid
$3,709 in medical bills for tenants—however, $3,609 of this was
added to the tenants' accounts, so it came back, plus interest, at
settling time. Landlords customarily paid only those medical
bills they thought they could collect later from the tenant, with
interest.[18]

It was by citing his own financial difficulties that the planter
could most successfully defend himself against those who regarded him as personally responsible for the decrepitude of the
system in which he, too, was caught up. American individualism,
flavored by its strongly moralistic outlook, kept many onlookers
from seeing the misery of the cotton belt as the product of im-
personal social forces, making them interpret it instead as the
just results of somebody's "badness." If they adjudged the tenant
to be "good," then the landlord's "badness" must be the cause
of the difficulty. Or—a step above this in sophistication—if the
landlord was not thought of as being wicked, he was portrayed

17. Jackson, "Economic and Social Analysis," pp. 71–81; U. S. Department of Agriculture, "Farm Tenancy," p. 13; Blalock, "Plantation
Operations," p. 38.
18. *Ibid.*

as being almost as poor as his croppers and tenants, with taxes and mortgages taking his every penny. He was not bad but helpless.

This belief was not strictly true, either. There were planters who went bankrupt, just as there were many bankruptcies and much unemployment in other lines of endeavor during those drab years; but the typical planter was in a respectable enough economic situation. The social columns of small-town newspapers carried abundant evidence of the gentleman farmer's pleasant life. Tyronza's J. E. Emrich, for example, was somehow managing to send his daughters Sara and Dorothy to Kansas State College and the University of Tennessee, and every now and then he could scrape up enough to take the whole family to Louisville to see the Kentucky Derby.[19] But let us not generalize from Planter Emrich. A good survey of representative Delta plantations in 1934 disclosed an average gross income of $10,774, about three-fourths of it from the sale of cotton. Average expenses totaled $6,271; of this amount, about $1,500 was paid for labor, the largest single item of expense. Ginning cost 15 per cent of total expenses, taxes 12 per cent, repairs 8 per cent. Lesser amounts went to pay for feed, seed, rent, fuel, insurance, interest, fertilizer, and so on, leaving a total net income of $4,743. This represented an 8 per cent profit on each dollar invested: not a bad profit, and not a bad net income by the standards of 1934, when physicians were averaging around $3,300, dentists $2,600, and lawyers—though figures vary widely —about $3,500 to $4,000. The plantation owners were not America's most poverty-stricken men. The larger plantations, which supported most of the sharecroppers, were of course doing far better than the average. Three typical giants, for example, made yearly gross incomes that ranged from $75,000 to $95,000; total expenses, including an extremely liberal depreciation allowance in one case, were $51,000 to $77,000, leaving a handsome net income in each case.[20]

19. "Tyronza," social notes in *Marked Tree Tribune*, March 21, 1935, May 7, 1936, May 28, 1936.

20. Blalock, "Plantation Operations," pp. 10–18; Milton Friedman and Simon Kuznets, *Income From Independent Professional Practice* (New York: National Bureau of Economic Research, 1945), pp. 69, 101; Jackson, "Economic and Social Analysis," p. 47. A WPA study arrived at an

Although their income was highly satisfactory, planters complained that it was fluctuating and uncertain, while the burden of their overhead was fixed and inescapable. And the worst of all these burdens was supposed to be the tax load. Actually property taxation was not only slanted by the planters in their own favor but was hardly enforced, anyway. "The assessed valuation of property is established almost entirely on the basis of the owner's statement of value. . .," wrote an Arkansas economist; "No effort is made to equalize valuation as between individual properties or between property types."[21] Although the assessed valuation of property was legally supposed to be 50 per cent of true value, rural real estate worth less than $600 was assessed at 57 per cent while properties worth $40,000 and over were assessed at only 20 per cent of true value. Land in the Delta, though the richest in the state of Arkansas, was assessed at the lowest percentage of value, and many thousands of acres of fertile Delta soil were not on the tax rolls at all. There was no fear that the state might crack down on such evasion, penalties being practically nil. In four plantation counties of northeastern Arkansas, Cross, Poinsett, St. Francis, and Woodruff, almost 200,000 acres of land had been tax-delinquent since 1931 and were scheduled for forfeiture to the state in 1933. Not a single acre was forfeited. In three counties, injunctions were in effect prohibiting tax-delinquent lands from being forfeited as state law provided, and the state had not even attempted to have these injunctions set aside! Drainage and levee taxes were 72.5 per cent delinquent and in many areas had simply been forgotten. The general property tax was even more farcical. Over a thousand persons in Poinsett County had bought auto and truck licenses, but not one vehicle appeared on the tax rolls. These rolls also revealed a grand total of two watches in the entire county. "We don't pay any taxes here on personal property unless we want to," explained a county resident. The result of

even higher estimate of net income per plantation: $8,071. See William C. Holley, Ellen Winston, and Thomas Jackson Woofter, Jr. *The Plantation South, 1934–1937,* WPA Research Monograph 22 (Washington: G. P. O., 1940), p. 36.

21. C. O. Brannen, "Tax Delinquent Rural Lands in Arkansas," Arkansas Agricultural Experiment Station Bulletin No. 311 (Fayetteville, Ark., November, 1934), p. 29.

all this was that in 1931, 1932, and 1933 Arkansas lost $3 million a year from not enforcing taxation. And a University of Arkansas economist concluded that "the elimination of penalties in tax collection has become characteristic not only of the property tax but of other taxes collected by the state."[22]

If it is true, then, that planters generally had an acceptable net income remaining to them after meeting their expenses, which were apparently much more bearable than was claimed, what was fundamentally wrong with the plantation system? Everyone, after all, agreed that the sharecroppers' plight was a symptom of more basic ills.

In the first place, the system drained the soil of its fertility by emphasizing the production of one staple soil-depleting crop, cotton. This weakness was less apparent in the fertile Delta than elsewhere, but even here the danger could be seen. Tenants knew they would not receive the benefits of planting soil-building crops; this would bring income to the landlord, not to them. And because cotton could readily be sold, bankers would extend credit on favorable terms to landlords who planted as much acreage to the crop as possible. So cotton was planted and the soil was weakened. Still another threat to the cotton economy was the increasingly sharp competition that it faced; synthetic fabrics like rayon were claiming an ever-growing share of certain markets. But the plantation system cannot be blamed for the appearance of cotton substitutes. Republican high tariffs closed European markets to Southern cotton, but the Hawley-Smoot tariff can hardly be considered a product of the plantation system, either. The real difficulty with the system itself was that it depended upon an obsolete combination of production factors. The cheap-labor formula for minimizing production costs was outmoded. Aside from the vicious cruelty of the cheap-labor formula, there was another objection. Other countries, their economies largely pre-industrial, could

22. *Ibid.*, pp. 34–35. For other information given in the preceding paragraph, see *Ibid.*, pp. 3–4, 24, 27–29; Estal E. Sparlin, "Inequalities in the Arkansas Property Tax Assessment System," Arkansas Agricultural Experiment Station Bulletin No. 369 (Fayetteville, Ark., January, 1939), pp. 4–9, 12, 23–25; "Personal Assessments a Farce," *Arkansas Gazette*, January 24, 1935.

utilize the formula with far greater success. India, Egypt, Brazil, the Soviet Union, Iran, China, and the Sudan all had cheaper labor and thus could produce cheaper cotton. During the 1920's and early 1930's their rapidly increasing production, combined with declining world consumption, began to represent a serious threat to Southern cotton growers. Cotton prices, reflecting the new situation, staggered weakly up to about twenty cents a pound in 1927, then began to fall inexorably to the 1932 lows of five and six cents. Planters, once living quite comfortably, were now "getting by"; sharecroppers, once subsisting, were now starving. And yet this crisis in the plantation system, though promptly recognized, was met only slowly, partially, and painfully, in a process that was still not complete decades later.

There appear to be two main reasons why the cheap-labor plantation system was so long in yielding to fundamental changes. The first reason was that the cheap-labor system, which was in reality a slave-labor system perpetuated with minor changes after the Civil War, had become an inextricable part of a whole complex of cultural attitudes. These attitudes stereotyped croppers as a good-for-nothing class on whom any systematic help would be wasted, and they underlay the various devices used to keep the tenant class too politically subservient to demand changes. Furthermore, these attitudes upheld the juggling of accounts and the denial of schooling that kept the tenants on the plantation; and the fertility typical of an impoverished peasantry kept them multiplying, depressing wages, so that they were far too numerous for other regions to absorb. Outmoded machinery can be replaced rapidly, but outmoded cultural patterns persist. And so the deplorably inefficient system perpetuated itself. Looking back at the period with twenty years' perspective, James H. Street declared:

For at least the period since the advent of the tractor the stultifying effect of southern social and economic institutions has been a greater factor than the existence of technical difficulties in explaining the slow rate of progress in the mechanization of cotton production and the lag in the general rationalization of southern agriculture as well. The over-riding circumstance in this process has been the availability of a routinized, poorly educated, and politically ineffectual rural labor force which for a long period rendered sustained inventive and developmental interest in labor-saving farm machines economically pointless.[23]

The second reason the plantation system managed to keep going was more simple. Its leaders, making use of their political power, bailed themselves out with government subsidies. This is the story of the cotton program of the Agricultural Adjustment Administration.

23. Street, *New Revolution in the Cotton Economy,* p. 34. On the crisis of the plantation system, see also Johnson, Embree, and Alexander, *Collapse of Cotton Tenancy,* pp. 34–45; Street, *New Revolution in the Cotton Economy,* pp. 30–34, 41–51; Broadus Mitchell, *Depression Decade: From New Era through New Deal, 1929–1941* (New York: Holt, Rinehart and Winston, 1947), pp. 181–85; Wilbur Joseph Cash, *The Mind of the South* (New York: Alfred A. Knopf, 1941), pp. 399–401; Henry Irving Richards, *Cotton and the AAA* (Washington: The Brookings Institution, 1936), pp. 11–13; Alexander, *Arkansas Plantation,* pp. 26–28. The author's understanding of the problem was also aided by an interview with Robert Watts (Pete) Hudgens, formerly Southern regional director and Associate Administrator of the Farm Security Administration, June 24, 1961.

# 2.

## "... By *Increasing Agricultural Purchasing Power*"

*P*lantation owners were not the only farmers desperately in need of help in 1932 and 1933. Realized net farm income in 1932 was only one-third of the 1929 level. And that, in turn, hardly reflected affluence; agriculture had never recovered from its slump after World War I. By the time Franklin Roosevelt took office, agricultural recovery ideas were legion. Many of these—such as taxing the "middleman" and achieving parity between agriculture and industry—developed out of the ill-fated McNary-Haugen bills of the late twenties. But the idea which became the heart of the New Deal approach to the farm problem was even newer: a "domestic allotment plan," advanced by Montana State College professor Milburn L. Wilson and enthusiastically accepted by Secretary of Agriculture Henry Wallace and Undersecretary Rexford Tugwell. They believed that by providing payments high enough to induce farmers to accept a reduced allotment of crop acreage, limitation of output—or "adjustment" of output, to use the approved word—could be achieved, with resulting salutary effects on the price level.

In the case of the AAA's cotton program, the fastest, most drastic "adjustment" of all was needed: in the summer of 1933 a huge carry-over of 12.5 million bales of United States cotton hung over the world market, more than the total consumption of American cotton had been during each of the previous three seasons; and with forty million acres planted, another bumper crop was in prospect.[1] There seemed to be only one way to avoid rock-bottom prices. The solution would be bitter but unavoidable: plow the cotton under and create scarcity in order to raise the price.

Few people defended the scarcity program in principle. The charges of critics like Norman Thomas, who wished "to create more wealth, not restrict production," and ridiculed "the pleas that we have too much cotton in a country where the children of the cotton growers can't have underclothes,"[2] seemed too simply sensible for rebuttal. The chieftains of the reduction program excused themselves only on grounds of necessity: "To have to destroy a growing crop is a shocking commentary on our civilization," agreed Secretary Wallace. His chief aide, Tugwell, claimed that "we used the only means at hand, under the competitive and money economy.... If idle acres, turned-under cotton and slaughtered little pigs constitute a symbol of sin, the indictment is against the whole system."[3]

There was one group, however, that approved the government program joyously. As Federal money came pouring into the cotton country in payment for the fiber that had been destroyed, as the smaller supply began to drive prices back uphill, the planters became even more dedicated Democrats than before. Praise for the party of scarcity and high prices was on every lip; one candid farmer avowed that the South was out "to get the Civil War debt back" and then some.[4] A delegation of Arkansas planters met in Little Rock to declare, "The tighter the government control the better . . . we never want to see a

1. Edwin Griswold Nourse et al., Three Years of the Agricultural Adjustment Administration (Washington: The Brookings Institution, 1937), pp. 70–75; James Harry Street, The New Revolution in the Cotton Economy (Chapel Hill: The University of North Carolina Press, 1957), pp. 43–44; Henry Irving Richards, Cotton and the AAA (Washington: The Brookings Institution, 1936), pp. 14, 74–79.

2. Quoted in New Leader, January 26, 1935, and Memphis Press-Scimitar, March 13, 1935.

3. Wallace is quoted in Nourse et al., Three Years of AAA, p. 87, and in Russell Lord, The Wallaces of Iowa (Boston: Houghton Mifflin, 1947), p. 362; Rexford Tugwell, "Nature and Agricultural Adjustment," Brookings, South Dakota, June 29, 1934, in "Speeches of the Undersecretary (1934)" folder, RG 16, N Arch.

4. Lord, Wallaces of Iowa, pp. 382–83.

relaxation of governmental control. The more inspectors Washington puts on the job, the happier we'll be!"[5]

Though the resulting rise in cotton prices was significant—about four cents a pound—the benefit payments were more directly a blessing from the government. For the acreage plowed up in 1933—from 25 to 50 per cent of the planted crop—the planter received an amount usually equal to about six to eight cents a pound. From the landlords' viewpoint, there seemed to be only one difficulty with the plow-up terms: the payments for a tenant's plowed-up acreage were supposed to be split with him in proportion to his interest in the crop—50–50 in the case of sharecroppers, 75–25 in favor of a "third and fourth" tenant.[6] Landlords were highly dissatisfied, and when the 1934–35 cotton contract terms were drawn up in early 1934 the landlord-tenant benefit distribution ratio was changed in the landlord's favor. Benefits now were to be divided into "rental" and "parity" payments. The rental payment would provide 3.5 cents per pound of previous average yield on every acre withdrawn from production; the parity payment would be only a penny for each pound formerly grown. The entire rental payment went to the landlord; he only had to share the smaller parity payment in proportion to the customary interest in the crop. On acreage withdrawn from a sharecropper's little plot 4 of the 4.5 cents—the 3.5 rental plus half the parity—would go to the landlord. He thus got all but a ninth part of the government money, while in previous years he had received only half the return from cotton grown on the same acreage. In the case of a tenant paying, as was customary, a fourth of the cotton as rent, the landlord fared even better. The tenant would get three-fourths rather than half of the little parity payment, but the landlord still got all the government rental. Thus, on a tenant-farmed plot producing 200 pounds of lint cotton per acre, for a gross income of $20 per acre with cotton at a dime a pound, the landlord formerly would have received as rental $5.00 an acre. Now, getting a fourth of the parity payment plus all the rental—a total of 3.75 cents per

5. Carroll Binder, "Bankhead Bill Popular," *Chicago Daily News*, April 5, 1934.

6. Nourse *et al.*, *Three Years of AAA*, pp. 95–99, 300, 342; Richards, *Cotton and the AAA*, pp. 139–40.

pound—he would receive $7.50. Thus the New Deal ordained that the landlord should receive 50 per cent more money for not producing than for producing, while the tenant who once kept $15 per acre from the sale of ten-cent cotton should now get only $1.50, his three-fourths of the parity payment, a mere tenth of his former income.[7] The way this distribution of government money affected planter and sharecropper income in actual cases was easy to discover. On one plantation called "a very representative cotton farm" by researchers, the landlord's gross income increased under the AAA from $51,554 in 1932 to $102,-202 in 1934, while the average gross income of his tenants fell from $379 to $355. This study was conducted by the AAA's Cotton Section, which was so anxious to justify its program that it concluded from the above figures, "It is logical to infer that both the landlord and tenant have been greatly benefited by the Agricultural Adjustment Administration's Cotton Program."[8]

One might assume that planters would be content with the share of government money they were able to secure by terms of the contract. Such was not true, for a great many—perhaps a

7. This rank discrimination was found only in the AAA's cotton program, and it can undoubtedly be attributed to complete landlord control of that program. Even in the largely Southern tobacco program, tenants and sharecroppers received the same proportion of government money that they received from the sale of the crop. There were two categories of tenants that were supposed to get part of the rental payment, however, under the cotton program: cash tenants—there were few in the cotton belt —and so-called "managing" share tenants, both of which were entitled to half of the rental in addition to their share of the parity. Since the decision as to whether a tenant was a "managing" one was largely the landlord's decision, no great number of tenants fell into this category either. On the division of payments, see Nourse *et al., Three Years of AAA*, pp. 95–99; R. A. Ballinger, "Important Provisions in the 1934–1935 Cotton Acreage Reduction Contract," University of Oklahoma *Current Farm Economics* series, Vol. 6, No. 6 (December, 1933), inside front cover; Margaret B. Bennett to Paul Appleby, January 14, 1935, Folder 467, Solicitor's File, RG 16, N Arch; Richards, *Cotton and the AAA*, pp. 140, 146.

8. AAA Cotton Section and University of Arkansas College of Agriculture, "Arkansas Plantation Survey, 1935," Tables 7, 8, p. 8, in L-TS, RG 145, N Arch. Other surveys corroborated these findings: see Mordecai Ezekiel to Henry Wallace, March 5, 1935 (Memorandum, "Distribution of Increased Cotton Income"), L-TS, RG 145, N Arch; Howard R. Jackson, "An Economic and Social Analysis of Three Cotton Plantations in Arkansas in 1934" (Master's thesis, University of Arkansas, 1937), pp. 10, 48, 52–55, 60.

majority[9]—of them were able to claim their tenants' pittances as well. From the beginning of the program, there were many ways in which enterprising landlords could do this. If the illiterate and powerless tenant could be induced to make his mark at the bottom of a long form laden with small print written in legalese, only the landlord and the government knew that the tenant had waived his right to government money. Often landlords, signing their cotton contracts, simply forgot to mention having any tenants. And if by chance a check did arrive payable to both tenant and landlord, the AAA thoughtfully provided a form authorizing the planter to cash it—and, by implication, keep the money—without the worker's endorsement.[10] Indirect methods could also be used. After passage of the Bankhead Act requiring, in effect, that only that amount of cotton could be marketed for which Federal bale tags were made available, planters forced tenants to turn over their tags—in the Arkansas Delta, for example, the AAA's own survey disclosed that 77 per cent of all tenants had been intimidated into this illegal but seldom penalized act.[11] Or, again, without evading the law, planters could now demand payment of previously forgotten debts, or simplest of all, raise the tenant's rent by the amount of his AAA check.[12] Particularly prone to victimization

9. Nourse *et al.*, *Three Years of the AAA*, p. 342; interview with Sam Bledsoe, formerly of AAA's information staff, July 10, 1962; Calvin B. Hoover, "Human Problems in Acreage Reduction in the South," personal report to Henry A. Wallace and Chester C. Davis (Durham: Duke University, March, 1934), p. 8; D. P. Trent to Chester Davis, December 28, 1934, L-TS, RG 145, N Arch.

10. Seth Thomas to Cully Cobb, March 18, 1935, folder 466-B, Solicitor's File, RG 16, N Arch; Nourse *et al.*, *Three Years of the AAA*, pp. 342–43; Hoover, "Human Problems," pp. 7–8. The tenant had to sign the form mentioned, but any planter could think of many ways to convince the tenant that signing it was necessary.

11. D. P. Trent to Chester Davis, December 28, 1934, L-TS, RG 145, N Arch; and *Arkansas Gazette*, November 20, 1934.

12. Carroll Binder, "Federal Benefits . . . ," *Chicago Daily News*, April 9, 1934; Rodney Dutcher, "Freezing Out . . .," Memphis *Press-Scimitar*, April 22, 1934; Rosie Morelock, "A Step Out of the Government Slavery," *Commonwealth College Fortnightly*, May 1, 1936 (Commonwealth College Papers, University of Arkansas, Reel 2). Regarding the question of whether AAA benefits could be claimed by landlords as payment for debt, the Solicitor of the Department of Agriculture first answered "yes" in the South, and then "no" in the North only two years later, with no change in law or administrative ruling to explain the con-

were tenants who managed their own farms—"managing share tenants"—who were supposed to receive, in addition to their share of the small parity payment, half of the large rental payment as well. This composed a prize too large to be ignored, and the tenant's loss of it was common.[13]

Planters could divert their tenants' money with clear consciences, generally, because they seldom regarded such action as "cheating." Tenants were seen as such childlike, dependent, improvident persons that it was the landlord's prerogative to make all decisions for them. Claiming the AAA benefits, Wilbur J. Cash observed in *The Mind of the South*, was "not felt as constituting dishonesty at all, but as being simply a part of the natural right of the man of property to claim all revenues over and above what was required to feed and clothe the workmen after the established standard."[14] One large Southern cotton planter reported to friends in the AAA, "Most of us, I think look upon those rulings which call for the division of the 'payment' with the cropper as little more than a gracious gesture."[15]

It soon became apparent that the AAA cotton reduction program involved an even greater problem than benefit sharing. A tenant merely cheated out of his money would at least be able to live on his income from cotton, but if his little plot was taken entirely out of production, he would have nothing. And this personal disaster struck thousands, as plantations gradually shifted from the use of sharecroppers to the use of day labor. The AAA played a triple role in this process: first, it enlarged the pool of labor available for such work by cutting acreage out

---

tradiction: see Seth Thomas to Cully Cobb, March 10, 1935, and Mastin White to Whitney Gilliland, January 19, 1937, both in folder 466–B, Solicitor's File, RG 16, N Arch; and, in connection with the first of these rulings, Cully Cobb to Chester Davis, January 5, 1935, folder 467, Solicitor's File.

13. Hoover, "Human Problems," pp. 7, 10; Richards, *Cotton and the AAA*, p. 144; Harold Hoffsommer, "The AAA and the Cropper," *Social Forces*, XIII (May, 1935), 498.

14. (New York: Alfred A. Knopf, 1941), pp. 395, 397–98.

15. Thad Snow, "Report," n.d. [December, 1936], stapled under cover of Louis C. Gray to Mordecai Ezekiel, April 1, 1937, in "Tenancy (1937)" folder, RG 16, N Arch. See also Hoover, "Human Problems," p. 8; Richard Hofstadter, "The Southeastern Cotton Tenants Under the AAA, 1933–1935," (Master's thesis, Columbia University, 1938), pp. 34, 36.

from under sharecroppers; second, by enriching the planters, the AAA made it more profitable for them to pay labor with cash than with a share of the crop; and finally, since the AAA required that benefits be shared with sharecroppers but not with wage laborers, it created a positive monetary inducement to change the workers' status.

According to AAA rulings, no direct change-over from tenants to wage workers was permitted. But there were many ways a friendly county agent could help a planter avoid such inconvenient regulations. The least respectable way to do this was to misinform the tenants. If told that they would have to accept the status of wage laborers for the next year, few of them would know that their status supposedly could not be changed. Often they would become angry and move, hoping—usually in vain— to find a crop elsewhere. Or they would agree to the change, and once the verbal contract was made, the AAA would never interfere with it. Or the plantation could be leased to a son or other relative, and although the AAA required any lessee or purchaser to undertake all the obligations of the old owner, there was no way for sharecroppers to keep up to date on such rulings: all they could do was accept the new landlord's assertion that he planned to farm with day labor. Any planter who could convince his friend, the county agent, that it was "impossible" to keep all of his tenants could comply with the AAA cotton contract simply by allowing those displaced to stay on in their shacks, living by growing a subsistence garden. This would make the landlord feel kind and law-abiding, and it would save him the trouble of sending a truck all the way into the nearest town when he wanted day labor at chopping time and picking time. Another way for the planter to reduce the status of his workers was to do it gradually. Each year workers who were nominally sharecroppers or tenants would find their acreage reduced, until finally they would be spending most of their time and making most of their money on wage work offered elsewhere on the plantation. Soon the fiction of "sharecropping" could be dropped without notice, or as the "sharecroppers" moved away they could be replaced with squatters available for wage work during the peak seasons.[16]

16. On sharecroppers becoming wage workers, see Seth Thomas to

By the end of 1934 switching workers from the relative security of sharecropping to the highly seasonal, insecure wage
worker status was too obvious to deny. "The practice is rather
general throughout the cotton belt," AAA's D. P. Trent admitted
privately while issuing public denials.[17] As croppers became
wage workers, their former plots—listed as separate farms by
the Census Bureau—became incorporated into the planter's
own lands, and the trend was reflected in the census figures.
Throughout the Delta there was a fall in the number of farms,
but a large rise in the size of them. Mississippi County was
typical: the number of 20- to 49-acre farms fell by almost a
fourth, but 500- to 999-acre farms rose 136 per cent and those of
1,000 acres or more increased by 375 per cent. Between 1930
and 1935, the number of tenant-operated farms in Arkansas declined for the first time since the Civil War. Among Negroes,
because they were mainly in the plantation country and in the
lower tenure categories, there was an even greater drop than
for tenants in general. "Population changes in the lowland part
of the state seem to have been dominated by the crop reduction
program," concluded one agricultural economist; ". . . tenants
and croppers apparently had left their farms."[18]

How many tenants did the AAA displace? The answer is impossible to give precisely, not only because the process was so
often gradual and partial, but also because there were other

---

Chester Davis, April 23, 1935, p. 7, in folder 466–B, Solicitor's File, RG
16, N Arch; Norman Thomas, *The Plight of the Share-Cropper* (New
York: League for Industrial Democracy, 1934), pp. 27–29; Arthur F.
Raper, *Preface to Peasantry* (Chapel Hill: The University of North Carolina Press, 1936), p. 252; "Displaced Tenant Family," p. 25, L-TS, RG
145, N Arch; Donald C. Alexander, *The Arkansas Plantation, 1920–1942*
(New Haven: Yale University Press, 1943), pp. 57–59; Richards, *Cotton
and the AAA*, p. 145. For a dissent from this consensus, see Frey and
Smith, "Influence," *Rural Sociology*, I (December, 1936), 501.

17. D. P. Trent to Chester Davis, December 28, 1934, L-TS, RG 145,
N Arch.

18. William H. Metzler, "Population Trends and Adjustments in Ar-
kansas," Arkansas Agricultural Experiment Station Bulletin No. 388 (Fay-
etteville, Ark., May, 1940), pp. 49–53; see also J. A. Baker and J. G. Mc-
Neely, "Land Tenure in Arkansas: I, The Farm Tenancy Situation,"
Arkansas Agricultural Experimental Station Bulletin No. 384 (Fayetteville,
Ark., 1940), pp. 18, 19–25, 30; Frey and Smith, "Influence," *Rural
Sociology*, I (December, 1936), 497–500.

forces at work. The high rate of Southern rural reproduction had historically produced a population surplus, but in the Depression years industrial outlets for this surplus were blocked. The cotton tenant's tradition of moving from one landlord to another in midwinter persisted, with disastrous results. The tenant who moved knew nothing of the reduction program, typically, and had no idea why a new tenancy was now impossible to find. "There was plenty of work," said one, "and what I don't understand is why it ain't that way now, 'cause the land is still here."[19]

In spite of all complications, some general evaluation of the AAA's effect on tenants is possible. For one thing, the sheer extent of the program was certain to force substantial displacement. The aim was to retire well over one-third of the South's cotton acreage, and, as Fred Frey and T. Lynn Smith remarked, "There are few people gullible enough to believe that the acreage devoted to cotton can be reduced one-third without an accompanying decrease in the laborers engaged in its production."[20] In some areas the goal of 33 per cent reduction may have been reached. The over-all achievement was less; there were 35 million acres planted to cotton in 1932, about 26.5 million in 1934–35. Man-hours needed for cotton production fell from nearly 3 billion to only 2.25 billion—a 25 per cent decrease. There was a proportionate reduction in the total cash return to labor, despite AAA pittances. A study which reached fairly typical conclusions could "state with authority" that the AAA had caused unemployment, displacing at least 15 and probably 20 per cent of all sharecropper families. Most of those displaced sought Federal relief, and those who conducted the relief program found that 16 per cent of the ex-tenants who came to them gave the AAA program as the reason they had been driven off the land. This figure might be too small, because few tenants knew much about the AAA or the reasons for their landlord's decisions. Brooks Hays, soon to become a noted Congressman, knew a well-informed attorney who estimated displacement at

19. Quoted in Brooks Hays, "Memorandum for Mr. [Paul] Porter," n.d. [1935], in L-TS, RG 145, N Arch.
20. Frey and Smith, "Influence," *Rural Sociology*, I (December, 1936), 489; Thomas, *Plight of the Share-Cropper*, pp. 12, 27.

40 per cent, most of it because of the reduction program. And Richard Hofstadter, soon to become a noted historian, stated bluntly, "I have not found a single responsible observer of conditions in the South who does not report that the AAA was the cause of a substantial amount of displacement."[21]

A development of major importance was occurring. Just as surely as the Republicans had allowed the plantation South to survive after a brief post-Civil War interlude of democratic reconstruction, so now the Democrats were preserving the planters of the South at the expense of their tenants. "It may come to be," observed the Southern sociologist Rupert Vance, "that the greatest efficiency of the Southern planters consists in securing government subsidy to uphold a system that might otherwise break down of its own weakness.... With one hand the cotton landlord takes agricultural subsidies and rental benefits from his government, with the other he pushes his tenants on relief. ... in the South when the government salvages the landlord it creates almost as great a problem of displaced and dispossessed tenants whose only hope is further demands on the Federal treasury."[22]

A generation later, the sons and daughters of those displaced and dispossessed tenants crowded the ghettoes of Northern cities, and the problem was more acute and more visible than ever before. But nobody, in 1934, possessed the gift of prophecy, and who was there to protest the policies of the New Deal in the cotton South? The tenants themselves could not; they were uninformed and disfranchised. The Republicans could not; they were uninterested and discredited. Norman Thomas spoke out, but he seemed more aware of the AAA's scarcity rationale than its contribution to mass unemployment. And Erskine Cald-

21. On the extent of displacement, see Hofstadter, "Southeastern Cotton Tenants," p. 95; Brooks Hays, "Memorandum for Mr. [Paul] Porter," n.d. [1935], in L-TS, RG 145, N Arch; W. T. Wilson and W. H. Metzler, "Characteristics of Arkansas Rehabilitation Clients," Arkansas Agricultural Experiment Station Bulletin No. 348 (Fayetteville: June, 1937), pp. 14–15; J. T. Sanders, "Lessons from the Old Cotton Program . . .," Oklahoma Current Farm Economics Series, Vol. 9, No. 1 (February, 1936), p. 35; Frey and Smith, "Influence," Rural Sociology, I (December, 1936), 497–500.
22. Rupert Vance to William Watts Ball, September 15, 1934, William Watts Ball Papers (Durham, N.C.: Duke University).

well was writing, but the characters he created were more humorously lusty than pathetically victimized.

Who was there, indeed, to serve as the voice of the share-cropper? In early 1934 there was no such voice. But, in the Arkansas Delta, where the cotton program was working quite thoroughly and typically, there lived two young Socialists who were infuriated by what they saw. One of them, Henry Clay East, tough, stocky, and outspoken, scion of an old local family, ran a gasoline station and was respected as a shrewd, honest businessman. The shy, skinny proprietor of the dry cleaners next door to East's filling station had been a radical longer; Harry Leland Mitchell—H. L., or Mitch, as his friends called him—had had some pretty peculiar ideas when he came to Tyronza six or seven years previously. Even before he had graduated from high school in Halls, Tennessee, he had been interested in some of the ideas that Bob LaFollette had promoted during his third-party presidential campaign in 1924. About the same time, Mitch encountered Upton Sinclair's *Letters to Judd,* and by the time he left high school religious and economic orthodoxy were far behind. So lost to all propriety was he that he even began questioning the fundamental truths of segregation and white supremacy, and whenever he encountered another questioning mind he would attempt to make a convert. Clay East was one of these. East was so angry about the depression that he overcame his initial hostility to socialism long enough to read the books by Upton Sinclair that Mitchell brought him. Soon Clay was admitting to Mitch that Sinclair's ideas impressed him. He decided to subscribe to Oscar Ameringer's militantly Socialist newspaper, *The American Guardian,* published in Oklahoma City, and soon East was ready to convert others. Not a single salesman who entered his service station could leave with an order unless he agreed to subscribe to *The American Guardian* first. Then, before East would renew each order, the salesman had to pass a stiff oral exam designed to reveal how thoroughly he had been reading the paper.[23]

23. On the background of East and Mitchell, see the transcript of Mitchell's recorded interview for the Columbia University Oral History Collection, STFU Papers and elsewhere (referred to hereafter as Oral History MS). The author has also gained valuable information from vari-

In 1932, Norman Thomas, Socialist candidate for President, spoke in Memphis. East and Mitchell drove over to hear him, were greatly impressed, and returned to Tyronza ready to establish a Socialist party local there. Having officially become Socialists, the first tasks they saw before them were to build membership and to decide on a program that would have some relevance to the miserable plight of the sharecroppers and tenants that crowded the Delta. A few tenants, some of them Negroes, joined the Socialist party, and Clay East managed to recruit some businessmen and a number of skilled workers. This heterogeneous little band, observing the first New Deal relief programs in Tyronza, saw how readily the local planters gained control of them and used them solely for taking care of the planters' "best" tenants and foremen during the off season. This relieved the planters of part of their "furnish" burden and did almost nothing to alleviate the destitution of the masses of rural unemployed. Mitchell and East organized a mass meeting of the needy at the town's Odd Fellows lodge, where an "Unemployed League" was created to fight planter control of the relief and works programs. The League failed to make the program's leadership any more democratic, as it turned out, but it did obtain widespread aid for those who most needed it.[24]

Having achieved its immediate purpose, the Unemployed League dissolved. This, unfortunately, left an organizational vacuum in the area at the very time Mitchell and his friends were beginning to perceive the vastly greater threat posed by the AAA to the workers of the Delta. They became convinced that if they could compile specific proof of what they saw daily, they could show the nation that the AAA was not only creating scarcity but eliminating farm employment and encouraging dishonesty. The first man they sought out was Dr. William Amberson, a Memphis professor of physiology, a fellow Socialist, and a close friend of Paul Porter, executive assistant to AAA chief Chester Davis. Amberson presented the idea to Norman Thomas himself, who approved enthusiastically and agreed to finance

ous letters and interviews of East and Mitchell, 1961–1970, especially East to the author, n.d. [June, 1962].

24. Oral History MS, pp. 10–18; interview with Mitchell, December 3, 1961.

the survey. The results were published in a booklet bearing the simple title, *The Plight of the Share-Cropper.* The facts were shocking, but they were accurate, and were accepted—privately, of course—even by some AAA officials.[25]

While the data were being compiled, Amberson, Mitchell and their associates invited Thomas to come examine Delta conditions for himself. Thomas was happy to make the trip. Once, while having lunch with Clay East, Thomas told him that while it was good to have more people in the Socialist party, what was needed in the Delta was some sort of organization of the tenants and sharecroppers—a union, perhaps.

A sharecroppers' union! Such a thing was not entirely unheard of, but successful ones—had there been any of those?[26] And how could people as poor as the dispossessed of the Delta ever hope to bargain with their employers?

But then, there was Dr. Amberson's friendship with Paul Porter to remind Mitchell and East that pressure on the AAA might be possible. Having returned Norman Thomas to the railroad depot in Memphis, the two young men drove back across the river, talking excitedly all the way to Tyronza.

25. Paul W. Bruton to Jerome Frank, May 21, 1934, folder 466, Solicitor's File, RG 16, N Arch. On the Amberson-Mitchell-East survey, see Thomas, *Plight of the Share-Cropper,* p. 33 and *passim.*; Jonathan Daniels, *A Southerner Discovers the South* (New York: Macmillan, 1938), pp. 81–87; Oral History MS, p. 21.
26. For previous attempts to form agricultural unions, see Stuart Jamieson, *Labor Unionism in American Agriculture,* Bureau of Labor Statistics Bulletin 836 (Washington: Government Printing Office, 1945), pp. 303–5. On Thomas's suggesting the new union, see Oral History MS., pp. 19–20. The role of Thomas and the Socialist party is somewhat exaggerated, in the author's opinion, in M. S. Venkataramani, "Norman Thomas, Arkansas Sharecroppers, and the Roosevelt Agricultural Policies, 1933–1937," *Mississippi Valley Historical Review,* XLVII (September, 1960), 225, and in Jerold Auerbach, "Southern Tenant Farmers: Socialist Critics of the New Deal," *Labor History,* VII (Winter, 1966), 3.

# 3.

# The Sharecroppers
# and the Split in AAA

*U*ntil 1935, the Agricultural Adjustment Administration was a house divided against itself, with tension constantly growing between the Extension Service conservatives, to whom the AAA was essentially a farm strike designed to force prices up, and the younger urban reformers, who demanded an attack on the entire problem of rural poverty. During 1934, the two groups became so bitterly estranged that the AAA's ultimate attitude toward sharecropper problems could be established only after the victory of one side or the other.

Seemingly, the initial advantage lay with the agricultural liberals. Their chief advocate was Rexford Guy Tugwell, a tall, handsome, sophisticated professor in his early forties, whose close relationship with President Roosevelt could have been decisive in the sharecropper controversy were it not for the fact that, as Undersecretary of Agriculture, Tugwell was outside the semi-autonomous AAA and could take no direct part in its battles. His many outside duties as a leading New Deal spokesman also hindered his support of the AAA reformers.[1]

1. Arthur M. Schlesinger, *The Coming of the New Deal*, Vol. II of *The Age of Roosevelt* (Boston: Houghton Mifflin, 1959), pp. 29, 34; "Unofficial Observer" [Literary Guild of New York], *The New Dealers* (New York: Simon & Schuster, 1934), pp. 75, 85–92; Russell Lord, *The Wallaces of Iowa* (Boston: Houghton Mifflin, 1947), p. 403.

Within the AAA, perhaps the most potentially powerful of the liberals was Jerome Frank, leader of its young reformist lawyers. Born in New York, educated in Chicago, Frank had been recommended by Harvard's Felix Frankfurter for the highest legal post in the Department of Agriculture, but a political mistake made him General Counsel of the AAA instead. Frank, a quick, slender, dapper, smallish man, was the author of several professional articles and the book *Law and the Modern Mind.* In his Georgetown home in Washington, he and his wife, a poet and playwright, entertained such friends as Carl Sandburg, Max Eastman, and Sherwood Anderson.[2] To Jerome Frank the AAA was far more than a price-raising device; he insisted that government aid should "go in fair and equitable proportion to actual producers of agricultural commodities, including sharecroppers. . . . The [Agricultural Adjustment] Act refers first and foremost to producers who contribute the labor incident to the production."[3]

The AAA's novel Consumers' Counsel, established to keep AAA marketing agreements from favoring producers over consumers, was another stronghold of the liberals. Frederic C. Howe, "lean, full of zip and humor at the age of sixty-six," one of the old Wilsonians, headed the Counsel and staffed it with men who were as zealous as he in protecting the consumer's pocketbook.[4] One of the more energetic of these aides was a hearty, audacious ex-journalist named Gardner (Pat) Jackson, a man with abundant charm for his friends and disdain for his enemies, a man who was soon to become one of the chief assets of the Southern Tenant Farmers' Union. His wealth was inherited, and perhaps also his sympathy for the disadvantaged: his father, William Sharpless Jackson, a wealthy Colorado banker and railroad president, had married an unusually brilliant

2. "Unofficial Observer," *New Dealers*, pp. 96–98; various interviews with Gardner Jackson, 1961–62; *Who's Who in America*, Vol. XVIII (1934–35), p. 559; Schlesinger, *Coming of the New Deal*, pp. 49–52.

3. "Suggested basis for preparation of statement of policy with reference to landlord-tenant relationships," attached to memo, Robert K. McConnaughey to D. P. Trent, September 15, 1934, in L-TS, RG 145, N Arch.

4. "Unofficial Observer," *New Dealers*, pp. 67–68; Lord, *Wallaces of Iowa*, pp. 396–398, 403.

and perceptive woman, Helen Hunt, author of the famous indictment of United States Indian policy, *A Century of Dishonor.*
When she was dying, she asked Jackson to marry her like-
minded niece. This he did. To this marriage Gardner Jackson
was born, in Colorado Springs in the fall of 1896. At Amherst,
the influence of Alexander Meiklejohn further stimulated his
progressive sympathies, and during the 1920's he devoted most
of his time to the crusade for Sacco and Vanzetti.[5] To Jackson,
service in the AAA represented, at the moment, the best way
he could fight for the victims of the status quo.

On the other hand, no matter how many men such as Jackson
one may find in an organization, the prognosis for their success
is always dim if their superiors strongly disagree with them. At
the helm of the AAA, for example, stood Chester Davis, solid,
respectable, responsible only to Wallace and antagonistic only
to disturbances. Though born on an Iowa farm, Davis's entire
career had been spent as an agricultural journalist, administrator, and lobbyist rather than as a farm operator. One of the
first "agribusinessmen," he was staid, conservative, and almost
humorless—except when he was, in the words of an admirer,
"blowing up outbursts of bombast or excesses of agitation with
a quiet laugh."[6]

Davis's mode of operation was well illustrated by his response to the first report of sharecropper unrest that reached
him. Early in 1934, a thoroughly orthodox Extension Service
official, Dover Parham Trent, became so alarmed over evidence
of sharecropper victimization that he suggested that Davis or
Wallace might make a "very frank and positive public statement
. . . that there is evidence to indicate that many thousands of
share tenants and share-croppers are being denied their rights
and their equitable share of the benefits . . . , that the Government has an obligation to see that these benefits actually go to
those for whom they are intended and that the Government
does propose to meet this obligation fully and fearlessly by

5. Murray Kempton, *Part of Our Time* (New York: Simon and Schuster, 1955), pp. 43–45, 52; interview with Gardner Jackson, August 14,
1961.

6. Lord, *Wallaces of Iowa*, pp. 400–401; "Unofficial Observer," *New
Dealers,* pp. 99–102.

protecting tenant farmers to the fullest possible extent."[7] Davis considered Trent's private memorandum, and then had him prepare a second statement, this one for public use. The second statement claimed that only a tiny minority of landlords would ever exploit their tenants—and, alas, "it is doubtful if any plan might be devised which would prevent a certain amount of such practice," because "no . . . cotton adjustment program can change human nature."[8]

That Davis was capable of such responses could be traced, at least partially, to the fact that he was such an orderly man: in matters affecting the cotton reduction program, he consulted, naturally enough, with men who "knew" the South: men like the county agents. Officials, in other words, who represented the planters. The foremost among these was the head of the Cotton Section, Cully A. Cobb, who, like Davis, had been primarily a farm journalist. The son of a Mississippi Baptist preacher, the Rev. Napoleon Bonaparte Cobb, he remained "sort of the Southern preacher type," as a friendly associate remembered him—or "the epitome of the Southern mint-julep drinking, back-slapping, guffawing planter," in the eyes of a more hostile contemporary. Large, affable, ponderous and oratorical when speaking or writing, he came to believe that his opposition in the AAA was Communist inspired.[9] Perhaps this feeling originated from Cobb's first attempt to discover the sources of sharecropper unrest, when he asked a trusted county agent to tell him about the Amberson-Mitchell-East sharecropper eviction survey and received the following telegram in reply: "DOCTOR WILLIAM R. AMBERSON ON STAFF MEDICAL DE-PARTMENT UNIVERSITY OF TENNESSEE CHIEF OF POLICE REPORTS

7. D. P. Trent to Chester C. Davis, February 15, 1934, in Cotton Production Control Folder, AAA Production Control Program Reports, RG 145, N Arch.

8. "Statement of the Results of Cotton Program . . .," n.d. [February, 1934], Cotton Production Control Folder, AAA Production Control Program Reports, RG 145, N Arch.

9. Interviews with Gardner Jackson, June 30, 1961, and Sam Bledsoe, July 10, 1962; Rodney Dutcher, "Freezing Out of Sharecroppers Revealed," Memphis *Press-Scimitar*, April 22, 1936; *Who's Who in America*, Vol. XVIII (1934–35), p. 559; David Eugene Conrad, *The Forgotten Farmers* (Urbana: University of Illinois Press, 1965), pp. 114–15.

HIM FULL FLEDGED COMMUNIST HAS MADE NUMBER EFFORTS TO
START UPRISINGS AMONG NEGROES ALL THREE INDIVIDUALS LOCALLY
REGARDED VERY DANGEROUS"[10]

Though forewarned, Cobb nevertheless decided to send an
investigator, E. A. Miller, to the Arkansas Delta. Miller arrived,
refused to look at Clay East's card file of eviction evidence, and
went out to learn the truth from the plantation owners. Unanimously, they declared all their tenant houses were full. This
satisfied Miller that nobody had been evicted, that no large
families had been replaced with small ones, that no whites had
been replaced with more docile Negroes, and that all the miserable occupants of the tenant houses had crops to farm despite
the AAA reduction. Miller called on H. L. Mitchell and told
him—according to Mitchell—that he should abandon agitation,
because "the landlords are all your friends and these sharecroppers are a shiftless lot. There is no use of being concerned
about them as they don't really count. They are here today and
gone tomorrow."[11]

But Cobb and Miller were not to have the last word on the
problem. Their impressions were quickly eclipsed by the appearance of "Human Problems in Acreage Reduction in the
South," a monograph written with care and scholarly accuracy
by Calvin B. Hoover of Duke University and the AAA economics staff. The Hoover report—directed expressly to Administrator Chester Davis—exposed the cheating, expressed grave
doubts about features of the 1934–35 program then underway,
and, in general, corroborated the substance of the journalistic
exposés which were appearing with increasing, and embarass-
ing, frequency at the time the report appeared early in 1934.
Whatever Davis might have felt, the document convinced Secretary Wallace that tenants were being victimized; he kept this
conviction from inspiring any sudden Secretarial crusades, how-

10. W. M. Landess to Cully Cobb, March 10, 1934, in Norcross Folder,
L-TS, RG 145, N Arch.

11. William R. Amberson to Paul Appleby, November 21, 1934, and
H. L. Mitchell to R. F. Croom, April 8, 1936, both in STFU Papers;
Norman Thomas, *The Plight of the Share-Cropper* (New York: League
for Industrial Democracy, 1934, pp. 11–12; Cully Cobb, "Procedure . . .
Tenant-Landlord Relationships in Arkansas," n.d. [1934]; E. A. Miller to
Cully A. Cobb, March 19, 1934, both in Norcross Folder, L-TS, RG 145,
N Arch.

ever. Instead, he simply admitted in press conferences, briefly and in passing, that the situation of the tenants left something to be desired.[12]

Wallace publicly minimized the problem because he was reluctant to supply enemies of the New Deal with ammunition, but he saw to it that the Hoover report stimulated much soul-searching in the privacy of AAA offices. First it had to be decided who would initiate the necessary action. Over Cully Cobb's protests, even before the Hoover report appeared, a Committee on Violations of Rental and Benefit Contracts had been set up including representatives of the General Counsel and the Comptroller in addition to one from the Cotton Section. In May a Compliance Section was established, ostensibly to check up on withdrawn acreage, but with its jurisdiction so vague as to overlap that of the Committee on Violations. Still later in the year Jerome Frank, leader of the AAA liberals, successfully urged the establishment of a Committee on Landlord-Tenant Relationships. Yet none of these three committees was assigned to investigate the Hoover report disclosures. A new investigating committee, appointed especially for the task, was set up with Extension Service veterans J. Phil Campbell and D. P. Trent at its head. Formation of the committee was accompanied by an official statement that the AAA "recognizes very clearly that some displacement of labor has resulted from the adjustment program."[13]

Nevertheless, Chester Davis was sure that the Campbell-Trent investigators should begin with two fundamental principles in mind. In the first place, he told them, "it is not intended that the [Agricultural Adjustment] Act should be used in an

12. Paul H. Appleby to John P. Davis, April 3, 1934, "Negroes (1934)" folder, RG 16, N Arch; Calvin B. Hoover, "Human Problems in Acreage Reduction in the South," personal report to Henry A. Wallace and Chester C. Davis (Durham: Duke University, March, 1934), *passim*; "Cotton-Crop Cut Injures Tenants, Admits Wallace," *New Orleans Times-Picayune*, May 3, 1934; Lord, *Wallaces of Iowa*, p. 376.

13. Paul W. Bruton to Jerome Frank, May 21, 1934, Folder 466, Solicitor's File, RG 16, N Arch; see also Alger Hiss, "Memorandum of Conference . . . July 3, 1934," in "Tenancy (1934)" folder, RG 16, N Arch; Paul A. Porter, "Acreage Adjustment and Agricultural Labor," May 10, 1934, in Agricultural Labor folder, Calvin Hoover Papers, RG 145, N. Arch.

effort to deal with deep-seated social problems." (Davis might have been unaware that this statement denied the avowed purpose of the act as stated in its preamble and as understood by those who drafted and supported it.) Second, the AAA would not "undertake to dictate the usual and normal relationships and tenure arrangements" in the South, said Davis, implying that tenants should get all the payments due them, but should not expect the AAA to defend them against a change in status. Secretary Wallace fully agreed with Davis.[14] Apparently both men had forgotten Section 24 of the AAA's 1934–35 administrative rulings:

Change in Status of Tenant.—No 1934 and 1935 Cotton Acreage Reduction Contract . . . will be accepted if it shall *appear* that there exists between said landlord and tenant any lease, contract, *agreement, or understanding* . . . the effect or purpose of which is:

(a) To cause or obligate . . . the tenant or the share cropper to pay over . . . his share of any payment . . .; or

(b) *To change the status of any tenant for 1935* . . .; or

(c) To reduce the tenant's or the share cropper's proportionate share of the crops . . .; or

(d) To increase the rent to be paid by the tenant . . .; *of if there is any reason to believe* that the landlord has adopted *any device or scheme of any sort whatever* for the purpose of depriving a tenant of any kind or a share cropper of his share of such payments or of *any other right under such contract.*[15]

From his erroneous premises, Davis quite logically derived certain specific instructions for his "investigators." They were to work hand-in-glove with the planters and county agents "who have had charge of the cotton adjustment program in the states and counties. . . . The work which you are to do in investigating and adjusting difficulties must be done in such a way as not to reflect unfavorably upon the work which has already been done by these local leaders. . . . *Nothing must be*

14. Chester C. Davis to "District Agents and Others . . .," May 5, 1934; AAA Press Release, "Conference Called on Cotton Contract Compliance," May 2, 1934, both in L-TS, RG 145, N Arch.

15. United States Department of Agriculture, AAA, "Administrative Rulings . . . 1934 and 1935 Cotton Acreage Adjustment Plan," (Washington: G. P. O., February, 1935), Sec. 24, p. 12. Italics mine. See also United States Department of Agriculture, AAA, "Cotton Regulations Pertaining to Option-Benefit, Benefit, and Option Contracts . . ." (Washington: G. P. O., July, 1933), Art. II, Sec. 209.

*done which might cause them to feel that their actions are being questioned,"* Davis instructed. Furthermore, he advised, no "small minority should be permitted to cast a cloud upon the whole program and bring criticism upon the South and upon the Agricultural Adjustment Administration. . . . The work which you are to do is as much for the protection of the committeemen, county agents, landowners and . . . the Agricultural Adjustment Administration" as anything else, Davis concluded.[16]

With Chester Davis calling for a whitewash, the result was a foregone conclusion. His instructions were obeyed explicitly by the field representatives; the ones in Arkansas reported that they began their "investigation" at the office of the state Extension Service, which "suggested the territory which should be investigated first, made out an itinerary for the work and instructed the county agents. . . . Both the county agents and the county committeemen were very friendly toward the investigations. The county agents provided office facilities and clerical help . . . and were present in person when the majority of cases were investigated." The real trouble, these "investigators" hinted, was the union organization that was getting under way in the Delta that summer: "Most of these complaints came from certain counties where agitators had attempted to stir up trouble."[17] Except for the union, the croppers would be in fine shape, said a warehouse operator. "All of them that I know are . . . paid out of debt, has some money left . . . The thing, in my opinion, that has created a disturbance up there and made it necessary to move more sharecroppers than usual has been due to the propaganda of H. L. Mitchell . . . telling them first that they were mistreated and that they were not getting their proper share of government rent. . . . That, of course, created a situation in which some of those fellows were not desirable tenants."[18]

Although the government "investigators" knew as well as the warehouse operators that the whole matter had been provoked

16. Davis to "District Agents and Others . . .," May 5, 1934, in L-TS, RG 145, N Arch; Xerox copy in possession of author. Italics mine.
17. J. Phil Campbell *et al.*, "Report of Adjustment Committee on Investigation of Landlord-Tenant Complaints," September 1, 1934, in L-TS, RG 145, N Arch.
18. F. D. Russell, testimony to legislative investigating committee, February 18, 1935, CCP, Reel 1.

by agitators, they had to be fair enough to call on the agitators. The one that saw Clay East was W. J. Green, who

first was wined and dined by the planters for several days, the colored people reported this to me, well one morning he came to my station and said that he would like to talk to me alone. . . . He then said that he was interested in violations of the contract only. I told [him] by God to come back at ten in the morning and I would have them for him. . . . The following morning he came marching in with a bunch of landlords several of which were county commissioners, I handed him a typewritten paper with eleven specific cases where planters had empty houses in which families had lived the year before, I gave the exact number of families they had the previous year, the number at that time, the location of the farm and the owner. Mr. Green began reading these off, most all of these men were present. . . . Green told these men that the contract meant just what it said and that they had better get things straightened out. He left for Memphis that afternoon and reported to the paper mentioned [the *Commercial Appeal*], that no violations were found.[19]

Because the AAA was extremely sensitive to criticism, it is quite possible that Green gave a false report to the *Commercial Appeal*. But he did tell the truth, as he saw it, to his superiors. "Many of the conditions mentioned are no doubt true," he admitted, "although it is only natural for these [STFU] men to give examples of extreme cases in the work which they are doing." Other Arkansas "investigators" were either less honest or more closely supervised than Green. "The charges [were] found to be without foundation," reported one. "There were instances of eviction of undesirable tenants . . . but in all cases the landlord was justified." Another investigator explained that "the parties complaining . . . were the type who intended to 'get all they could out of the Government' and who had the wrong conception of the AAA program."[20] By now, obviously, the "right" conception of the program was Chester Davis's and Cully Cobb's.

The Campbell-Trent Committee on Violations continued its "investigations" well into the next year, but by the fall of 1934 the pattern of its "disclosures" was evident. Of 1,457 complaints

19. Clay East to the author, n.d. [received August 14, 1961].
20. W. J. Green to Cully A. Cobb, March 5, 1935, in STFU folder, L-TS, RG 145, N Arch; Campbell *et al.*, "Report . . .," September 1, 1934, L-TS, RG 145, N Arch.

investigated to that time, 1,040 were called "unjustified," with no remedial action whatever. (In Arkansas 346 of 477 were so labeled; in Mississippi 54 of 65.) Only twenty-one AAA contracts were revoked, eleven of them in Arkansas. The results of the "investigations" were hailed by everybody in the South but the tenant farmers. "Here is an investigation that should certainly have been impartial and fair," said the *Arkansas Gazette*. "The report wholly refutes charges that were made last spring of the eviction of thousands of tenants and sharecroppers."[21] Chester Davis himself echoed the *Gazette*. After setting up the machinery of the "investigation" in such a manner as to guarantee the results, he felt perfectly free to use these results in at least one effort to convince Secretary Wallace that tales of evictions were phony.[22]

What was actually phony, the *denial* that tenants were being widely victimized, probably derived less from Davis's specific instructions to his "investigators" than from the fact that "investigation" of each complaint was wholly in the hands of the county agent-Extension Service network. In other words, the planters were investigating themselves. When a tenant first complained, therefore, "the complainant was asked to discuss his case with the county committee"; this was enough to discourage all but the most foolhardy or most outrageously cheated sharecroppers. Then, if the committee decided not to dismiss the complaint but to call in the AAA field investigator, the investigator's orders were to consult "the state director of extension and others connected with the cotton program." Leaving to go into the county, "he arrived without any public announcement. . . . He first discussed the matter fully with the county agent and the county committee in order to get as much firsthand information as possible." If the tenant was not yet scared off, he was made to confront his landlord "in order to discuss the circumstances in the case." If, after all this, the tenant's complaint was still thought by his planter-judges to be serious enough to merit action, some kind of compromise settlement

21. Campbell *et al.*, "Report . . .," September 1, 1934, L-TS, RG 145, N Arch; *Arkansas Gazette*, August 25, 1934, August 27, 1934.

22. Interview with Sam Bledsoe, July 10, 1962; Chester Davis to Henry Wallace, December 26, 1934, in Norcross folder, L-TS, RG 145, N Arch.

was sought.[23] Only if the planter refused to accept even a compromise was his AAA contract revoked. After the contract was canceled, of course, the AAA had no authority to protect a "successful" complainant from the wrath of his landlord.

This discriminatory procedure was not only satisfactory to Davis and the Cotton Section, but to Secretary Wallace himself. Indeed, to Wallace this delivery of the tenants to the planters was democracy of the purest hue. "If these county associations, composed of the farmers themselves, were subordinated to a local machinery operated from Washington," said he, "we might lose much that has been developed . . . toward a democratically administered machine for dealing with agricultural problems."[24] Wallace apparently did not know that over half the farmers of the South were tenants and that almost none of them were on AAA boards. The county committees, like the county courthouses, were possessions of the oligarchy that ran the South with one-party irresponsibility.

Had Davis and Wallace read their mail, including the scrawled notepaper messages, they would have realized this fact. One cropper told AAA officials he could hardly believe they were serious in telling him to deal with the local committee: "Even the committee has done that," he protested, "and we cannit get results by replying to thim fer they ar crooked the Bunch." Wrote another, "I would suggest to not let the County Agent look after this matter as he is a staunch friend to Polk [the allegedly unfair landlord]. Will you please not let Mr. Polk or the County Agent see this letter as Mr. Polk is a dangerous man."[25] The county agent in this case was no exception; most of them sided with landlords quite openly, and at least one, C. C. Morris of Corsicana, Texas, told the AAA that he thought tenants had no right to any part of the benefit payments. County agents generally acted as defense attorneys for accused planters,

23. *Ibid.*; Campbell *et al.*, "Report . . .," September 1, 1934, L-TS, RG 145, N Arch.

24. Henry A. Wallace, speech on cotton program over WMAL, January 23, 1934, script in "Speeches of the Secretary (1934)" file, RG 16, N Arch.

25. W. W. Winter to the Department of Justice, October 23, 1934, folder 1316, Solicitor's File, RG 16, N Arch; Paul W. Bruton to Jerome Frank, Supplement A, May 21, 1934, folder 466, Solicitor's File, RG 16, N Arch.

while their friends on the committee were judge and jury. In one typical case, the final report of the committee—which found for the landlord—was signed by the same committeeman who had submitted a signed statement in support of the landlord's case and who was himself accused of violations by his own tenants. (AAA's Legal Section, examining the evidence in this particular case, decided that the tenant's position should have been upheld.[26] But there was nothing that could be done to change the decision.)

This county committee discrimination was open enough for reporters to see even on brief trips into the area. One who discovered abundant evidence of cheating noted that "the AAA here [Memphis] has been powerless to correct that, because its local representatives usually are plantation owners."[27] These planters, another journalist observed, "have been in the habit of exploiting the economic, social, and political weakness of their tenants [and] they cannot be expected suddenly to mend their ways in the spirit of the New Deal. Tenants have no representation on these boards. . . . It is not surprising that the luscious fruits of the New Deal should fall largely into the hands of the powerful planters."[28]

Following the victory of the conservatives in the Campbell-Trent "investigation," the Legal Section liberals began gradually to turn to the wording of the AAA Cotton Contract itself in their effort to protect sharecropper rights. Section 7 of this contract, which had to be signed by every cotton planter in the South as a condition of receiving benefit payments, required the landlord to

. . . endeavor in good faith to bring about the reduction of acreage contemplated in this contract in such a manner as to cause the least possible amount of labor, economic and social disturbance, and to this end, insofar as possible, he shall effect the acreage reduction as

26. C. C. Morris to Mordecai Ezekiel, January 9, 1935, and Ezekiel to Morris, January 14, 1935, in "Tenancy (1935)" folder, RG 16, N Arch; Exhibit "B," contract no. 71–056–476, and Exhibit "C," contract no. 71–056–714, attached to Margaret B. Bennett to Jerome Frank, February 4, 1935, folder 465, Solicitor's File, RG 16, N Arch.
27. Rodney Dutcher, "Freezing Out of Sharecroppers Revealed," Memphis *Press-Scimitar*, April 22, 1936.
28. Carroll Binder, "Federal Benefits Intended to Aid Tenant . . . Went to Landlord," *Chicago Daily News*, April 9, 1934.

nearly ratably as practicable among tenants on this farm; *shall, insofar as possible, maintain on this farm the normal number of tenants and other employees; shall permit all tenants to continue in the occupancy of their houses on this farm,* rent free, for the years 1934 and 1935, respectively (unless any such tenant shall so conduct himself as to become a nuisance or a menace to the welfare of the producer); during such years shall afford such tenants or employees, without cost, access for fuel to such woods land belonging to this farm as he may designate; shall permit such tenants the use of an adequate portion of the rented acres to grow food and feed crops for home consumption and for pasturage for domestically used livestock; and for such use of the rented acres shall permit the reasonable use of work animals and equipment in exchange for labor.[29]

Administrator Davis, sadly accepting the proposition that there was no way to enforce the "insofar as possible" clauses, comforted Wallace and himself with the thought that the very next clause provided for "all tenants to continue in the occupancy" of their shacks—and it was provided that this "shall" be done, not "shall, insofar as possible." This was a perceptive observation. Unfortunately, by Davis's literal interpretation of the contract this clause would be as meaningless as the one preceding it. For it plainly stated that "all tenants," not "all persons," were entitled to remain in their shacks. And if a person no longer had a crop, if the landlord no longer found it possible to keep him as a tenant, then he no longer *was* a tenant and consequently was no longer protected by the clause to which Davis attached such importance. Only if the two crucial clauses were interpreted in the context of the whole paragraph—and thus enforced—could tenants be protected.

What did the contract really mean, then? As controversy grew more heated, as the conservative-liberal battle lines were drawn more tightly, both sides sought out the man who had drafted Section 7: wealthy Oscar Johnston, manager of the AAA Cotton Pool and of the British-owned Delta and Pine Land Company, a huge plantation near Scott, Mississippi. Johnston insisted that the paragraph was only "a proviso morally obli-

29. Henry Irving Richards, *Cotton and the AAA* (Washington: The Brookings Institution, 1936), pp. 140–41, and J. F. Cox to C. B. Baldwin, April 11, 1934, in L-TS, RG 145, N Arch, both contain the full text of Section 7 of the cotton contract. Italics mine.

gating landowners," not one intended to be legally enforceable.[30] Cobb and the conservatives enthusiastically agreed. They were willing to make only one concession: they would grant that the same number of tenants had to be kept, but not the same tenants. When the Legal Section argued that this protected "tenancies, not tenants," the conservatives merely shrugged. The AAA's lawyers, they felt, had no right to tell farmers what a contract meant.[31] On this issue the battle within the AAA was finally to be joined.

The occasion for the showdown was provided by Hiram Norcross, a planter from Tyronza, Arkansas, who was so notorious among his tenants that many, in desperation, joined the Southern Tenant Farmers' Union. Norcross then decided that all his union tenants had to go, but he first went to County Agent R. L. McGill to find out if there would be any legal difficulty involved. McGill assured him—and also told STFU attorney C. T. Carpenter—that "if Mr. Norcross sees fit, he might move all of the tenants off his place and the only concern that we might have would be that he replace them with an equal number." AAA's W. J. Green confirmed McGill's advice. "The cotton reduction contract does not prevent the landlord from renting the land to another person in 1935," he told H. L. Mitchell.[32] Norcross proceeded to pass out the eviction notices. Writing from a hotel in Kansas City, he told the AAA that "it is of vital importance to every landlord whether he has the right to select who shall be a tenant," and by long-distance telephone he or-

30. Oscar Johnston to Chester Davis, January 26, 1935; Johnston, statement quoted in C. T. Carpenter, Brief for Appellants Winburn West *et al., vs.* H. Norcross, Appellee, in the Supreme Court of Arkansas, n.d. [1934].

31. Margaret Bennet to Henry Wallace, January 12, 1935, Folder 467, Solicitor's File, RG 16, N Arch; "Memorandum to Mr. McConnaughey, Assistant Chief, Benefit Contract Section," January 7, 1935, L-TS, RG 145, N Arch; William R. Amberson, "The New Deal for Share-Croppers," *Nation*, February 13, 1935, pp. 185–87; Cully Cobb to Chester Davis, February 6, 1935, L-TS, RG 145, N Arch.

32. Transcript of H. L. Mitchell's recorded interview for the Columbia University Oral History Collection, STFU Papers and elsewhere (referred to hereafter as Oral History MS), pp. 8–9, 12–13, 21; W. J. Green to H. L. Mitchell, October 17, 1934, in Commodity Stabilization Service Records, RG 145, N Arch.

dered his lawyers to kick out of their cabins all of the evictees
who had not yet moved.[33]

C. T. Carpenter drew up a brief for the evicted tenants and
presented his case against Norcross in the Poinsett County
Chancery Court. As he had expected, the case was lost, and he
appealed it to the Supreme Court of Arkansas. Carpenter held
it to be "a well-recognized rule of law that where it is the intent
of the parties to a contract to benefit thereby a third party and
there is adequate designation of the third party to be benefitted,
and privity exists between the promisees and the third party,
such third party may sue at law for damages, or in equity to
specifically enforce the contract."[34]

Even as Carpenter was appealing the lower court decision,
he was also trying to secure administrative action from the AAA.
The editor of the Memphis *Press-Scimitar*, Edward J. Meeman,
joined Carpenter in the appeal, attempting to have Henry Wallace himself force the AAA to take action against Norcross. Both
men believed, as Carpenter put it, that landlords "will stop
their high-handed course the minute they realize that the Department will enforce its contract."[35]

There was additional pressure from the agricultural liberals
themselves. Wallace's chief aide, Paul Appleby, again demanded that AAA actively protect tenants; "the worst indictment of the Bankhead Bill [which enforced AAA cotton reduc-
tion] has been its effect on the sharecropper and tenant farmer,"
said Appleby, adding that this calamity had been foreseen,
warned against, and finally illustrated dramatically by the
Norcross case. Paul Porter, the AAA's chief publicist, told Jerome Frank that papers across the country had carried the news
that the Norcross evictees had been afforded no remedy when
they appealed to their local AAA committee, because Norcross

33. Hiram Norcross to Paul Appleby, January 5, 1935, in Norcross
folder, L-TS, RG 145, N Arch.
34. C. T. Carpenter, Brief for Appellants Winburn West *et al.*, *vs.* H.
Norcross, Appellee, in the Supreme Court of Arkansas, n.d. [1935], STFU
Papers; *Modern News* [Harrisburg, Ark.], March 29, 1935; *West v. Nor-
cross*, 190 Ark. 667, 672 (1935).
35. C. T. Carpenter to Jerome Frank, January 11, 1935, and Mary
Connor Myers to Frank (telegram), January 18, 1935, both in folder 467,
Solicitor's File, RG 16, N Arch; Edward J. Meeman to Henry A. Wallace,
December 24, 1934, in Norcross folder, L-TS, RG 145, N Arch.

himself was chairman of it. Obviously the evictions had been for union membership, Porter said, calling on Frank to act.[36] A field representative of the landlord-oriented Committee on Violations, who didn't believe that the contract could possibly be used to protect all tenants from eviction, nevertheless called on the AAA to "let it be known in no unmistakable terms, that it would not interpret the mere fact of joining a union . . . as constituting a tenant a nuisance or menace."[37] But most landlords knew little of the conflict within the AAA, so they remained quite open about their feelings. Typical was R. B. Snowden of Hughes, Arkansas; "should my own tenants 'unionize' against me," he commented, "I would carefully prepare to get along without tenants . . . unionizing my tenants will certainly destroy the mutual understanding which exists in most cases between tenants and their landlords."[38]

Through all of this, Jerome Frank had showed remarkable restraint. If the interpretation of a contract is not a lawyer's business, nothing is; yet for the better part of a year representatives of the Cotton Section and the Committee on Violations had been maintaining that a contract provision aimed at minimizing labor displacement really meant almost the opposite, legally—that a landlord could evict as many tenants as he wanted to, provided he replaced them. It was said in defense of this position that it kept displacement as low as any other contract interpretation could; if the same *number* of tenants were kept, certainly there could be no *net increase* in the number of rural unemployed. This argument, unfortunately, overlooked the fact that a single man could be substituted for a large family, the fact that a new tenant could be allotted so small an acreage that despite his nominal tenant status he was really a casually employed wage worker, the fact that a simple legal

36. Paul Appleby to Cully Cobb, December 27, 1934, L-TS, RG 145, N Arch; Paul Porter to Jerome Frank, January 3, 1935, folder 465, Solicitor's File, RG 16, N Arch.

37. Lafayette Patterson to Victor Christgau, January 22, 1935, folder 467, Solicitor's File, RG 16, N Arch.

38. Hughes is quoted in the Memphis *Press-Scimitar*, February 14, 1935. Evidently this landlord-tenant "mutual understanding" was something mystical, like the "sacred doctor-patient relationship" that would have been destroyed by public medical care in the 1960's, according to the physician's union.

document could substitute paper tenants for real ones, and the fact that benefit checks could very easily get "lost" in the shuffle as old tenants moved out and new ones moved in. All this assumed that new tenants would actually be brought in to replace evicted ones. Since other provisions of the contract had been evaded so widely, there must have been a few instances in which evicted tenants were never replaced.

For some time, Frank attempted to win others to his view of what the contract required, without insisting on it. Margaret Bennett kept persuasively presenting the Legal Section's conception of the contract to the Committee on Violations; but every time she did so, she was voted down by the Committee's Cotton Section and Comptroller's Section representatives. Finally, with the Norcross case before the Arkansas Supreme Court, she, too, appealed directly to Secretary Wallace: "Nothing could be more effective in stopping this [public] criticism and in indicating to the public that the Secretary is, in fact, attempting to carry out the declared policy of the Act (that is, to increase not only the price of agricultural commodities, but also the purchasing power of *all farmers*) than a declaration by the Secretary at this time that an effort will be made to enforce paragraph 7 and participation by the Secretary in the Norcross litigation."[39]

At the same time, Frank finally decided to insist that *all* legal matters, rather than all legal matters except for Section 7 of the cotton contract, be handled by the Legal Section. With the Norcross case revealing the weakness of Cully Cobb's law practice, "my offhand opinion is that such legal interpretations by the Cotton Section will not affect the legal obligations of the landlords under Paragraph 7," said Frank. "I assume that . . . the legal opinion of the office of the General Counsel will be accepted rather than the legal opinion of representatives of the Cotton Section and the Comptroller's Office."[40] Thereupon he turned the question over to his subordinates for consideration

39. Margaret Bennett to Henry Wallace, January 12, 1935, folder 467, Solicitor's File, RG 16, N Arch; "Memorandum to Mr. McConnaughey," January 7, 1935, L-TS, RG 145, N Arch.
40. Jerome Frank to Henry Wallace, January 12, 1935, and Frank to William E. Byrd, January 14, 1935, both in Norcross folder, L-TS, RG 145, N. Arch.

in detail, in order to formulate the first official interpretation of the Section.

There was another reason for the long-postponed decision: the Southern Tenant Farmers' Union had sent a delegation to Washington to place the issue directly before the AAA. It was all very well to be suing landlords and making publicity down in the Delta, but the union leaders knew that nothing could take the place of direct confrontation. So Mitchell, with the Tyronza leader, Alvin Nunnally, and the two Marked Tree local presidents, E. B. McKinney and Walter Moskop, began driving to Washington. They spent 48 hours on the road, got lost in a convict work camp, and arrived barely in time to attend a meeting of agricultural labor leaders arranged by Pat Jackson. Very early the next day, after much needed sleep, the STFU leaders went to the Department of Agriculture to present Dr. Amberson's letter of introduction to his old friend Paul Appleby. Appleby greeted them warmly and scheduled an immediate meeting with Wallace.

The Secretary of Agriculture was polite, a sympathetic listener, but noncommittal.[41] He did promise another investigation of the STFU charges, but, his view of the "democratic" local AAA committees being what it was, he seemed to feel that the sharecropper spokesmen could benefit from a session with Cully Cobb and his men. This last meeting was approximately as friendly and productive as one could expect. Cobb dwelt at length on the fact that none of the STFU leaders had any personal grievance against the AAA. This fact seemed to impress the cotton spokesmen more than anything else; "summed up," they told each other, "two of the delegates, Mitchell and Moscop, were not farmers; one McKinney, colored, had no grievance, and one, Nunnally, a sharecropper, had been asked to vacate, due mainly [to factors beyond the AAA's control]."[42]

Unlike the Cotton Section, the Legal Section managed to grasp the idea that the STFU delegates were speaking not for themselves but for thousands. Now that Wallace had promised

41. Oral History MS, pp. 31–34; Mitchell, unsigned first person MS, n.d., pp. 7–9, STFU Papers.
42. W. J. Green, "Report of Conference . . . held in Mr. Cobb's Office January 10, 1935," and W. J. Green to Cully Cobb, March 5, 1935, both in STFU folder, L-TS, RG 145, N Arch.

another investigation, Jerome Frank was ready to make it a real one. Cobb knew of Frank's determination and could see the showdown coming. Even before the union representatives arrived, he had tried to select an attorney of his own for any possible forthcoming investigation. This expedient failed. William Byrd, Davis's assistant, agreed with Appleby that "a complete and unbiased report must be made immediately by representatives of the Administration other than the Cotton Section," and Cobb's attorney was rejected.[43] But Frank, to make the new investigation credible, wished to avoid bias on the opposite side as well. The Legal Section contained many liberals and radicals whose preconceptions might have influenced their findings: Miss Bennett, Robert McConnaughey, or Frank Shea, to name only the few most closely involved with the sharecropper issue. Instead, Frank chose to appoint the impartial Mrs. Mary Connor Myers, a Bostonian with red hair, a firm jaw, and no past connections with the liberal "agitators" in AAA. On the contrary, one of her strongest recommendations for employment had come from one of George Peek's conservative associates who praised her for being "particularly well informed on administrative law."[44] A further indication that Frank wanted nothing more or less than the truth was his full agreement that Mrs. Myers's inquiries should be conducted in secret.

As soon as Mrs. Myers arrived in the Delta she rented a small office in Marked Tree, in the same little brick building in which Carpenter had his office. She agreed to have STFU members show her what had happened, and began touring the area with them. She was profoundly shocked by the condition of the sharecroppers. At the same time, she was impressed with their kindness and courtesy, their fortitude under trying conditions, and the extent to which they had been almost completely denied knowledge of their rights under the AAA reduction program.

43. William E. Byrd to Paul Appleby, January 9, 1935, in L-TS, RG 145, N Arch; Cully Cobb to Jerome Frank, January 5, 1935, Frank to Victor Anderson, January 8, 1935, Anderson to Robert K. McConnaughey, January 9, 1935, and Jerome Frank to Henry Wallace, January 12, 1935, all in folder 467, Solicitor's File, RG 16, N Arch.
44. "Southern Sharecroppers Are Real Forgotten Men," *Philadelphia Inquirer*, March 6, 1935, clipping in CCP, Reel 1; Charles J. Brand to Henry Wallace, September 1, 1933, Mary Connor Myers folder, RG 145, N Arch.

With difficulty she kept her reactions from being noted by reporters, but she sent a confidential telegram to Jerome Frank: "HAVE HEARD ONE LONG STORY HUMAN GREED . . . SECTION SEVEN ONLY ONE SECTION CONTRACT BEING OPENLY AND GENERALLY VIOLATED . . . MAILING MILD SAMPLE AFFIDAVIT TONIGHT . . . CROPPERS MUCH HIGHER CLASS THAN I EXPECTED AND ALL PATHETICALLY PLEASED GOVERNMENT HAS SENT SOME ONE TO LISTEN TO THEM. . . ."[45] Mrs. Myers secured hundreds of scrawled statements from cheated sharecroppers and tenants. This one came from Booker Lamberth, Frank James, and Bill Gougey: "at cotton picking time he [landlord C. E. Hughes] brought some blank sheet of paper for us to sing [sign] ant told us we had to sing them or not sell cotton . . . our pardie [parity] money we have not got it." From Mack Cutler: "They gave one half of the corn and ordered [me] to Move." From Charles Davis: "I plowed up 6 acrease of Cotton. And I Dident get No pay For it . . . I dident get no Lotmon [allotment] Book I Dident No What My Lotmon Wase an I Dident get no [tax exemption] tags." Oscar Horton: "I mde or Ginn 10. Bales of cotton all of Which was sold I have never had no Govenmt Book and dont no Just What my allotment Was." Charles Smith: "I Never Got no Govermet Tags they Sold my cotton Without my Signiture to it Also Charge me 10 dollars Per acre for 5 acres of corn Land." Harry McDaniels: "I have not got my Paritie Payment as yet and I has not heard from it." L. K. Funches: "This is Cerify that I Did not get any Tags for my cotton." Frank Woodard: "he Never give me no Lotment or tags and I have not got my Parity Mony he said that he did not Know any thing a bought it." Henderson Bentley: "Mr H N. Norcross is a out lower [outlaw] the way he is treated some Family White and Collard and Dear Secretary [Wallace] we Need Some help and it don't do no good for us to See the county committee for he tole us if Mr Norcross says move to move for them was Mr Norcross Houses . . . Dear Secretary Look for the poor labor and help us out for the land lord ar gantes us." Austin Williams: "We all here

45. Mary Conner Myers to Jerome Frank, January 18, 1935, folder 467, Solicitor's File, RG 16, N Arch; Herbert Barnes, "Conditions in South Beyond Words, Said," *Farmers National Weekly*, February 15, 1935; interview with Howard Kester, July 17, 1961; H. L. Mitchell, first person MS, n.d., p. 12; Oral History MS, pp. 38–39.

Signed our Rights from us . . . the Land Lords told us that we
Would hafter Sign or we coulden Get our cotton Ginned . . .
Please Dont Mention My Name." And there were many, many
others.[46]

Mrs. Myers had unlocked Pandora's box. She herself had seen
conditions in only one area, but newspaper hints that the AAA
had actually sent an impartial investigator into the field provoked responses elsewhere in the South. An attorney from Dy-
ersburg, Tennessee, expressing hope that there had been a
change of heart in the AAA, sent in a petition from fifty-two
managing share tenants alone who had been cheated. A Kennett, Missouri attorney assured the AAA that he had no personal axe to grind: he had more eviction cases than he could
handle. A "wholesale moving program" was going on, he reported, and the situation was becoming so serious that the local
Kiwanis club had formed a committee to try to get Federal
emergency aid for the evictees.[47]

It was widely understood at the time that the secrecy sur-
rounding Mrs. Myers's trip to the Delta was only to facilitate
her investigation. There was no doubt in anyone's mind that her
findings would be disclosed and acted upon. "If she finds the
fire, Secretary Wallace will put it out," the *Press-Scimitar* editorialized. The United Press told the nation that there would be
full disclosure of the results, and that if Administrator Davis
"concurs in Mrs. Myers' findings, he may proceed against vio-
lators for return of sums distributed to them in AAA benefit
payments on their promise of contract compliance."[48] But Mrs.
Myers returned to Washington, submitted her report—and nothing happened. Someone reported that Davis had been heard to
say it was "too hot" to release, and "hot" it must have been: so

46. These handwritten statements, which are only a few of those Mrs.
Myers collected, are in a manila envelope in folder 467, Solicitor's File,
RG 16, N Arch.
47. E. R. Slaughter *et al.*, petition to the Secretary of Agriculture, n.d.
[Feb., 1935]; Bert Hodge to Mary Connor Myers, February 8, 1935; Seth
Thomas to W. J. Green, March 9, 1935; W. R. Proffer to Mary Cannon
[*sic*] Myers, February 12, 1935; clipping from Kennett *Missourian*, February 8, 1935, all in folder 466–B, Solicitor's File, RG 16, N Arch.
48. "Wallace Will Put It Out," editorial in Memphis *Press-Scimitar*,
January 21, 1935; United Press dispatch in Memphis *Press-Scimitar*, February 9, 1935.

"hot" that a Bureau of Labor Statistics economist couldn't see a copy despite his assurances that "I shall treat it with the greatest confidence," and that it would only be used for the confidential briefing of a few high Department of Labor officials.[49] There is little evidence that the report got any farther than Chester Davis himself—although he told the author that it was passed along to the Cotton Section, as it may well have been. This, though, is not the most surprising thing about the suppression of the Myers Report; the fact is that over thirty years later the report still did not appear in the National Archives. Virtually all other papers relating to landlord-tenant matters are there, each in its proper place, but the Myers Report is missing.[50]

The suppression of the report caused an immediate outcry, ranging from the *Press-Scimitar*'s meek opinion that it was "too bad" Davis decided to withhold it ("Suppression is not the way to cure social evils") to the angry blasts of Drew Pearson. Pearson, in his syndicated "Washington Merry-Go-Round" column, said that the Senate might be asked to pass a resolution calling on Davis to submit the report; Gardner Jackson and several liberal Congressmen were behind the suggested move. Jackson organized a rather impressive demonstration of STFU members before the Department of Agriculture building, and Norman Thomas printed another edition of *The Plight of the Share-Cropper*, this time with an explicit challenge to print the Myers Report. Protest mail deluged AAA offices.[51] In response to the protests, the AAA implied that Mrs. Myers had investigated only a few specific cases, the results being withheld temporarily

49. Oral History MS, pp. 38–39; George Marshall to Mary Connor Myers, February 28, 1935, and Myers to Seth Thomas, March 2, 1935, both in folder 467, Solicitor's File, RG 16, N Arch.

50. The Chief of the Social and Economic Branch of the National Archives has told me on two occasions (Jane F. Smith to the author, August 21, 1962, and July 2, 1965) that years of searching on behalf of a number of interested scholars have failed to disclose a copy of the Myers Report. Chester Davis, however, in a letter to the author, August 7, 1962, furnished a clue regarding the mystery: the report, wrote Davis, "was a guided propaganda move . . . certainly was not a responsible finding," and cannot be found today probably because "the report just wasn't that important."

51. Memphis *Press-Scimitar*, February 22, 1935; Drew Pearson, "Washington Merry-Go-Round," *Arkansas Gazette*, March 10, 1935; copy of Thomas, *Plight of the Share-Cropper*, and attached memos in Thomas folder, L-TS, RG 145, N Arch.

pending legal action. The truth of the matter was that no legal action was apparently ever contemplated, let alone initiated. Furthermore, Mrs. Myers had not limited herself to investigation of one or two plantations; she had spoken with hundreds of sharecroppers on dozens of plantations across two counties.[52]

In keeping the lid on the report, some anxious bureaucrats became nearly paranoid: the Solicitor of the Department of Agriculture, for example, angrily charged that Mrs. Myers had violated the secrecy order by taking copies of the report home with her. At this, the long-suffering lady lawyer exploded. "My connection with this sharecropper situation has been the most humiliating professional experience I have had," she said, explaining that she had been told desks could be broken into and files were not safe enough, so consequently she should take copies of the document home with her where they could be locked up. With her explanation, she turned over her last copies of the report and announced she was "delighted to see the last of" it.[53] But that was not quite the last of it. Chester Davis asked her to submit a memo "of not more than two or at the most three pages in length giving in the most concise form possible your reasons why the report should or should not be made public."[54] Mrs. Myers did so. Her answer, like the report itself—and these two alone, apparently, of all the AAA records—does not appear in the National Archives.

The best summary of the lessons taught by the Myers Report suppression was given by a journalist who concluded, "It is clear that Wallace has no intentions of taking any steps likely to conflict with the interests of the planters. If he moves at all it will be as a result of the mass movement on the part of the Southern small farmers and tenants themselves."[55]

Meanwhile, even as Mrs. Myers left for Arkansas, Jerome

52. For some of the replies to those who protested, see J. P. Wenchel to Henry Schnautz, May 22, 1935, and many similar letters in folder 467, Solicitor's File, RG 16, and in "Mary Connor Myers" folder, L-TS, RG 145, N Arch; H. L. Mitchell to R. F. Croom, April 8, 1936, STFU Papers.
53. Mary Connor Myers to Seth Thomas, March 8, 1935, in folder 467, Solicitor's File, RG 16, N Arch.
54. Chester Davis to Mary Connor Myers, March 11, 1935, folder 467, Solicitor's File, RG 16, N Arch.
55. Herbert Barnes, "Conditions in South Beyond Words, Said," *Farmers National Weekly*, February 15, 1935.

Frank was taking further steps to remind the Cotton Section of certain limitations on its legal powers. At that time—mid-January, 1935—Chester Davis was absent on business and Victor Christgau was Acting Administrator. In this capacity, he officially informed Cully Cobb that the proper interpretation of Section 7 of the cotton contract was a legal question. "Please, therefore, hereafter," said Christgau, "submit all letters, telegrams, memoranda and proposed instructions to County Agents or others, whether oral or written, covering legal questions, to the General Counsel and advise the personnel of your section of this request."[56] It should be emphasized that there appeared to be nothing particularly revolutionary about this directive. Had there been anything unusual about the idea of lawyers settling legal matters, Christgau—who was *not* dismissed in the coming purge—would hardly have risked insubordination in the absence of his superior. Furthermore, the order seems to have been accepted even by the conservatives. There was no immediate outcry, and an official of the generally conservative Commodities Division supported Christgau, recommending "that the answers of the Cotton Section relating to these questions be reviewed by the Legal Section before they are sent forward" to agents in the field.[57] Planters protested this procedural change in the strongest terms,[58] but their outcries were lost in the growing concern over Mrs. Myers's dispatches from Arkansas. Every word she relayed to Frank was a blow to the old interpretation of the contract and a spur to the AAA's young lawyers working on the new official interpretation.

In the meantime, certain immediate changes could be made. First, the procedure for adjusting tenant complaints could be overhauled. In view of Mrs. Myers's findings, "it is doubtful whether the local committees as now constituted, being frequently composed of landlords only, are competent to pass on

56. Victor Christgau to Cully Cobb, January 14, 1935, copies in folder 467, Solicitor's File, RG 16, and in Box 30 (Cotton Acquis.-Admin.), RG 145, N Arch.

57. D. S. Myer to Cully Cobb, January 19, 1935, folder 466–B, Solicitor's File, RG 16, N Arch.

58. See for example, American Cotton Cooperative Association, N. C. Williamson, telegram to Henry Wallace, January 16, 1935, folder 467, Solicitor's File, N Arch.

such questions," Frank said, insisting that a special Landlord-Tenant-Labor Committee be established to take over the judicial function of the local AAA committees.[59] Second, the AAA could intervene in the STFU's Norcross case. For a time it appeared that the only controversy regarding such intervention would concern means—Alger Hiss, Frank's leading assistant, argued for AAA participation in the suit, while Oscar Johnston, the cotton pool manager, maintained that the AAA could do no more than revoke Norcross's contract.[60] The Cotton Section was definitely on the run; not even Johnston was fully defending the Cully Cobb viewpoint. Somebody remembered that Dr. Calvin Hoover, author of the AAA report on labor displacement, had stated that he didn't think the cotton contract obligated landlords to keep the same tenants on hand. But now Hoover met fact to face with a delegation of Arkansas landlords in Wallace's office and told them flatly that his personal feeling was never meant to be binding and that he would defer to any contrary opinion from the Legal Section. (Paul Appleby had shown Hoover some of Dr. Amberson's documentation of cheating and evictions in the Arkansas Delta. Hoover found Amberson "quite reasonable. I would agree with a good deal that he says.")[61] So complete was the eclipse of the conservative forces that a rumor got through to the *New York Times* that Chester Davis himself was on the way out. His viewpoint, it was said, was too much like that of a few big-business oriented NRA officials whose days were also numbered.[62]

59. Jerome Frank to Robert McConnaughey, January 25, 1935, folder 467, and "Administrative Order" draft, n.d. [February 4, 1935], folder 465, both in Solicitor's File, RG 16, N Arch. As members of the proposed committee, Frank suggested himself, Dr. Calvin Hoover, John B. Payne (a moderate), and either D. P. Trent or Victor Christgau, with Cully Cobb in an advisory capacity. The committee would, of course, appoint field representatives to do the actual investigations.
60. Alger Hiss to Jerome Frank, January 26, 1935, and Oscar Johnston to Chester Davis, January 26, 1935, both in L-TS, RG 145, N Arch.
61. Calvin Hoover to Henry Wallace, February 5, 1935, folder 466–B, Solicitor's File, RG 16, N Arch, and Hoover to Paul Appleby, January 8, 1935, in "Tenant Farmer Correspondence" section, Calvin Hoover Papers, RG 145, N Arch.
62. "Find Dereliction by Code Officials," *New York Times*, January 28, 1935.

Meanwhile, work on the first official interpretation of the contract was completed, and the opinion—largely the work of Alger Hiss and Francis M. Shea—was submitted by Shea on Monday, February 4, 1935. The opinion was primarily based on the clear intent of Section 7 as a whole, but it emphasized that part of the Section which provided that the landlord "*shall* permit *all* tenants to *continue* in the occupancy of their houses on this farm, rent free." The decision was that the cotton contract required all tenants, not just the same number of tenants, to be kept on the plantations. Evictions were to be only for cause.[63] Upon its promulgation, the interpretation would have marked the final defeat of the Davis-Cobb forces on the sharecropper question. The crisis was no longer coming; it had arrived. Still, in the three weeks that had elapsed since Victor Christgau had served Frank's cease-and-desist order upon the Cotton Section, no sign had come from Davis that he planned to contest the Legal Section's action.

But the Administrator of the AAA was not asleep. Even as Legal Section typists were clacking out the Shea opinion, Davis was going outside of the AAA, working with his ally Seth Thomas, Solicitor of the Department of Agriculture. Thomas's opinion was that tenants did not have to be kept *as tenants*, but they did have to be permitted to remain on the landlord's property.[64] Davis ignored the latter half of Thomas's opinion, seized on the first part, and went in to force a showdown with Secretary Wallace.

The AAA chief demanded that either the liberals go or he go. He went far beyond the sharecropper issue, demanding the resignation or demotion of liberals prominently associated

---

63. Francis Shea to R. K. McConnaughey, February 4, 1935, L-TS, RG 145, N Arch. My emphasis on "*shall*," "*all*," and "*continue*." In regard to the possible "nuisance or a menace" loophole, Shea cautioned: "Personal likes or dislikes of the owner are not grounds upon which he may properly invoke the proviso. Nor should he be permitted to rest the discharge of tenants or croppers on charges of threats or agitation which cannot be shown to involve immediate destructive action." See also William R. Amberson, "The New Deal for Share-Croppers," *Nation*, February 13, 1935, pp. 185, 186.

64. Seth Thomas to Henry Wallace, February 6, 1935, folder 466–B, Solicitor's File, N Arch.

with other pro-labor, pro-consumer efforts. Wallace capitulated, though he apparently prevailed on Davis to reduce the number of those on the "must-go" list. The next morning, the day after Shea's opinion had been issued, the dismissal letters appeared on key desks throughout the AAA. Frank was out; so was Shea, but not Hiss (although he later resigned, along with Victor Christgau). Lee Pressman had pushed for labor standards in marketing codes, so he got one of the letters. The Consumers' Counsel had been a nuisance, insisting on full inspection of all books and records of the big processors that benefitted from marketing agreements, so Frederic Howe was demoted and his indiscreet assistant, Pat Jackson, was fired.[65]

The next day Secretary Wallace publicly explained why he had dismissed the very men who had been fighting for what Wallace liked to claim were his own goals. "It was an exceedingly trying conference for Wallace," wrote a sympathetic eyewitness. "He was gray-faced and haggard. I never saw at any press conference so many plainly hostile representatives of public opinion, with barbed questions prepared, planted. Wallace was sad and uneasy; his guard was down; his questioners were clamorous and loud. It was not a pleasant occasion." Wallace relied mainly on Administrator Davis, who was also present. Davis explained that the "reorganization" had been "for an efficiently operating organization in the Triple-A. . . . I think it is important to have in the key positions in the Triple-A men who have some familiarity with farm problems and who have a farm background."

"Chester has now made the speech I halted in the midst of making," Wallace immediately added. The changes were only made "for the greatest possible harmony" in the AAA, the Secretary said.

The newsmen kept demanding the *meaning* of the purge. "You can't have the ship listing right and then left," the pale

65. *New York Times*, February 6, 1935; Wallace's recollections of the showdown are in his "No Final Answer to the Farm Problem," *U. S. News & World Report*, January 8, 1954, p. 42, and in Conrad, *Forgotten Farmers*, pp. 146–51. Previous published accounts fail to establish the direct connection between the Norcross Case, the Myers Report, the Legal Section interpretation, and the purge.

Secretary finally confessed. "It must go right straight along. Straight down the middle of the road."[66]

It soon became clear to those interested in the "reorganization" just why Davis knew he could use the sharecropper issue as the basis of his "they-go-or-I-go" stand. The New Deal political coalition was heavily dependent upon cotton state spokesmen in Congress; in particular, the support of Senate Majority Leader Joseph T. Robinson of Arkansas and of Mississippi's Pat Harrison, chairman of the Senate Finance Committee, was indispensable. Surely we may assume that Chester Davis reminded Wallace of that fact when they met in his office on that cold Monday afternoon. Senator Robinson's attitude was particularly important. He saw copies of every important paper that left the Department of Agriculture, so Norman Thomas was told by his highly-placed friends in Washington, and surely nothing that would affect Arkansas could be done without Robinson's acquiescence. And that faithful planter organ, the *Memphis Commercial Appeal*, published a report that "the dismissals [in the AAA] came about as a result of a protest by Senator Robinson, Representative [William J.] Driver [of Arkansas] and a delegation of Arkansas planters." Chester Davis himself gave this as his reason for demanding the purge: "If the contract had been so construed . . . Henry Wallace would have been forced out of the Cabinet within a month. The effect would have been revolutionary."[67] Davis did not say so, but pressure sufficient to demote Wallace, one of President Roosevelt's leading heirs-apparent, could, under the circumstances, have come only from the oligarchy that controlled a strategic part of the nation and of the Democratic party. Davis was not necessarily correct in his assumptions, but he believed he was. And evidently he convinced Wallace, too.

Rexford Tugwell had been away from Washington, recuperating from an illness, when the axe fell; hurrying back, he

66. Lord, *Wallaces of Iowa*, pp. 406–7; *New York Times*, February 7, 1935, p. 2.
67. Interview with Norman Thomas, July 5, 1962; "Strange Allies," *Arkansas Gazette*, March 13, 1935; George Morris, "In Washington," *Memphis Commercial Appeal*, November 22, 1936; Davis is quoted in Lord, *Wallaces of Iowa*, p. 405.

suspected that his own job might be gone. He told Interior Secretary Harold Ickes "that he was definitely through in the Department of Agriculture," and that he would rather work under Ickes than with Wallace; with no liberal support left, any Wallace reform attempts would be like trying "to take a broad jump from a bowl of jelly."[68] The sorrowful Tugwell went on to the White House for a talk with President Roosevelt. FDR assured Tugwell of his continued confidence, but told him that he had to support the Davis-Wallace action. "Mr. ROOSEVELT . . . doesn't care to know his Left from his Right," editorialized the *New York Times*.[69]

So it happened that in the winter of 1935, on the birthday of the Great Emancipator, the Secretary of Agriculture emancipated Southern tenants from their homes. He sent a telegram to the Memphis Chamber of Commerce: "SECTION SEVEN OF COTTON CONTRACT DOES NOT BIND LANDOWNERS TO KEEP THE SAME TENANTS. . . . THAT IS THE OFFICIAL AND FINAL INTERPRETATION OF THE SOLICITOR OF THE DEPARTMENT OF AGRICULTURE AND NO OTHER INTERPRETATION WILL BE GIVEN."[70]

The Secretary was a kind man, a gentle man who had to find some means of explaining away what he had done. So he strengthened his previous belief that sharecropper misery was chargeable to conditions far more fundamental than anything the AAA could touch. "Neither the AAA programs nor any relief program," he said, "can really come to grips with the fundamentals of these conditions. At best, anything we might do either through the AAA or relief would be temporary palliatives."[71] Wallace never seemed to realize that not even Jerome Frank asked anything of the AAA but "temporary palliatives." Nobody asked the AAA to cure everything, but there were those who hoped it would remedy what it could. Failing that, the

68. Harold L. Ickes, *The Secret Diary of Harold L. Ickes: The First Thousand Days, 1933–1936* (New York: Simon & Schuster, 1953), pp. 292–93, 302–3.

69. "Reorganized AAA," editorial, *New York Times*, February 7, 1935.

70. Henry Wallace to Memphis Chamber of Commerce, February 12, 1935, folder 466–B, Solicitor's File, RG 16, N Arch.

71. Henry Wallace, "The Problem of Farm Tenancy," statement on the Bankhead Bill, March 5, 1935, folder 466–B, Solicitor's File, RG 16, N Arch.

Administration at least could have refrained from worsening the situation.

However, once Wallace had sent his telegram, he refused to believe that conditions were getting worse at all. He drove himself to accept the Davis-Cobb fancy that rising cotton prices meant there was no such thing as a tenancy problem, and he never allowed himself to see the total irrelevance of the price level to the problems of labor displacement and income distribution. Once, in Atlanta, he tried to meet the charge of sharecropper evictions head-on: "What are the facts? One is that the number of people on farms in the South *increased* 1,250,000 from 1930 to 1935." Wallace assumed that all of these people were better off because of the increase in the South's total cotton income; this, he said, has "helped almost all producers, whether landlord or tenant." By 1937, he was telling an assemblage of cotton magnates at Memphis that "the solution of the sharecropper problem . . . and almost every problem that has drawn the attention of reformer and sociologist to the South, lies largely in one thing. We must enable the South to earn a bigger income."[72] The cotton barons may well have been generous with their applause, for they knew which Southerners would be getting the "bigger income" of which Wallace spoke.

After the 1935 Wallace telegram, that epitaph to liberalism in the AAA, the attitude of the entire Department of Agriculture changed. A myth developed that the purged men had been impractical dreamers whose removal was necessary to avoid catastrophe. "The AAA has suffered at times," economist John D. Black wrote, ". . . from a desire of some of its staff to hasten

72. Henry Wallace, "The Cotton Program Carries On," speech at Atlanta, April 13, 1935, text in "Speeches of the Secretary (1935)" folder; Wallace, "Common Aims in Agriculture," speech at Tuskegee, Ala., September 10, 1936, text in "Speeches of the Secretary (1936)" folder; and Wallace, "Charting the Course for Cotton," speech at Memphis, October 1, 1937, text in "Speeches of the Secretary (1937)" folder; all above folders in RG 16, N Arch. Ironically, just as the wealthier Southern planters received more New Deal money than the poorer tenants, the wealthier Western and Midwestern farmers received far more than the poorer Southern and Northeastern ones. Complete figures have been computer evaluated by Leonard J. Arrington of Utah State University, "Western American Agriculture and the New Deal," Organization of American Historians convention, Los Angeles, April 17, 1970.

too much the coming of the millennium, from a failure to reckon sufficiently the hard realities of human nature, of group pressures, . . . and even the limitations of their own wisdom."[73] Black's view became the accepted one in the Department. The millennium-rushers had been likeable enough, some felt, but all were agreed that their advanced views would have ruined the AAA. Wallace himself came to believe that Frank's opinion "was not only indefensible from a practical agricultural point of view but also bad law."[74]

Wallace's "bad law" charge can be met by comparing the relative merits of Jerome Frank's legal training with that of Henry Wallace and the Cotton Section. But what of the other indictment, the common charge that the liberals were attempting to overthrow the whole plantation system? Assuming the accusation is true, would it really have been impossible to achieve? The Depression was a great earthquake that loosened the roots of many well established institutions, and none of these was so little defended or so obviously outmoded as the plantation system. NRA undermined the institution of competition and continued reversing the old trustbusting attitude toward large corporations; were these institutions more decadent than the plantation system? The Securities and Exchange Commission substantially abridged the freedom of Wall Street; would reform of the cotton economy have been more earth-shaking?

These questions are moot, however, for the AAA liberals were not trying to overhaul the entire plantation system. In the controversy over Section 7, they were not even trying to improve it. *They were merely trying to make sure that AAA crop reduction did not worsen the situation, and for this they were fired.*

But the magnitude of the liberals' proposals, exaggerated as it was in the minds of Wallace, Davis, and Cobb, was not the only objection of the conservatives. Being practical men, they assumed that the success of the cotton program was entirely

73. John D. Black, supplementary statement in Nourse *et al., Three Years of AAA*, p. 504. A similar viewpoint is implied in Conrad, *Forgotten Farmers*, pp. 152–53; Lord, *Wallaces of Iowa*, pp. 404–6; and in Nourse *et al., Three Years of AAA*, p. 345.
74. Wallace's diary, as quoted in Schlesinger, *Coming of the New Deal*, p. 79.

dependent upon landlord support and that the proposed changes, whatever their merits, would have jeopardized that support. Grant the first part of this assumption and the second part is still highly doubtful. What would the Legal Section have required of landlords? Not that they keep exactly the same tenants; only that they show cause for any evictions. "Even were an attempt made to enforce paragraph 7," Margaret Bennett had pointed out, "a producer could, of course, evict a sharecropper who neglected his crop, or who was destructive of the producer's property, or who created a serious disorder on the plantation, or in any other way became a 'nuisance or a menace to the welfare of the producer.' "[75] Were these terms, then, so onerous as to threaten landlord cooperation with the AAA? Let it be remembered that the cotton South began to worship the AAA and the Bankhead Act as cotton proceeded to double in price;[76] let it be remembered that the prohibitive tax on excess production also played a large part in the success of the cotton reduction program. These circumstances, which accounted almost entirely for landlord compliance with the program, would have remained unchanged with the adoption of the Legal Section interpretation of the contract. On their own tracts, farmed with wage labor, landlords would still have continued to receive all of the increased cotton income and all of the benefit payments, plus half or more of the cotton crop proceeds and 80 to 90 per cent of the AAA money from their sharecropper-farmed tracts. Are we to assume that planters would sabotage a program so overwhelmingly favorable to them, so heartily approved by them, simply out of anger at being made to show cause for evicting tenants?

The author cannot believe that Southern landlords were quite that selfish and vindictive.

75. Margaret Bennett to Henry Wallace, January 12, 1935, folder 467, Solicitor's File, RG 16, N Arch.
76. For evidence of overwhelming support for the cotton program, see Richards, *Cotton and the AAA*, pp. 186ff.

# 4.

# *Collective Bargaining or Public Relations?*

*U*ntil the Norcross suit precipitated the explosion in the AAA in early 1935, the Southern Tenant Farmers' Union was an abandoned orphan. Struggling in obscurity, linked to Norman Thomas by an occasional letter, living on the incomes from their businesses, H. L. Mitchell and Clay East tried to puzzle out what a sharecroppers' union should be. Would it prove possible to organize workers as little educated, as totally at the mercy of their employers, as the "croppers" of the Arkansas Delta? What methods could be used in the almost unprecedented task?

A few principles were immediately apparent: a sharecropper union demanded sharecropper leadership, which small businessmen Mitchell and East were continually trying to discover and promote. So eager were they, during the STFU's first years, that some of their "leadership" discoveries were disastrous. J. O. Green, for example, wanted to make the union a uniformed Fascist force; W. H. Stultz tried to turn it over to the planters as a company union; and Walter Moskop became convinced that Mitchell was stealing money and therefore tried to assassinate him.[1]

1. On the Green case: J. O. Green, letter to the editor, *Memphis Commercial Appeal*, September 26, 1936; *The Sharecroppers Voice*, August, 1935; H. L. Mitchell affidavit; transcript of Mitchell's recorded interview for the Columbia University Oral History Collection, STFU Papers and elsewhere (referred to hereafter as Oral History MS), pp. 47–48.

As the union grew, excellent sharecropper leadership appeared, but in the difficult, obscure days of 1934 it was still necessary to use nonfarmers frequently. East and Mitchell worked particularly closely with friends in the Arkansas Socialist party: "Uncle Charley" McCoy, a former machinist from Trumann, promoted the STFU among white tenants and offered his home for planning sessions; rail-thin, talkative J. R. Butler, a self-educated country schoolteacher, inundated all proceedings with a mish-mash of ideas drawn from Populist, Wobbly, and other midwestern radical sources; and, of course, Dr. William Amberson was always ready to drive over from Memphis to counsel prudence and recommend procedures most likely to win acceptance with his friends in the AAA and the national headquarters of the Socialist party.[2] Only the decision to protest the AAA's impact on tenant farmers, however, owed much to Socialist influence, and even that was an issue which, very largely, had been brought to Socialist attention by the Arkansas radicals rather than vice-versa.

All the other significant demands and characteristics of the infant STFU derived principally from the knowledge and background of its founders rather than from their New York allies. The union's Constitution, for example, largely Butler's work, began with a class-struggle statement such as even the AFL Constitution included; it went on to recommend establishment of "one big union of all agricultural workers," IWW-style, in

---

On Stultz, Mitchell's Oral History MS, pp. 47–48, is inaccurate: see Stultz, Walter Moskop, Jack Fies, and Ed Pickering, telegram to Clarence Senior, April 25, 1935; Jack Fies to Norman Thomas and Jack Herling, April 25, 1935, Senior to Roy Burt, April 26, 1935, Senior to Norman Thomas, April 29, 1935; Howard Kester to Thomas, Senior, and Herling, April 30, 1935, and other correspondence, all in S P Arch, Duke; W. H. Stultz to Cully Cobb, May 22, 1935, Commodity Stabilization Service Records, RG 145, N Arch; *Marked Tree Tribune*, June 13, 1935; *The Sharecroppers Voice*, July, 1935. On Moskop's attempt to shoot Mitchell: Kester to Thomas, May 30, 1936, Mitchell to Ward Rogers, June 20, 1936, Evelyn Smith to Dr. William Amberson, June 30, 1936, all in STFU Papers; Oral History MS., pp. 60–61.

2. Oral History MS, pp. 24–28; Clay Fulks, "A Tribute," *Commonwealth College Fortnightly*, February 15, 1936, CCP, Reel 2; Evelyn and Charles McCoy to H. L. Mitchell, October 9, 1936, and J. R. Butler to Oliver Peterson, June 10, 1937, both in STFU Papers; interview with Mitchell, December 3, 1961.

order to replace tenancy with occupant-ownership and eventually "a cooperative order of society."[3] Mitchell, more radical but also more practical, drew up a "Program for Action" aimed squarely at the AAA, though the Norcross suit was months in the future and the union leaders still had no clear idea how they could attempt governmental redress. In the STFU's infancy, Mitchell's chief contribution to success was probably his intimate knowledge of the area, gained during years of delivering dry cleaning to the planters and tenants. He knew them so well that when a cropper told him which planter was his boss, Mitchell usually could predict the worker's grievance. Healthily fearful of the planters and riding bosses, Mitchell insisted on secrecy: "You are cautioned not to travel to and from meetings in large crowds. Go one or two at a time in different directions. Avoid the highways and roads as much as possible. . . ."[4] Clay East was equally impressed by the vulnerability of the union, but he was able to do something more positive about it: as town constable of Tyronza, he had a badge, a gun, and a respected name, all of which bought months of grace before the planters finally resorted to force.[5]

The STFU founders were also aware that uneducated people could be best approached for revolutionary action through their existing values and institutions. These, in Arkansas in 1934, were few. "I was just like all the other people over in Wynne," said white cropper Myrtle Moskop, "when they first started talking about union, I thought it was a new church."[6] This was

3. STFU, "Constitution, By-Laws, etc., of the Southern Tenant Farmers' Union," Searcy, Arkansas, July 26, 1934, STFU Papers. Compare with such documents as the 1892 platform of the Populists, the IWW preamble, and the AFL Constitution in Henry Steele Commager (ed.), *Documents of American History* (6th ed.; New York: 1958), II, 143, 337, 412.
4. "How to Conduct a Union Meeting," in H. L. Mitchell, Official Notice to Members of Community Councils, Union Officials, and National Executive Council Members, n.d. [August, 1935]; interviews with H. L. Mitchell, December 3, 1961; Howard Kester, July 17–18, 1961; J. R. Butler, July 22, 1962; Mitchell, "Instructions to Organizers," No. 1, n.d. [1934], STFU Papers.
5. Oral History MS, p. 20–B; interview with H. L. Mitchell, December 3, 1961; Clay East to Sheriff Howard Curlin, August 30, 1934, copy in possession of East.
6. "Croppers Leave for Eastern Arkansas," *Commonwealth College*

logical; sharecroppers knew of nothing else one joined. For-tunately, there were many clergymen like Ward Rodgers, a militant young Vanderbilt graduate with a black mustache and booming voice, and E. B. McKinney, the unpredictable but charismatic leader of Marked Tree's Negroes, to make the tran-sition from church to union easy. Identification of the planter with Pharoah was traditional with Southern black men; Scrip-ture could be used to support organizing speeches as well as sermons; and churches were commonly the only buildings avail-able for meetings of any kind. Even Norman Thomas, when he came to the Delta, fell into the shout-and-respond pattern of rural Southern preaching: "The only approach is for the work-ers to organize (ORGANIZE, the congregation repeats without breaking the rhythm) and stick together (STICK TOGETHER/ Yes, sir / Hallelujah) Stick together, the white man and the black man (PRAISE GOD) and seek justice in our union (UNION! / You're right, brother Thomas / Amen!)"[7]

Because enthusiastic hymn-singing seemed to bind funda-mentalist congregations more closely than anything else, STFU organizers were quick to adapt favorite hymns to secular pur-poses. In the eighteenth century, Charles Wesley, complaining that the Devil had all the good tunes, took them out of the tav-erns into the Methodist chapels; in the twentieth century the IWW and the STFU took them back out again, creating songs for the workers of the 1930's and the students and black people of the 1960's. Two Negroes, old A. B. Brookins and young John Handcox, and one white man, the radical Presbyterian Claude Williams, were most active in adapting and promoting such rousers as "We're Gonna Roll the Union On," "It's a Wonderful Union"—formerly "Give Me That Old Time Religion"—and "Raggedy, Raggedy Are We." But by far the most successful

*Fortnightly,* July 1, 1936, CCP, Reel 2. The statement probably should have been attributed to Myrtle Lawrence, a much more articulate STFU member.—H. L. Mitchell to the author, November 26, 1968.

7. Memphis *Press-Scimitar,* March 14, 1935; September 18, 1936; *Arkansas Gazette,* March 14, 1935; Marvin Sanford, unpublished MS on the STFU, n.d. [1938]; H. L. Mitchell, typed unsigned MS, n.d., Sec. II, p. 7, and Ansley Garrette, Minutes of meeting of Shiloh local, April 20, 1936, all in STFU Papers.

was a song derived from an old camp meeting favorite, "Jesus
Is My Captain." As "We Shall Not Be Moved," it has become an
American folk classic:

> The union is a-marching,
>> We shall not be moved,
> The union is a-marching,
>> We shall not be moved.
> Just like a tree that's planted by the water,
>> We shall not be moved.

"We Shall Not Be Moved usually began with 'So-and-so is our
leader,' etc.," Lee Hays of the Weavers recalled, "and of course
we sometimes picked the wrong so-and-so to be the leader."[8]
But no matter; the song itself furnished the gleaming ideal.
"That song i Do believe sprung from our Lips with the voice of
God," wrote J. W. Washington. "it re[mem]bered my mind Back
to the time when Moses was Leading the childrens of Isrel. i believe that Was Handed Down for this Day for some of us are
getting shot and some getting beaton."[9]

What might have been the union's greatest problem became,
because of the nature of STFU goals and leadership, quite min-
imal. It could be argued that within the STFU America's greatest problem, that of race relations, was solved as well as any
realistic observer could expect. The union's history furnishes a
lesson in interracial understanding that represents one of its
greatest legacies to those who study the past to find clues for
action today. To be sure, an interracial policy might have been
expected in the STFU, given the beliefs of its founders. But
carrying this ambitious doctrine into practice was quite another
matter, and East and Mitchell were prepared to tread carefully.
Racial antagonisms seemed of little importance, however, to

8. Lee Hays to the author, n.d. [September, 1962]; Pete Seeger to the
author, June 2, 1962; John Greenway, *American Folksongs of Protest*
(Philadelphia: University of Pennsylvania Press, 1953), pp. 16–17, 223;
Commonwealth College, "Commonwealth Labor Songs," (Mena, Ark.,
1938), pp. 5–7. STFU songs have been recorded, with helpful notes, on
"The Original Talking Union," Folkways album no. FH-5285, "Gazette,"
Folkways album no. FN–2501, and "American Industrial Ballads," Folk-
ways album no. FH–5251.

9. J. W. Washington to H. L. Mitchell, January 19, 1936, STFU
Papers.

the members of the very first locals formed. At the STFU's initial meeting in the Sunnyside schoolhouse on Fairview plantation, those present agreed that people who face the same problems must not be divided by race. The workers on the next plantation organized—Sloan's, near Tyronza—reached the same conclusion. Both of these locals, however, were composed of people who worked side by side and knew each other as individuals; under such circumstances, prejudices were not applied. But when word of the STFU reached Marked Tree, a town too large for blacks and whites to know each other intimately, the race issue could no longer be sidestepped.

At this point, STFU leaders decided that a bit of ideological backtracking might help them storm the citadel. So they organized a Negro local and a white local, and poor whites who might otherwise have hesitated now rushed to join. The defeat of principle was only temporary; in the first place, the only building in Marked Tree large enough to seat the hundreds of members was a Negro lodge hall. At first, the Negro local met on different nights from the white local, but when the Negro leaders invited white members to their meetings it was hard for the whites to refuse—and they could hardly tell the Negroes to sit at the rear of their own lodge hall. Soon, as Mitchell said, "the only way you could tell which local was meeting was by which set of officers were on the platform."[10] Among the Negro officers there was one, in particular, who was impressive. Whites would turn and tell Mitchell, "You know, that nigger's got more sense than any white man here."

"That nigger," the president of the Negro local, was Edward Britt McKinney. McKinney, called Britt or E. B. by his friends, was a bald, garrulous preacher, addicted to hyperbole—which may have been one of the sources of his effectiveness. Though willing to work with whites, he was race-conscious, having been influenced by Marcus Garvey's Negro nationalism, and "his people" remained primarily the Negro union members. But it was probably his own idea that segregation could be overcome by inviting the whites to the Negro meetings. His leadership

10. Interview with H. L. Mitchell, December 3, 1961; Marvin Sanford, unpublished MS on the STFU, n.d. [1938]; Oral History MS, pp. 81–83; typed MS, no title, n.d. [1935?], in the STFU Papers.

was undoubtedly one of the major reasons the two Marked Tree locals grew together instead of remaining apart; the white leader, Walter Moskop, was intelligent enough, but he was an embittered man with few strong qualities of personal leadership. Besides, there was a question of status. Moskop had been a bootlegger, while McKinney was a preacher.[11] And in Arkansas, a dark brown Man of God may sometimes have rated a bit higher than a light tan purveyor of booze, though the services of both were probably in equal demand.

After the success of the two-local tactic in Marked Tree, the STFU felt free to adopt it elsewhere. Without feeling that he was surrendering to white ignorance, Mitchell could cheerfully advise inquirers, "Of course it is quite all right for the two races to organize into separate locals just so long as they are all in the same union and fighting for the same things."[12] The STFU leaders knew that once there was widespread comprehension of what "fighting for the same things" meant, the irrationality that underlay the demand for two locals would begin to fade away. Men like Mitchell, East, Butler, and McKinney were perfectly willing to be pragmatists. To reach and convince whites who would otherwise be antagonized, they used white organizers; to gain the confidence of Negroes fearful of being exploited, they used black organizers. For the same reasons, they were careful to balance officeholders by race. In other words, the STFU was cognizant of race only to the extent necessary to create a movement in which race would become unimportant. Although the two-local tactic and population imbalance on some plantations kept many locals all-white or all-black, the abundance of biracial locals and the fact that all important action was taken at integrated mass meetings demonstrate how thoroughly the STFU solved the prejudice problem—in a union that, like the Deep South itself, was from half to two-thirds black.[13]

11. Interviews with Howard Kester, July 18, 1961; Claude Williams, August 18, 1962; J. R. Butler, July 22, 1962. Butler told the author he thought McKinney may have developed his powers of persuasion as an agent sent North by planters after World War I to convince Southern Negroes they ought to return to Ole Massa.

12. H. L. Mitchell to Lee Munday, July 21, 1937, STFU Papers.

13. Ward Rodgers in *Modern News* [Harrisburg, Ark.], February 15, 1935; Leon Turner to Mitchell, August 18, 1936; Mitchell to J. E. Cameroon, January 11, 1936; J. R. Butler to Edwin L. Clarke, November 25,

There may have been some racial differences in the union, because the Negroes, having occupied the doormat position in the plantation economy for generations, had learned the survival value of docility and close social organization. The whites, in sharp contrast, almost all new to the plantation system, were fiercely individualistic, unfamiliar with organized enterprise, and considerably (if surprisingly) less literate than the Negroes. There were occasions even after they had joined the union that they hesitated to commit themselves to united action. Mitchell himself once said that "intimidation moves were generally more successful against the whites than the Negroes. The latter have more sense of organization and the value of organization, a greater sense of solidarity." Black union leaders like Will Davis begged for white support: "The negros is ready to orginize in fact they are the only ones that is willing to strike if [of] corse they are afraid to under take to Do any thing By their selves and they cant Do nothing By their selves."[14]

To summarize, so-called "racial" differences were never more than interesting but understandable generalizations to active STFU members; or, at most, prejudices were inherited superstitions that must influence tactics but need not interfere with strategy. The STFU never allowed interracial action to be postponed so long through fear of treading on traditions that their antagonists became emboldened by delay. Instead, they were convinced that "most of the trouble arising between the races is directly rooted in the problem of bread and jobs and economic security. It is not primarily a problem of color"[15]—nor of "deeply-rooted traditions, removable only by education over a long period of time." Holding this belief, they eschewed pussy-footing and egg-treading; they plunged immediately into the task of revealing to both races their common goals, and they organized both races into a common effort as rapidly as possible.

---

1938; Butler to Marvin Sanford, October 8, 1938, all in STFU Papers. See also George Sinclair Mitchell, "The Negro in Southern Trade Unionism," *Southern Economic Journal*, II (January, 1936), 30, 33.

14. Interview with Howard Kester, July 18, 1961; Marvin Sanford, unpublished MS on the STFU, n.d. [1938]; Will Davis to J. R. Butler, June 19, 1937, STFU Papers.

15. STFU, Statement to [Arkansas] Governor's Commission on Farm Tenancy, n.d. [August, 1936], STFU Papers.

With its racial policy established and its foundations firmly laid in the Arkansas Delta, the STFU "personality" was already quite clear by the end of 1934. Remaining extremely unclear, however, were the methods the union might best use: collective bargaining? public relations? A third alternative, seeking administrative action from the Federal government, appeared most promising until Chester Davis threw the sharecropper supporters out of the AAA.

During the cold months of early 1935, when it still appeared that the agricultural liberals had a chance in Washington, the forces of law, order, and respectability in Arkansas began an anti-STFU campaign of violence that did much to determine the union's ultimate choice of strategy.

It began on a chilly weekday afternoon in the middle of January, with a number of landlords and lawmen sprinkled among the hundreds of farm tenants gathered in Marked Tree's town square to hear STFU spokesmen tell of Henry Wallace's promise to begin an investigation of AAA operations in the Delta. When E. B. McKinney was introduced as "Mr.," a disapproving murmur rustled among the crowd, which was further upset when McKinney claimed to have received telegrams of support from various un-Southern places; "including European countries," the offended T. C. Brigance remembered—"Russia included. He stressed Russia." Brigance became even angrier when Ward Rodgers "talked along there about the people starving to death and of the awful conditions of the people that were there and just that general line of Communistic talk."[16] After the meeting, Prosecuting Attorney Fred Stafford arrested Rodgers for "criminal anarchy," and Sheriff J. D. DuBard confiscated his letters and papers. Since they included mention of the Communist party's United Front campaign, they were passed along to the newspapers; headlines such as the *Marked Tree Tribune's* "Letters Show Ward Rodgers Active Field Agent on U. S. Pay for Socialist-Communist Combine" forced him out of his Federal relief job as an adult educator.[17] Then came the formal part

16. T. C. Brigance, Testimony to Arkansas Legislative Investigating Committee, February 18, 1935, CCP, Reel 1; Oral History MS, pp. 34–35.
17. Oral History MS, pp. 35–36; Howard Kester to Norman Thomas,

of Rodgers's punishment: as a holiday mood prevailed, with spectators tossing candy to the seven planters, four businessmen and a sharecropper who made up the jury, Justice of the Peace J. C. McCroy convened his "court" in a vacant store. After Prosecutor Stafford reminded the party that "Rodgers is an organizer for the Communist Party and is advocating racial equality right here in Arkansas," the jury took ten minutes to find him guilty. McCroy sentenced him to six months in jail and fined him $500 and court costs.[18]

Rodgers was easily the union's best white speaker and organizer; with his arrest, Mitchell again began looking for help. He decided the best place to find it would be at Commonwealth College, whose militant director, Lucien Koch, twenty-seven, "the youngest college president in the country," had promised assistance. Commonwealth, a radical labor college in western Arkansas, had begun in 1914 as a socialist colony called Llano, in the Antelope Valley north of Los Angeles. Its members had moved to a settlement they called Newllano in Louisiana, amid many crises and schisms, before 1925 when they found their permanent home ten miles west of Mena in Arkansas's Ouachita Mountains. The intellectually respectable staff, which received no salaries, was soon charged by the Arkansas American Legion with receiving "money from Moscow," a charge personally denied by FBI chief J. Edgar Hoover. But, in response to the Depression, the college's curriculum moved steadily leftward; it soon offered courses in Russian history but not American, in Marxism but not capitalism or liberalism. A student strike to make the college avowedly Communist was beaten by Director Koch, however, and with this demonstration of independence the college continued to receive donations from such supporters

February 2, 1935, SP Arch, Duke; Kester, "Revolt in Arkansas," *Student Outlook*, n.d., p. 5, clipping in STFU scrapbook, STFU Papers; *Marked Tree Tribune*, January 31, 1935; Memphis *Press-Scimitar*, January 17, 24, February 9, 1935.

18. *Marked Tree Tribune*, January 24, 31, 1935; F. Raymond Daniell, "Arkansas Violence Laid to Landlords," *New York Times*, April 16, 1935, p. 18; *Modern News* [Harrisburg, Ark.], January 25, February 15, 1935; Oral History MS, pp. 38, 41; Memphis *Press-Scimitar*, January 17, 1935. Rodgers was freed on appeal.

as Sherwood Anderson, Harvard's Law Dean Roscoe Pound and economist Sumner Schlichter, labor historian John Commons, H. L. Mencken, John Dewey, Justice Louis D. Brandeis, and Albert Einstein.[19]

In response to Mitchell's call, both the Socialist and the Communist factions at the college drew up a United Front agreement for pro-labor action, and, led by Koch, sent volunteers to aid the STFU. Koch's idea was to tell as many sharecroppers as possible of the AAA anti-eviction contract and the attempts being made to have it enforced. At a Negro church near Gilmore, Koch and Young Communist Leaguer Bob Reed were interrupted by Jake Lewis and other lawmen who beat them, then took them to the county jail where the sheriff's men beat them some more. Sheriff Howard Curlin explained to the press that the two men had been addressing a mixed meeting at a Negro church.[20] The next day Koch, undaunted, took three STFU and Commonwealth people to Lepanto, where City Marshal Jay May, on the pretext that their presence constituted "disturbing the peace," jailed all of them for three days in a tiny, stinking, freezing cage later condemned by the county grand jury as "entirely unfit for human beings."[21]

When two British women's leaders, one of them the wife of noted Labourite Aneurin Bevan, successfully spoke in the area, it appeared that more famous visitors might be immune from attack; there was therefore no great fear when Norman Thomas himself, after a well-publicized interview with Arkansas's conservative Governor Futrell, again entered the Delta to blast

19. On Commonwealth College, see William Henry Cobb, "Commonwealth College: A History" (Master's thesis, University of Arkansas, 1962), Chap. V; and Cobb, "Commonwealth College Comes to Arkansas," *Arkansas Historical Quarterly*, XXIII (Summer, 1964), 99–122; *Commonwealth College Fortnightly*, July 1, 1935, October 15, 1935, November 15, 1936, and entire Reel 3, CCP.

20. *Arkansas Democrat*, n.d. [February 3, 1935?], and J. D. DuBard, testimony to Arkansas Legislative Investigating Committee, February 18, 1935, both in CCP, Reel 1; H. L. Mitchell, sworn affidavit, n.d. [April, 1936?], STFU Papers, referred to hereinafter as "Mitchell affidavit"; Howard Kester, "Revolt in Arkansas," *The Student Outlook*, n.d., clipping in STFU Papers.

21. Mitchell affidavit; "Delegation Back with Lynch Rope," *Commonwealth College Fortnightly*, February 15, 1935, CCP, Reel 2; *Marked Tree Tribune*, October 8, 1936; Memphis *Press-Scimitar*, February 4, 1935.

the AAA. At Trumann, Gilmore, Marked Tree, and Lepanto, Thomas encountered hostility but no open violence. Then he went to the hamlet of Birdsong, just inside Mississippi County, which, according to its leading newspaper, had "a citizenship of refined, hospitable, patriotic people . . . who are willing to go to the uttermost to preserve liberty and Christion [*sic*] civilization in the earth." The refined, hospitable people who met Thomas were deputies and riding bosses, most of them reekingly drunk. They hustled Thomas off the platform, beat lesser members of his party to the ground, and later sent a sharecropper named Clayton Taylor, who had seemed too friendly with the Socialist leader, to the county prison farm for a year.[22]

The violence was only beginning. Clay East and Mary Hillyer of the League for Industrial Democracy were soon driven out of Marked Tree; on March 21 night riders drove by the cabin of old A. B. Brookins, who had barely recovered from an earlier savage beating, and riddled his home with gunfire. Another union leader, W. H. Stultz, fled the Delta under threat of death. Soon the comfortable middle-class home of STFU attorney C. T. Carpenter was hit with bullets; and shortly after E. B. McKinney returned from a speaking tour, his home, too, was shot through and two of his sons wounded. Meanwhile, several STFU meetings in Negro churches were disrupted and most of the members clubbed, without respect for sex or age. An attempt to murder John Allen, black STFU secretary on the notorious Twist plantation in Cross County, narrowly failed. But after Allen escaped to Memphis one woman who refused to help law officers find him was pistol-whipped so brutally that her ear was severed. After it became known that most of the STFU leaders had fled to Memphis, abandoning the homes they had known for years, the *Marked Tree Tribune* offered another of its inimitable headlines: "Citizens Ask Reds to Leave."[23]

22. Mitchell affidavit; "Norman Thomas Visits the Cotton Fields," n.d., [1935]; First STFU press release, n.d., [1935?]; and STFU statement to the [Arkansas] Governor's Commission on Farm Tenancy, n.d. [August, 1936], all in STFU Papers; *The Sharecroppers Voice*, March, 1936; F. Raymond Daniell, "Arkansas Violence Laid to Landlords," *New York Times*, April 16, 1935, p. 18; *The Osceola Times*, November 30, 1934, March 22, 1935.
23. *Marked Tree Tribune*, March 28, 1935; Memphis *Press-Scimitar*, March 22, 1935; Mitchell affidavit; STFU statement to the Governor's

Governmental response to the violence was boredom, so far as the union leaders could tell; it was typified by the AAA's answer to Carpenter, who wrote Rexford Tugwell with some heat about the shooting at his home, and two months later received a two-sentence reply expressing "our genuine desire to be of assistance."[24] But there were two Washington responses, much more provocative ones, that unfortunately remained unknown at the time. One was Henry Wallace's. Perhaps guilt-ridden about the AAA purge and the violence afterward, he was so stung by continual protests from Northern liberals that at one point he drafted an angry reply to Norman Thomas: "If there is bloodshed in eastern Arkansas during the next year, it would be my opinion that the socialists and others who have come in from the North will be largely responsible." Tugwell's face must have blanched as he thought of seeing that in newsprint; he persuaded Wallace not to send it.[25] The second interesting response—if a response was all it was—was the triumphant Cully Cobb's. Flushed with victory in the cotton contract fight, Cobb contended that the union was "the real problem" in the Delta, and that meetings of all the Delta county agents should "be called quietly" in order "to prevent a recurrence of what has happened."[26] At the same time, in order to disseminate "the truth" about the STFU, a meeting of all area law officers was called by regional prosecuting attorney Denver Dudley, a union-baiter who could assure voters that he had had "more felons sent to the penitentiary and electrocuted than by any other during the same period; yet . . . the criminal court costs

---

Commission on Farm Tenancy, n.d. [August, 1936]; "Black Terror in Arkansas," n.d. [March, 1935], both in STFU Papers. STFU members were reported killed during the period of violence, but I have been unable clearly to authenticate these reports.

24. C. T. Carpenter to Rexford Tugwell, April 5, 1935, and Tugwell to Carpenter, June 7, 1935, both in Commodity Stabilization Service records, RG 145, N Arch.

25. Henry Wallace, rough draft of reply to Norman Thomas, n.d., stapled with Thomas to Wallace, April 16, 1935, and M. Huss, memo to Rexford Tugwell, n.d., in "Tenancy (1935)" Folder, RG 16, N Arch.

26. Cully Cobb to Chester Davis, February 13, 1935, and Cobb, J. Phil Campbell, and W. J. Green to Davis, February 14, 1935, both in L-TS, RG 145, N Arch.

to the counties has averaged considerably less."[27] No evidence of what Cobb told the county agents and Dudley told the lawmen can be found; we know only that violence intensified immediately thereafter—if a coincidence, one worth noting.

The Socialist party's reaction was so emphatic that it has distorted everything previously printed about the STFU. Although Mitchell had written frequently to Clarence Senior in Chicago and Norman Thomas in New York, Socialist headquarters had sent its supposed puppet little advice and almost no money throughout 1934. Then, suddenly, Ward Rodgers was arrested and became "the hottest thing we have in court;"[28] making his case a *cause célèbre,* Senior prodded national Negro leaders, radical farm spokesmen, newspapers, and Congressman Usher Burdick to come to the aid of the STFU, "which is run by Socialists."[29] Norman Thomas, who had always been deeply interested in the union, and his chief aides, who hadn't, hurried to the Delta to pay Attorney Carpenter's expenses[30] and try to encourage the sharecroppers. When the AAA liberals were fired and the violence increased, so did the publicity, and the half-truth of a "Socialist Tenant Farmers' Union" took shape.

The Socialists were hardly the only radicals and progressives who, amid violence in Arkansas and defeat in Washington, discovered the STFU. Through the Socialist party, the STFU acquired an extraordinary aide, Howard Kester, and through Kester, a clergyman, the left wing of national Protestantism was reached. Kester, a Virginia Presbyterian, was a close associate of theologian Reinhold Niebuhr and Walter White of the Na-

27. *Jonesboro Daily Tribune,* May 22, 1936; *Arkansas Gazette,* February 12, 1935; *Modern Times* [Harrisburg, Ark.], February 15, 1935.

28. Clarence Senior to J. Clark Waldron, January 22, 1935, SP Arch, Duke.

29. *Ibid.*; National Headquarters, Socialist Party, to all local and branch secretaries, February 6, 1935, Senior to Jack Sullivan, January 23, 1935, Senior to Howard Kester, February 5, 1935, Senior to Milo Reno, February 6, 1935, Senior to E. V. Schultz, February 6, 1935, Senior to Walter White, February 6, 1935, and Senior to Rep. Usher Burdick, January 29, 1935, all in SP Arch, Duke.

30. Norman Thomas to C. T. Carpenter, January 25, 1935, and J. Clark Waldron to Clarence Senior, March 17, 1935, both in SP Arch, Duke; Memphis *Press-Scimitar,* February 1, 1935; *New Leader,* January 26, 1935, clipping in STFU scrapbook, STFU Papers.

tional Association for the Advancement of Colored People, and was admired by hundreds of his colleagues in the Fellowship of Reconciliation and the Committee on Economic and Racial Justice.[31] Immediately upon his arrival in the Delta early in 1935, the rugged, stocky "Buck" Kester began helping with everything from executive decisions to organizing locals, often at great personal hazard. Accustomed to the companionship of intellectuals, he could nevertheless communicate unerringly with tenant farmers—as in the ritual he developed for union meetings, "The Ceremony of the Land." "Commenting on the ceremony," a friend reported, "Mitch says that Buck would have made a swell Ku Klux organizer."[32] As for his national influence, within one week in 1935 Kester received commitments of aid from an officer of The Council for Social Action of the Congregational and Christian Churches of the U.S.A., a member of the Department of Religion at Smith College, and the dean of Howard University's School of Religion—all personal friends.[33] On a more regular basis, Willard Uphaus, head of the National Religion and Labor Foundation, contributed money to the union and aided it with publicity,[34] as did Kester's colleagues in the Southern Conference of Younger Churchmen, an organization which regarded capitalism as anti-Christian and aimed to eliminate "the system's incentives and habits, the legal forms which sustain it, and the moral ideals which justify it."[35] The union also found supporters in the Congregational and Christian church, the Methodist church,[36] and many other Prot-

31. Interviews with Howard Kester, July 17–18, 1961; Committee on Economic and Racial Justice, "Who's Who of Howard Kester," n.d., STFU Papers. Niebuhr, who in the 1930's was still concerned with the secular world, was expected by his Socialist compatriots to stimulate support for the STFU among his students at Union Theological Seminary. Clarence Senior to Reinhold Niebuhr, February 6, 1935, SP Arch, Duke.

32. Aaron Levenstein to Sidney Hertzberg, December 15, 1936, STFU Papers.

33. Ralph Harlow to Howard Kester, December 20, 1935; Harold O. Hatcher to Kester, December 21, 1935; Benjamin Mays to Kester, December 26, 1935, all in STFU Papers.

34. Willard Uphaus to Howard Kester, December 16, 1935; Uphaus to H. L. Mitchell, April 12, 1936, both in STFU Papers.

35. Southern Conference of Younger Churchmen, "Report of the Committee on Resolutions," Second Annual Conference, Chattanooga, n.d., STFU Papers.

36. The Sharecroppers Voice, January 1, 1936.

estant denominations. On occasion, ministers who perceived the sharecropper struggle in religious terms came to the Delta to photograph union activities or write about them for their churches.[37]

Although church support accentuated its characteristic religious orientation, the union was defended with equal zeal by many other types of organizations. The STFU had so many facets that when it was pinched, a dozen divergent organizations felt sympathetic twinges. Most obviously, other radical farm movements felt strong kinship with the union; its heavy Negro membership accounted for the interest of Negro associations, while defenders of civil rights were angered by the continual arbitrary arrests of its members. Reporters and students were attracted because a tenants' union was unique. The Socialist party, an ideological ally, publicized the union's tasks and trials through its League for Industrial Democracy lecture circuit, which circulated prominent speakers southward and then brought them north again to tell eager audiences of their experiences in the Delta. Dr. Amberson was a popular writer for *The Nation*; Reinhold Niebuhr could always get space in *The Christian Century*.[38]

The National Association for the Advancement of Colored People invited both Ward Rodgers and Howard Kester to its 1935 national convention in St. Louis, where they won many additional friends for their union. "Howard Kester was really the sensation of the convention," Rodgers reported.[39] Kester's friend Walter White maintained his correspondence with STFU leaders and was responsible for securing NAACP representation at the union's next convention.[40] Other black organizations extended their friendship, notably the National Negro Congress, an association centered in the Chicago areas where McKinney often spoke. Although the Congress eventually came under

37. H. L. Mitchell to Clarence Senior, July 8, 1935, SP Arch, Duke.

38. Interview with Howard Kester, July 17, 1961. Amberson wrote articles under his own name as well as at least one, "The Cropper Learns His Fate," for Mitchell and Butler (*Nation*, September 18, 1935, p. 328). Amberson to Clarence Senior, September 4, 1935, and Mitchell to Senior, September 9, 1935, SP Arch, Duke. See the bibliography for Amberson and Niebuhr articles.

39. Ward Rodgers to Clarence Senior, July 5, 1935, SP Arch, Duke.

40. Walter White to Howard Kester, December 26, 1935, STFU Papers.

Communist party control, it began as an independent liberal
effort under the sponsorship of such men as Ralph Bunche and
A. Philip Randolph. Its Executive Secretary, John P. Davis, was
sympathetic to Communist elements in the Congress, but chose
to invite Mitchell to serve as chairman of an NNC farm committee rather than one of the Communist party's farm spokesmen.[41]

With the arrest of Ward Rodgers, the American Civil Liberties Union (ACLU) began a long period of activity on behalf of
the union, publicizing terrorization of its members and defending them legally. In New York, the ACLU set up an Auxiliary
Committee for the Defense of Ward Rodgers, uniting its own
support of the STFU with that of the League for Industrial Democracy, the Fellowship of Reconciliation, the Socialist Committee for the Promotion of Labor Defense, various trade unions,
and other organizations.[42] Members of these groups composed
the nucleus of what became the Workers' Defense League,
which, under the sponsorship of the Socialist party, raised funds
for the legal defense of arbitrarily imprisoned members of the
STFU and other labor unions. "So long as the poorest sharecropper suffers under the whip-lash of the 'planters' law,'" cried the
League, "none of us are free."[43]

The most indispensable outside aid was financial. The union
could not possibly have continued the 1934 practice of supporting itself on the pittances its destitute members could spare for
dues. Luckily, and largely through the influence of Norman
Thomas, Northern fund-raising organizations finally came to
the rescue as expenses for legal fees and relief began to mount
in 1935. Over three-fourths of STFU income that year was provided by the Strikers Emergency Relief Committee, in which
Thomas and Jack Herling were especially active, and by the
American Fund for Public Service. The latter foundation, sometimes known as the Garland Fund, was later discredited by its

41. John P. Davis to H. L. Mitchell, January 29, 1936, STFU Papers;
Max Kampelman, *The Communist Party vs. the C.I.O.* (N.Y.: Frederick
Praeger, 1957), pp. 56–57; Wilson Record, *The Negro and the Communist
Party* (Chapel Hill: The University of North Carolina Press, 1951), pp.
153–61.
42. ACLU, Press Release, February 8, 1935, STFU Papers.
43. Workers' Defense League, "To Establish Justice" (N.Y., 1940),
p. 16.

support of Communist-front causes and by the dominance of Communists on its board of directors, who were once reported lukewarm toward the STFU because they feared it was too anti-Communist. The balance of the union's 1935 income came from individuals and organizations such as the ACLU, the Socialist party, and the Church Emergency Relief Fund of the Federal Council of Churches of Christ in America. Dues payments added up to less than $500.[44] This would have surprised critics like James Robertson, a Cross County prosecuting attorney who charged that the STFU "collected $35,000 in dues last year from ignorant Negroes and white people."[45] In the winter of 1935–36, the financial outlook brightened as individual friends of the STFU began forming, in a few Northern cities, special committees to aid the STFU or agricultural workers generally. The money-raising effectiveness of these aid committees was directly proportional to the ambition and aggressiveness of their leaders, and consequently the Washington Committee to Aid Agricultural Workers, with the untiring Gardner Jackson at its head, became the most successful. Jackson secured sizable contributions from such well-known figures as Justice Brandeis and columnist Drew Pearson;[46] Archibald MacLeish also gave to the STFU.[47] Jackson himself was unstinting in his largesse, supporting his family entirely on his own earnings and using his considerable inheritance to finance organizations which he felt were fighting for human betterment.[48] Many other wealthy individuals granted large sums to the union, realizing that its stand was not against wealth but against the arbitrary and harmful use of wealth. There was Mrs. Ethel Clyde of the Clyde steamship family and Mrs. Esther Fisk Hammond,

---

44. H. L. Mitchell, "The Southern Tenant Farmers' Union in 1935," official report, n.d. [January, 1936], p. 13; Mitchell to Clarence Senior, September 30, 1935; Senior to Mitchell, October 1, 1935, both in SP Arch, Duke; Mitchell, expense statement to American Fund for Public Service, April 21, 1936, STFU Papers.
    45. Quoted in *Arkansas Gazette*, September 26, 1935.
    46. Interviews with Gardner Jackson, August 14, 1961, June 30, 1962; H. L. Mitchell to the author, July 17, 1961.
    47. H. L. Mitchell to Archibald MacLeish, June 17, 1936, STFU Papers.
    48. H. L. Mitchell to Gardner Jackson, December 26, 1935, August 26, 1936, and others, STFU Papers; various conversations and interviews with Jackson.

heiress to the Fisk fortune, who just "adored" Norman Thomas but wouldn't contribute to the Socialist party because she didn't like to give to organizations—except when one like the STFU caught her fancy.[49]

Welcome as such contributions were, forcibly as they demonstrated how powerful outside support could be, Mitchell disliked having his union serve primarily as a pet for philanthropists. Despite the social and economic helplessness of the STFU, its leaders were convinced that it had to become "a real union," complete with geographically widespread membership, formal recognition by employers and the labor movement, and the ability to strike successfully as a means to such recognition.

Expansion of the STFU beyond the Delta was aided by a fortuitous accident. In Muskogee, Oklahoma, a rough-hewn character named Odis Sweeden, mainly Cherokee and thoroughly unique, was preparing to leave his outhouse when an item on the newspaper fragment he tore off caught his eye. The story made the STFU sound interesting, so Sweeden decided to organize some locals around Muskogee. Afforded a great deal of autonomy, Sweeden built each Oklahoma local around the immediate needs of its members. He was extremely persuasive, but occasionally there were setbacks such as he and Mitchell met when addressing a group of Choctaws near Durant. The STFU spokesmen explained that poor Negroes and white men wanted the red men to join them in getting land for the workers. "Indian already organized," the Choctaw chief replied; "when white man and black man get ready to take back the land, we join them." The meeting was over.[50]

Until Sweeden's Oklahoma locals began proliferating, STFU leaders felt more optimism looking in the opposite direction,

49. Clarence Senior to Norman Thomas, November 30, 1936, SP Arch, Duke. Mitchell, heading a sharecropper delegation that passed through Santa Barbara, where Mrs. Hammond lived, planned to visit her, but when he "looked in a telephone book and found that about half of a page was given up to the Fisk Hammond estate . . . I lost my nerve. I just couldn't see myself taking these sharecroppers into such a mansion as that." Oral History MS, p. 101.

50. H. L. Mitchell, unsigned first person MS, n.d., Sec. II, pp. 15–16, STFU Papers; Oral History MS, p. 52; Mitchell to Norman Thomas and Clarence Senior, April 29, 1935, and Mitchell to Senior, June 4, 1935, both in SP Arch, Duke; *The Sharecroppers Voice*, July, 1935, September, 1935.

southeastward toward Alabama. Around Montgomery, a Share Croppers Union that seemed much like the STFU had been in existence since 1931, and its leader, Tom Burke, was eager to merge the SCU with the Arkansas union. Burke and his associates were Communists, but in 1935 there had occurred very few of the events which made Cold War anti-communism a staple item of the liberal creed. "Anybody going in your general direction looked awfully good to you," Howard Kester said.[51] To Mitchell, the quintessential pragmatist, the only sensible question to ask the Republican party, the Communist party, the Socialist or the Democratic party, was "what are you doing to help organize farm workers?" Therefore, Mitchell at first leaned even more toward the Communists than the Socialists: "I admired the CP., their ability to get things done, to publicize situations etc. and when ever it came to getting help in our difficulty, we were pleased to have anyone's aid."[52] In early 1935, when SCU leaders claimed to be doing well in Alabama, Mitchell was as warm toward them as toward their comrades at Commonwealth College and on the board of the Garland Fund; but that summer he went to Alabama and found that the SCU existed mainly on paper. His disappointment deepened when he discovered that "Tom Burke" was really Clyde Johnson, an itinerant Party worker with few roots among the people of the Black Belt. Publicly, Mitchell remained favorable toward the SCU, but to close friends he confided more and more doubts.[53]

There remained, however, the exciting prospect of joining in the formation of an agricultural workers' International (as

51. Interview with Howard Kester, July 17, 1961. On The Share Croppers Union, see Stuart Jamieson (ed.), *Labor Unionism in American Agriculture*, Bureau of Labor Statistics Bulletin No. 836 (Washington: G.P.O., 1945), pp. 292–97; John Beecher, "The Sharecroppers Union in Alabama," *Social Forces*, XIII (October, 1934), pp. 124–28.

52. H. L. Mitchell to Gardner Jackson, September 3, 1936, STFU Papers. This candid letter can be—and has been—used to bolster the very sensationalistic, and very inaccurate, accusation that Mitchell was once secretly a Communist. Actually, considered in its entirety, the letter explains that Mitchell only briefly was uncritical of the Communists, and then only because he was so idealistically non-ideological.

53. Clyde Johnson to H. L. Mitchell, n.d., [April, 1936], and Mitchell to Gardner Jackson, September 3, 1936, STFU Papers; interview with Leif Dahl, July 12, 1962; Mitchell to Clarence Senior, August 21, 1935, SP Arch, Duke.

unions with locals in both the United States and Canada are called). There was little chance—or little need, so it seemed—for the STFU to take the lead in forming such a large union, for the first steps were already being taken by Don Henderson, who had been dismissed from Columbia's faculty for allegedly spending more time on Communist party work than classroom work. Ideological ties remained less important to Mitchell than aid and ability: Henderson had experience working with radical farm and cannery unions in California and with New Jersey locals organized by Leif Dahl, a former student of his. However, though a brilliant theoretician and able administrator, he antagonized many of his closest associates by his autocratic manner. "You didn't work with Don Henderson, you worked for him," said Claude Williams.[54]

In the summer of 1935, beginning his campaign for a farm workers' International, Henderson set up a "National Committee for Unity of Agricultural and Rural Workers," and the STFU officially endorsed Henderson's periodical, *The Rural Worker*, at its next convention.[55] For several months, *The Rural Worker* kept noticeable espousal of the Party line at a minimum, giving STFU leaders little cause to regret their endorsement. Then, in the summer of 1936, Henderson and his comrades in the Share Croppers Union began calling for a plan of farm organization that, in keeping with the demands of Party orthodoxy, would recruit all farm owners and managers—including managing tenants—into one organization and all farm laborers—including sharecroppers—into another. This division was obvious, according to Marxist-Leninist logic. But in the Delta, a man might rapidly shift from one form of tenure to another; his status was often difficult to determine, as AAA discovered in the "managing share tenant" controversy; and, in any case, members of all tenure classes shared the same abysmal economic condition.

54. Interviews with Leif Dahl, July 12, 1962, Claude Williams, August 18, 1962; H. L. Mitchell, "Activities of Donald Henderson, Communist Specialist of Cannery and Agricultural Workers Union," n.d. [1947], STFU Papers; Kampelman, *Communist Party vs. C.I.O.*, p. 174.

55. Proceedings of the Second Annual Convention, p. 8; Donald Henderson to J. R. Butler, July 10, 1935, July 19, 1935, STFU Papers; *Commonwealth College Fortnightly*, January 15, 1936, CCP, Reel 2.

Appalled by the Communist disregard for cotton belt realities, STFU leaders began to doubt the wisdom of affiliating with anyone bound to obey higher authority so blindly. The divide-by-tenure policy was seen as "an effort to put the screws on the STFU,"[56] and Mitchell angrily told Henderson that "we do not look with favor upon the introduction of 'craft unionism' in the cotton fields . . . we are concerned with the needs of our people and do not intend to dissipate our efforts in following new lines or old ones."[57] Mitchell complained to Norman Thomas that "two or three centuries ago such people as Henderson were out hunting witches, and it is to be regretted that they are now engaged in attempting to organize farm laborers."[58] When Henderson made no satisfactory apology, the STFU Executive Council withdrew endorsement of his periodical. Finally, at the end of 1936, apparently because of pressure from Norman Thomas and Roger Baldwin, Henderson admitted the impropriety of calling editorially for the Communist policy. Although the STFU did not re-endorse Henderson's newspaper, Mitchell accepted his apology. As he had told Pat Jackson, "we certainly have more important things to do than to fight with CPer's. I am willing to work with them as long as they don't try to force their own policies on us. Thats all."[59]

Henderson lost only an endorsement by calling for the divide-by-tenure policy; the Share Croppers Union lost its last faint hopes for amalgamation with the STFU. When the SCU's *Southern Farm Leader* repeated the Communist line, Howard Kester and J. R. Butler attacked it editorially in the STFU's *The Sharecroppers Voice*, and Mitchell decided that consolidation of the

56. Sidney Hertzberg to H. L. Mitchell, August 11, 1936, STFU Papers.
57. H. L. Mitchell to Donald Henderson, August 12, 1936, STFU Papers.
58. H. L. Mitchell to Norman Thomas, November 17, 1936, STFU Papers.
59. H. L. Mitchell to Gardner Jackson, September 14, 1936; for other information on the disagreement and Henderson's apology, see STFU, National Executive Council, minutes of meeting, October 4, 1936; Jackson to J. R. Butler and Mitchell, July 28, 1936; Norman Thomas to Mitchell, December 7, 1936; Mitchell to Thomas, December 9, 1936; Henderson to Mitchell, December 21, 1936; Mitchell to Henderson, December 28, 1936, all in STFU Papers.

two unions was now "impossible . . . I can't trust people who change their entire program overnight on orders from a super organization."[60] Said he to one of the SCU leaders, "We cannot agree to the idea of destroying the STFU in compliance with the theoreticians of Union Square."[61]

Especially after his disillusion with the Communist unions began in the summer of 1935, Mitchell felt as much desire to compete as to co-operate with them. If the Communists seemed to block the STFU's geographical expansion, perhaps the STFU could surpass them in that *sine qua non* of a "real union," the power to strike successfully. Toward the end of August, 1935, STFU members were polled on the question of striking for a pay rate of $1 per hundred pounds of cotton. (The going rate was about forty to sixty cents.) The vote to strike was overwhelming; Mitchell announced it as 11,186 to 450, confessing privately that the "percentage is correct but the totals are stretched a bit for publicity purposes."[62] Naturally, no laborer dared picket his employer's fields or even tell him he was on strike; but thousands suddenly were confined in bed with the "mis'ry" or found it necessary to go fishing to replenish the family larder. To impress workers who were too afraid of their ridin' boss to risk such subterfuges, STFU leaders fabricated the story that scabs had been shot dead when they tried to go into the fields. The rumor spread wildly. Kester and Mitchell met a ragged hitch-hiker who said he was going over to Tennes-

60. J. R. Butler to Gardner Jackson, July 31, 1936, and Mitchell to Jackson, August 26, 1936, STFU Papers.

61. Mitchell to W. W. Martin, December 21, 1936, STFU Papers. The divide-by-tenure policy was not the Party's only misapplication of doctrine to cotton belt problems: making obeisance to the Soviet Union's solution of minority problems—giving each one its own constituent republic—the CPUSA decreed "self-determination in the South," i.e., that Negroes should rule a republic of their own in areas where they predominated numerically. The STFU knew that such a policy would simply exacerbate racial hostility among workers instead of diminishing it. Mitchell remembered a sharecropper named Matheny who, upon seeing some Communist literature advocating "Negro self-determination," became furious at the idea of setting up a "new country" in the good old U.S.A.—Record, *The Negro and the Communist Party*, pp. 109, *passim.*; Evelyn Smith to Lee Coller, February 16, 1938, STFU Papers; interview with H. L. Mitchell, December 3, 1961.

62. H. L. Mitchell to Clarence Senior, September 9, 1935, SP Arch, Duke.

see to work: "Theys a strike on over heah and 25 men already been killed for picking cotton."[63]

The planters had assured each other that labor would be plentiful in spite of the strike, "especially in view of Federal relief regulations denying relief to those persons refusing jobs."[64] A few days later the "plenty of farm hands" prediction was repeated,[65] but after that the planters and their newspapers fell silent as the strike took effect. Now, instead of propaganda, two croppers named Hez Redmond and George Fly were beaten with axe handles, fired upon, and evicted; numbers of laborers were charged with vagrancy and jailed in Cross County and elsewhere; organizer J. E. Cameroon was kidnapped and taken to the sheriff of St. Francis County, who, however, refused to imprison him.[66] In the village of Luxora one sleepy Sunday afternoon, union organizers George Andrews and Mr. and Mrs. Lee Moskop were arrested for "circulating hand bills urging cotton pickers to refuse to work" and held in the Blytheville jail for over a week.[67]

Partly to head off a possible revival of terrorism, but mainly because pay scales were actually raised by the strike to a new average level of seventy-five cents per hundred, the STFU called off the strike at the start of October. Although planters said they would have been paying the new rate anyway,[68] union members were jubilant. Referring to the meager results of SCU organizing, Mitchell told Claude Williams "the CP apparently made a failure where we succeeded" and added to Clarence Senior "they shouldn't be so cocky from now on."[69]

63. *The Sharecroppers Voice*, September, 1935; Mitchell, unsigned first person MS, n.d., Sec. II, pp. 17–18.

64. *Arkansas Gazette*, September 3, September 4, 1935.

65. *Ibid.*, September 8, 1935.

66. Mitchell affidavit; STFU, Statement to Governor's Commission on Farm Tenancy, n.d. [1936], both in STFU Papers.

67. *The Osceola* (Ark.) *Times*, September 27, 1935; *The Sharecroppers Voice*, October, 1935; *Arkansas Gazette*, October 2, 1935.

68. *Arkansas Gazette*, October 4, 1935.

69. H. L. Mitchell to Claude Williams, October 4, 1935, Claude Williams Papers; Mitchell to Clarence Senior, October 4, 1935, SP Arch, Duke. On the strike results and members' enthusiasm, see Mitchell, "The Southern Tenant Farmers' Union in 1935," official report, n.d. [January, 1936]; Oral History MS, pp. 49–51; *The Sharecroppers Voice*, October, 1935; *Commonwealth College Fortnightly*, October 15, 1935, CCP, Reel 2;

Mitchell was right: the strike was the union's greatest achievement in over a year of existence. It revived the interest of the STFU's sympathizers; Reinhold Niebuhr's Committee on Economic and Racial Justice, various branches of the Socialist party, and union locals across the country, responding to a request from AFL President William Green himself, sent in contributions for strike relief and support of STFU organizers.[70] More important, the union expanded phenomenally. "Over thirty new locals have been organized within the past 45 days," Mitchell wrote, "and many more will be during this month. Two were reported today."[71] Thad Snow, an ex-newspaperman whose social conscience had not evaporated when he became a plantation owner, invited STFU leaders to organize his tenants and informed them that his entire area—the Missouri bootheel— could be brought into the union. Socialists in the vicinity concurred. As Mitchell looked for an organizer who could take full advantage of the opportunity, his eye fell upon John Handcox, the bright young Negro poet and songster who sometimes called himself "John Henry." In the early months of 1936 Handcox organized dozens of Missouri locals as Planter Snow beamed and tried to convince his associates that unionism was a good thing.[72]

Surely, the STFU leaders thought, with even a plantation owner recognizing their union as a genuine one, the time had now come to appeal to the American Federation of Labor itself. With preparations already getting under way at Atlantic City for the 1935 AFL convention, the Socialists' Clarence Senior redoubled his efforts to secure STFU recognition there. Mitchell presented his case to the Federation's Frank Morrison, and Socialist party Labor Secretary Paul Porter was pulling strings

---

W. Carroll Munro, "King Cotton's Stepchildren," *Current History*, XLIV (June, 1936), pp. 66–67.

70. Oral History MS, p. 51; Elisabeth Gilman to Howard Kester, December 12, 1935; Will Hale, Jr., to H. L. Mitchell, September 14, 1935; Hilda Hulbert to Mitchell, February 2, 1936; Otto Jessen to Mitchell, February 9, 1936, all in STFU Papers.

71. H. L. Mitchell to Clarence Senior, September 31, 1935, SP Arch, Duke.

72. Oral History MS, p. 112; Clarence Senior to H. L. Mitchell, September 26, 1935, SP Arch, Duke; Mitchell to Eleanor Fowler, August 12, 1936, STFU Papers.

well before the convention began on October 7. With the ground carefully prepared, A. Philip Randolph secured approval of a resolution recognizing the STFU and calling for "sympathetic consideration to any request for assistance" from it.[73] But the reception accorded to STFU representative Howard Kester, in contrast, almost justified Senior's prediction of "a hysterical red scare" at the convention. "I was persona non grata," Kester remembered. "I met the various union leaders by having them try to shake me off." The Randolph resolution, he realized, did no more than admit the STFU existed.

As thoroughly as John L. Lewis later did, Kester realized that the unorganized American masses were being "seduced with fair words" at the convention. Every time a union leader reminded him disdainfully that a sharecropper union could never be a paying proposition it brought home to him the implications of the old observation that American trade unionism has been money-conscious and dues-conscious rather than class-conscious. The final blow was meeting William Green, whose comprehension of the STFU inspired Kester to agree heartily with a remark he later heard John L. Lewis make: "I have studied William Green's mind for 25 years and I reluctantly declare to you that there is nothing there."[74]

The convention disillusioned STFU leaders even more deeply than the Share Croppers Union had. If nothing could be done in the nation's capital, if philanthropy kept the union alive but achieved nothing for its members, the sharecroppers' only hope was to strike. Then, when a strike succeeded against all odds, only to produce nothing but a disdainful rebuff from organized labor, what next?

73. AFL, Report of Proceedings, 55th Annual Convention (Atlantic City, October 7–19, 1935), pp. 280–81, 588; H. L. Mitchell to Frank Morrison, September 16, 1935, SP Arch, Duke; Clarence Senior to Mitchell, October 1, 1935, SP Arch, Duke.

74. Interview with Howard Kester, July 17, 1961; Clarence Senior's "red scare" prediction is in his letter to H. L. Mitchell, October 8, 1935, SP Arch, Duke.

# 5.

## Gardner Jackson
## to the Rescue

*M*embers of the Southern Tenant Farmers' Union faced the end of the year 1935 with more than their usual trepidation. December always brought uncertainty because oral cropping contracts terminated at the end of each year, but in previous years the AAA had not yet affirmed the right of landlords to "move" tenants and perhaps make money in the process. By December, 1935, things had changed ominously.

The union could do little for sharecroppers who moved voluntarily, not knowing that the surplus of workers made unemployment their likely lot; but outright evictions still had to be fought somehow, despite the failure of the Norcross suit the year before. So, assembled in convention during the first week of 1936, STFU delegates first established a Central Defense Committee for legal protection, then enthusiastically welcomed two representatives of the Arkansas Department of Labor who both promised to help defend them against cheating landlords. Finally, the convention's climax was Mitchell's warning to C. H. Dibble, owner of a plantation near Parkin, that his property would be picketed if he continued the mass eviction of his sharecroppers. Dibble had been completely satisfied with his croppers, had even considered signing a collective bargaining contract with them, when a delegation of planters—so Mitchell heard—threatened to ostracize him and have his credit cut off if he continued to "encourage" the union. Dibble suddenly turned about-face, ordering almost one hundred persons to get off his property by January 16. There was no pretense that the threatened tenants were loafers. Dibble admitted that they were excellent workers, all paid out of debt—the union claimed Dibble even owed them money—and that their union membership with the sole reason for their eviction.[1]

Mitchell knew that suing Dibble might not produce results. The first thing to do, he felt, was to force the plight of the hundred evictees into the public eye. So he had organizers J. E. Cameroon and Wiley Harris organize them into a tent colony on a roadside near Parkin. Their misery, Mitchell knew, would be no greater than if they were scattered in unheated shacks across the countryside, but it would be in the open, and perhaps something might be done about it.[2]

Instead, the first reaction to the tent colony was a planter blacklist of STFU tenants; throughout the Delta literally thousands were driven from their homes. "I have never been so nauseated by this situation as on this trip," Dr. William Amberson declared after driving through the area. "The utter brutality and callousness with which the planters are throwing off families is beyond belief."[3] Within a month, a dynamite stick was thrown into the tent colony, but Cross County Sheriff C. M. Stacy flatly refused to investigate. "Just another publicity stunt," said he. Whereupon Mitchell told him, "If harm comes to these people as a result of your failure to do your duty, the Southern Tenant Farmers' Union will prosecute you in the courts of law

1. Herman Goldberger to C. H. Dibble, November 18, 1935, STFU Papers; H. L. Mitchell, unsigned first person MS, n.d., Sec. II, pp. 18–19; H. L. Mitchell, "The Southern Tenant Farmers' Union in 1935," official report, n.d. [January, 1936], pp. 6, 12; *The Sharecroppers Voice*, February, 1936; STFU, statement to Governor's Commission on Farm Tenancy, n.d. [1936].

2. H. L. Mitchell to J. E. Cameroon and Wiley Harris, January 13, 1936; Mitchell to Norman Thomas, January 16, 1936; telegram, John L. Lewis to Mitchell, January 17, 1936, all in STFU Papers.

3. William Amberson, memo to H. L. Mitchell and Howard Kester, n.d. [January, 1936], STFU Papers; see also Dorothy Day, "Sharecroppers," *America*, March 7, 1936, p. 517.

as an accomplice of whatever crime may be committed."[4] "Crime" was not an inappropriate word; elsewhere in STFU territory, criminal activity had already begun, and it was being committed by the law officers themselves.

On the night of January 16, 1936, a union meeting was in progress at St. Peter's Methodist Church near Earle, Arkansas. Though they should have known better, some of the members had brought shotguns along to scare away little boys who had been throwing rocks at the windows. In the midst of the meeting, deputies Everett Hood and Paul D. Peacher, without a warrant, stomped into the meeting to break it up. Everybody who could started running; James Ball grabbed his gun, reached behind the rostrum for the dues book, and immediately was beaten and kicked to the floor by Hood, who later claimed that Ball was preparing to shoot him and that if he, Hood, had done his duty he would have killed him then and there. After smashing Ball senseless, the two deputies threw the young Negro in jail and charged him with intent to kill. Then both lawmen returned to the church. Finding several persons still there, they opened fire, wounded two men in the back as they ran for their lives, and arrested three more. "Earle Deputy Attack Victim," cried the headline in the Jonesboro paper, and Sheriff Curlin said he would arrest six or seven other Negroes for "attacking" Deputy Hood.[5]

The deputies noticed that Willie Hurst had been the one person to see everything that happened, and they heard that he was willing to testify against them. Both of these men were feared and hated by Negroes in the area; they were excellent representatives of that "type of deliberate nigger-hazers and nigger-killers" Wilbur J. Cash was soon to describe in *The Mind of the South*: "men who not only capitalized on every shadow of excuse to kick and cuff him, to murder him, but also with malice

4. Memphis *Press-Scimitar*, February 25, 1936; *Arkansas Gazette*, February 26, 1936.
5. *Jonesboro Daily Tribune*, January 17, 18, 1936; Mitchell affidavit; Newell N. Fowler, Brief for Appellant James Ball in the Supreme Court of Arkansas, n.d., STFU Papers; STFU, Statement to Governor's Commission on Farm Tenancy, n.d. [August, 1936]; *Socialist Call*, February 29, 1936; Helen Norfjor, "A Southern Tenant Farmer and a Birthday Dinner," *Farmers' National Weekly*, August 7, 1936.

aforethought baited him into a show of resentment in order so to serve him."[6] And yet, when the two deputies tried to bully Hurst into signing a statement exonerating them, he refused. A few nights later, two men built like Hood and Peacher—but wearing masks, so nobody ever discovered who they were—burst into a home where Hurst was visiting and murdered him. No inquest was ever held, and the fatal bullet was kept by local authorities.[7] With his witness gone, Ball was sentenced by a landowning judge to seven years in prison; the Arkansas Supreme Court later graciously reduced the sentence to a year and reprimanded Deputy Hood for violating the right of free assemblage.[8] It was the only time the conviction of any STFU member was ever upheld on appeal to a higher court.

The day after Ball was beaten and arrested, Howard Kester, union attorney Herman Goldberger, and organizer J. E. Cameroon visited the tent colony near Parkin and then met with about 450 sharecroppers in the Providence Methodist Church, also near Earle. In the midst of the meeting, Deputy Hood came in at the head of a khaki-clad, grinning mob of planters and riding bosses—Boss Dulaney, Jerome Hood, L. L. Barham, Otis Belford, Frank Hill, and Ernest Richards were among those recognized. They immediately began slugging the sharecroppers with ax handles and pistol butts, guffawing loudly as they cracked the skulls of screaming women and children. Then they smashed the furniture and broke out the windows for good measure. As Deputy Hood shoved Kester out the door, he promised him that "There's going to be another Elaine Massacre, only the next time we'll kill whites as well as niggers." By the

6. Wilbur J. Cash, *The Mind of the South* (New York: A. A. Knopf, 1941), pp. 122–23.

7. STFU, Statement to Governor's Commission on Farm Tenancy, n.d. [August, 1936]; *The Sharecroppers Voice*, March, 1936, January, 1937; Mitchell affidavit. A minister who visited Hurst's widow to console her was threatened with a shotgun by her landlord and told to get out of her house, as he was "interfering with labor." When the minister protested that he was only doing his duty, the planter swore, waved the gun, and said, "I'd shoot you if you was Jesus Christ himself!" Philip Kinsley, "Farm Co-op Held Tillers' Answer to Landlords," *Chicago Daily Tribune*, February 15, 1937.

8. Fowler, Brief for Appellant James Ball; STFU, Statement to Governor's Commission; *The Sharecroppers Voice*, July, 1936, January, 1937.

time Kester could return to Memphis, his wife Alice was frantic with grief; she had been telephoned condolences on his death.[9]

Threats of a second Elaine Massacre were so widespread that the only question seemed to be how soon the slaughter would begin. An enterprising salesman named Miller offered to supply the STFU with machine guns, citing in his sales pitch the fact that he had just sold six automatic weapons to Mississippi County planters and that the union, as a consequence, would surely want to be prepared for defense.[10] (One wonders how many guns he told the planters he had sold to the union.) STFU meetings in the Delta either ceased or went underground entirely, but brutality to individual members continued. "Freedom of speech and assemblage are as completely flouted in Northeastern Arkansas as though the state were a part of Hitler's Reich," the union charged.[11]

As Howard Kester pointed out, STFU members "have been reared with a shotgun in their hands and . . . have been taught 'direct action' from the cradle up as the best method of settling disputes." Under the impact of beatings and intimidation, the patience of many must have been sorely tried, but *The Share-croppers Voice* appealed to members to maintain the union's record of nonviolence. Fortunately, the appeal was heeded, although members reacted in various ways. C. A. Withers of Ed-

9. Interview with Howard Kester, July 18, 1961; STFU, Statement to Governor's Commission; Mitchell affidavit; STFU press release, January 18, 1936; Mitchell and Howard Kester, letter in *The Nation*, February 12, 1936; *Commonwealth College Fortnightly*, February 1, 1936, CCP, Reel 2. A few months later Hood again revealed his lovable nature; as 78-year-old Jessie McBass was picking cotton, Hood drove up and announced, "I am just going to give you 24 hours to get out of Arkansas and you had better not be found in the state after that time or you will be found hanging from a limb. . . . I thought you told me you were not going to have anything more to do with that God-damned union." Hood told McBass's son to get his father out of the state before he was lynched. McBass got out. Jessie McBass, signed affidavit, October 14, 1936, STFU Papers.

10. Mitchell affidavit. It should be repeated that the original of this affidavit, which the author has relied upon heavily, was signed and notarized, and the STFU was prepared to bring it to court. Events mentioned in it are corroborated at every point that can be checked against other sources.

11. STFU, Statement to Governor's Commission; Dorothy Day, "Share-croppers," *America*, March 7, 1936, p. 517.

mondson angrily warned that "if they rade our meetting there may be some plnters Killed as well as union men."[12] On the other hand, Kelly Williams, leader of one of the Earle locals, began staying drunk; if he couldn't strike back, he was determined not to die sober.[13] Some STFU members may have heeded the panic-stricken voice of *The Southern Liberator*, a Negro newspaper which begged black sharecroppers to avert massacre by leaving the STFU. "If you have a just complaint to make pertaining to your working conditions," pleaded the oddly named *Liberator*, "take it to your boss and you will get more consideration than joining some Radical movement—DON'T BE AN INGRATE!"[14]

For white as well as black men, following the *Liberator*'s advice might have been necessary for survival had it not been for Gardner Jackson's work in Washington. After his dismissal from the AAA, he could easily have taken another government position or returned to journalism, but he preferred to devote his entire attention and fortune to the task of organizing farm workers. In the summer of 1935, already having sponsored such demonstrations as the STFU picketing of the Department of Agriculture, Jackson announced his establishment of a National Committee on Rural Social Planning, the purpose of which, according to the *New York Times*, was "to study problems arising from work of the resettlement administration and those expected under legislation like the Bankhead Farm Tenant Bill."[15] Formation of such a committee had been urged by Justice Louis D. Brandeis; President Roosevelt, too, assured Jackson that he was delighted to hear of the committee's formation and would be happy to permit use of his letters to Jackson for committee publicity. Except for a few active associates like Professor Rupert Vance of the University of North Carolina, the committee was really Pat Jackson. Before his organiza-

12. C. A. Withers to H. L. Mitchell, July 22, 1936, STFU Papers.

13. H. L. Mitchell, unsigned first person MS, n.d., Sec. II, p. 20.

14. *The Southern Liberator* [Forrest City, Ark.], February, 1936; a copy of this issue is in the STFU scrapbook, STFU Papers. See also *Marked Tree Tribune*, June 27, 1935.

15. *New York Times*, July 8, 1935, p. 4; interview with Gardner Jackson, August 14, 1961.

tion was six months old, Jackson had become the STFU's "authorized representative" in Washington.[16]

To keep STFU members alive, Jackson had to secure food as well as physical protection. Previously H. L. Mitchell had claimed considerable success in persuading local authorities to extend relief to evicted sharecroppers, even though the amount available was seldom more than a few dollars a month.[17] But in the winter of 1936 the magnitude of the problem and the prejudice of officials from the state level downwards made it clear that only Federal action could solve the problem. Shortly after the Little Rock convention, as Dibble kicked out his croppers, Mitchell and Howard Kester left for Washington, where they met with Jackson and Dorothy Detzer to plan their appeal to relief officials. Armed with up-to-the-minute reports from Dr. Amberson, who was collecting specific examples of relief refusal, Jackson and Kester conferred with Will Alexander and Brooks Hays of the Resettlement Administration and Aubrey Williams of the Works Progress Administration (WPA), which had supplanted FERA in 1935. Resettlement Administrator Rexford Tugwell attended one meeting and encouraged Alexander and Hays to do all they could for the STFU. Alexander assured Kester and Jackson that Resettlement had funds available for direct relief and, as a long-range solution, would try to place as many evictees as possible into Resettlement community projects. Tugwell, Alexander, and Hays then directed regional Resettlement Administrator T. Roy Reid to see that his Arkansas subordinates carried out their instructions.[18]

WPA official Williams was politely noncommittal at first, un-

16. Interviews with Gardner Jackson, August 14, 1961, June 30, 1962; National Committee for Rural Social Planning letterhead, and J. R. Butler and H. L. Mitchell, credentials of Gardner Jackson, both in STFU Papers.

17. H. L. Mitchell, "The Southern Tenant Farmers' Union in 1935," official report, n.d. [January, 1936], p. 9; Arthur Raper, *Preface to Peasantry* (Chapel Hill: University of North Carolina Press, 1936), pp. 254–59; W. T. Wilson and W. H. Metzler, "Characteristics of Arkansas Rehabilitation Clients," Arkansas Agricultural Experiment Station Bulletin 348 (Fayetteville, June, 1937), pp. 5–7.

18. William R. Amberson to H. L. Mitchell (telegram), January 27, 1936; Howard Kester to Mitchell and Amberson, February 21, 1936; Gardner Jackson, memo to Franklin D. Roosevelt, March 12, 1936; Jackson, telegram to Mitchell, March 2, 1936, all in STFU Papers; Norman Thomas to Clarence Senior, January 28, 1936, SP Arch, Duke.

til he made his own investigation of the extent of WPA aid in the Delta and discovered the STFU was giving him more reliable information than his own subordinates. Angrily Williams called in Arkansas WPA Administrator Floyd Sharp, a conservative typographical union leader who regarded skilled craft unions as the only respectable ones and had aided the state legislature in their attack on "radicals" the previous year. Sharp admitted that his office had refused to extend aid to the evictees, because twenty-five "reputable citizens" in Cross and Crittenden counties had pointed out that they had tents to live in and a few chickens and corn cobs to eat. ("No worker is a citizen, let alone reputable," commented the STFU.)[19] Williams informed Sharp that his "reputable citizens" were over-ruled, effective immediately.[20] However, neither Reid nor Sharp were able—or, perhaps, willing—to make local officials extend aid to union members. The sharecroppers continued to starve and shiver, and STFU leaders cried out against the defiance of orders. Gardner Jackson told President Roosevelt's secretary, Marvin McIntyre, that Washington officials "either frankly or tacitly admit that they cannot make the local and regional officials in Arkansas carry out" Federal policies, and he told Roosevelt himself that "the record justifies and calls for the removal of the local officials involved."[21] But nothing was done. No relief was given; no officials were dismissed.

Jackson had learned, however, that strong sympathy for the sharecroppers did exist at the top of the governmental pyramid; men like Aubrey Williams, Will Alexander, and, to a growing

19. *The Sharecroppers Voice*, February, 1936.
20. On the Williams-Sharp episode and Williams's promise to have changes made, see Gardner Jackson, memo to Franklin D. Roosevelt, March 12, 1936; Howard Kester to H. L. Mitchell and Dr. William Amberson, February 21, 1936; Aubrey Williams, telegram to Floyd Sharp, February 3, 1936; Jackson, telegrams to Mitchell, February 3, 1936, February 5, 1936, all in STFU Papers; interview with Howard Kester, July 17, 1961; *The Sharecroppers Voice*, February, 1936; Sharp, testimony to the [Arkansas] Legislative Investigating Committee, February 18, 1935, CCP, Reel 1.
21. Gardner Jackson to Marvin McIntyre, March 12, 1936; Jackson to Roosevelt, March 12, 1936; Norman Thomas, "President Roosevelt and the Sharecroppers," NBC radio script, March 26, 1936; Mary Hillyer to Harry Hopkins, March 25, 1936, all in STFU Papers; *The Sharecroppers Voice*, March, 1936.

extent, Henry Wallace, could be won over by specific statements, by detailed lists of evicted families and the names of planters who had beaten them up—"the passing of these lists around the departments has a definite effect," he explained to STFU leaders. He told them whom to contact in the AFL and in the United Mine Workers, and coached them on what to say to the president and to the Resettlement Administration. He wanted weekly reports from Arkansas and regular statements on the condition of the families in the tent colonies.[22]

Meanwhile, Jackson had begun discussing a congressional anti-terrorism resolution with Representatives Caroline O'Day and Vito Marcantonio of New York and Maury Maverick of Texas.[23] The Socialist party was seeking a very similar measure, which Marcantonio also was backing, along with Representative Thomas Amlie of Wisconsin and Senator Rush Holt of West Virginia.[24] In addition to anxiety over sharecropper maltreatment, other forces were at work. The American Civil Liberties Union and the Federal Council of Churches of Christ in America, led by Howard Kester's friend James Myers, had long demanded Congressional investigation of terrorism; Edward Levinson's exposé of management's finks and goons, *I Break Strikes!*, had just appeared; and Heber Blankenhorn led a number of National Labor Relations Board investigators who were increasingly convinced that the Wagner Act could be made viable only by Congressional exposure of those working to subvert it.[25]

At this propitious juncture, to consolidate the growing support for civil rights proposals, Jackson persuaded Mrs. Ethel Clyde, the wealthy steamship heiress, to finance a dinner at Washington's exclusive Cosmos Club and extend invitations to

22. Gardner Jackson to H. L. Mitchell, March 12, 1936, and others, STFU Papers.

23. Gardner Jackson to H. L. Mitchell, January 18, 20, 1936, February 12, 1936, March 12, 1936, and others, all in STFU Papers; Jerold S. Auerbach, *Labor and Liberty: The LaFollette Committee and the New Deal* (Indianapolis: Bobbs-Merrill, 1966), p. 62.

24. Clarence Senior to Jack Herling, February 10, 1936; Paul Porter to Herling, February 11, 1936; Herling to Norman Thomas and Clarence Senior, February 12, 1936, all in SP Arch, Duke. The Amlie resolution, H.R. 270, had been drafted by the AAA purgee Lee Pressman and was aimed even more specifically at the STFU's tormentors than the O'Day-Maverick-Marcantonio measure. See Auerbach, *Labor and Liberty*, p. 43.

25. Auerbach, *Labor and Liberty*, pp. 30, 32, 49–61.

the most active supporters of workers' rights guarantees. As guests arrived, they found that conversation centered around a beaten, bandaged sharecropper who had come with Howard Kester, who was making sure that his humble friend was seen by everyone. Only one person scoffed at Kester's "sinking to the level of propaganda," and Brooks Hays, not by any means the most radical guest present, immediately sprang to Kester's defense.[26]

Jackson had arranged the program with care. After Kester had related a few Arkansas incidents, the remaining speakers would lead up to John L. Lewis, who could be counted upon to present a thunderously eloquent exposition of labor's handicaps. Finally, Wisconsin's Senator Robert LaFollette, Jr., conscious of having inherited the mantle of progressivism and sympathetic to the current workers' rights agitation, would conclude. After the verbal pounding by Lewis, Jackson surmised, La Follette might promise definite action. It worked out perfectly. Lewis was never better: "Not until blood is flowing in the streets," he declaimed, "will Congress realize the menace to civil liberties!" LaFollette rose to the challenge, pledging personally to lead a full-scale congressional investigation of violations of workers' free speech and assembly.[27] Thus was born the famous LaFollette Committee investigation of violations of free speech and rights of labor, which filled newspapers in 1936 and 1937 with its disclosures of management's warfare against collective bargaining. As Pat Jackson told the author, "The LaFollette Civil Liberties Committee derived directly out of the STFU."[28]

26. Interview with Howard Kester, July 17, 1961; Transcript of H. L. Mitchell's recorded interview for the Columbia University Oral History Collection, STFU Papers and elsewhere (referred to hereafter as Oral History MS), p. 63.

27. Interviews with Gardner Jackson, August 14, 1961, June 26, 1962. Jackson gave almost the same version of Lewis's remark on both occasions, so the author feels that the clarity of Jackson's memory justifies writing Lewis's statement as a direct quotation. On the Cosmos Club dinner, see Auerbach, *Labor and Liberty*, pp. 46–47; Oral History MS, p. 63; H. L. Mitchell, unsigned first person MS, n.d., Sec. II, p. 20; interviews with Gardner Jackson, August 14, 1961, June 26, 1962; interview with Howard Kester, July 17, 1961.

28. Interview with Gardner Jackson, August 14, 1961. See also the judgement of LaFollette Committee historian Auerbach, *Labor and Liberty*, p. 32.

And yet the LaFollette investigation, though inspired in large measure by lawlessness against Southern tenant farmers, never got into STFU territory. After LaFollette introduced his resolution (Senate Resolution 266), it was returned to his Senate Committee on Education and Labor, and Jackson immediately moved to bring STFU evidence into the picture. Mitchell, responding to Jackson's appeal, promised that he and Kester would bring along no less than twenty-five signed affidavits, the wrapper from the dynamite thrown into the Parkin tent colony, the shell ejector from the machine gunning of McKinney's home, and a couple of beaten sharecroppers as well.[29] But then the political power of undemocratically elected Southern senators began to show itself. "LAFOLLETTE AND OTHERS DISPOSED TO PLAY OUR EVIDENCE DOWN FOR PURPOSES OF POLITICAL STRATEGY," Jackson wired Mitchell, "IN HOPE OF GETTING RESOLUTION THROUGH WITHOUT STIRRING UP SOUTHERN SENATORS."[30] Eventually Heber Blankenhorn's evidence of management attacks on labor's Wagner Act rights provided most of the impetus that carried LaFollette's resolution through the Senate.[31] LaFollette promised STFU leaders in 1937 that he would take his investigation into their area if only one more appropriation could be scraped through Congress,[32] but that "one more appropriation" never came. Ironically, John L. Lewis told Gardner Jackson that "we would never have been able to organize" the CIO without the spotlight thrown by the LaFollette committee on management-financed terrorism,[33] yet the little STFU had to struggle along without such aid.

With no relief, with no public investigation of the violence

29. H. L. Mitchell to Gardner Jackson, April 14, 1936; see also Mitchell to Jackson, April 2, 1936; Howard Kester to Mitchell, n.d. [April, 1936]; Jackson to Mitchell, April 6, 1936; Jackson to Kester, April 10, 1936, all in STFU Papers.

30. Gardner Jackson, telegram to H. L. Mitchell, April 14, 1936, STFU Papers.

31. Auerbach, *Labor and Liberty*, pp. 65–73. See also H. L. Mitchell to Gardner Jackson, April 14, 1936, STFU Papers. "I was much more impressed with Sen. [Lewis] Schwellenbach [of Washington]," said Mitchell, becoming discouraged with LaFollette's efforts.

32. Interviews with H. L. Mitchell, December 3, 1961; Howard Kester, July 17, 1961.

33. Interview with Gardner Jackson, August 14, 1961.

directed against them, STFU members had to fear for life itself. Now, in Washington, Jackson and Norman Thomas were trying to stave off another Elaine Massacre. Supporting their pleas, Rexford Tugwell assured President Roosevelt that "bloodshed of some kind is expected by everyone."[34]

Accordingly, Roosevelt brought up the question of Arkansas terrorism at the next cabinet meeting, Friday, March 6, 1936. Jackson had been talking to his friends in the Labor Department, and Secretary of Labor Frances Perkins suggested that a Federal mediator be sent to the Delta. Members of the cabinet nodded approvingly, and the president appeared to agree. But then Vice-president John Nance Garner, "Cactus Jack" from Texas, interposed an objection: "It would embarrass Joe Robinson [the Senate Majority Leader from Arkansas]. We ought not to do anything without taking it up with him. He's up for re-election this fall, and that's a very delicate situation in Arkansas."[35] Always conscious of political amenities, Roosevelt agreed with Garner that a Federal investigation would be embarrassing. Instead, FDR directed Tugwell to contact Senator Robinson and enlist his support for some kind of state action to reduce the likelihood of bloodshed. Robinson, though strongly opposed to the STFU and loyal to the cotton planters, was even more loyal to the Democratic party and to Roosevelt, the Party's chieftain. He agreed with Tugwell to put pressure on Governor Futrell to appoint a committee which would receive Federal funds if necessary to carry out its task: to investigate the terrorism and recommend steps to stop it.[36] Tugwell also composed a reply to Norman Thomas, to be sent over Roosevelt's signature, telling him of FDR's "suggestion" that Futrell name an investigating committee. But, added Tugwell, the STFU's tribulations "seem to me beyond the scope of Federal interference." Reveal-

34. Rexford Tugwell to Franklin D. Roosevelt, March 10, 1936, in response to Roosevelt's memo to Tugwell, March 2, 1936, both in OF 1650, FDR Library.

35. Drew Pearson and Robert S. Allen, "The Washington Merry-Go-Round," in *Arkansas Gazette* and other newspapers of March 17, 18, 1936; Gardner Jackson, telegram to H. L. Mitchell, March 4, 1936; Jackson to Mitchell, March 12, 1936, both in STFU Papers.

36. Rexford Tugwell to Franklin D. Roosevelt, March 10, 1936, OF 1650, FDR Library.

ingly, the president refused to sanction such a remark; he crossed it out of the rough draft, and sent his answer to Thomas without it.[37]

Since individual acts of terrorism had not stopped the STFU —the union claimed that seventy-one white and fifty-two Negro tenants applied for membership in the Earle locals immediately after the raids by Deputy Hood[38]—the union's leaders never knew why there had been no massacre, despite the failure of either Federal or state governments to take action. There was a rumor that "a number of influential people" had contacted Delta sheriffs and warned them of the consequences to Arkansas of a mass bloodletting, but, not knowing of the Tugwell-Robinson-Futrell contacts, union officials had no idea who the "influential people" were.[39]

Inexplicably saved from liquidation, the STFU continued to take courage from Jackson's work in the nation's capital. Beginning a campaign of his own to organize a nationwide farm labor union, he succeeded in having Henry Wallace himself address an initial conference in Washington. With Communists organizing many of the country's most effective unions, there could be no question of refusing to work with them; Mitchell and Kester were concerned only that Jackson distinguish bona fide locals from such "paper" ones as the Alabama Share Croppers Union.[40] Surely, the least that STFU leaders could do to assist Jackson's organizing efforts, so they believed, was again to demonstrate their organization's viability as "a real union." Had they not scored an impressive victory in the previous fall's cotton picking strike?

And so, as chopping time approached—the period in spring

37. [Rexford Tugwell], "Suggested Reply to Attached Telegram," n.d. [March 12, 1936], and Franklin D. Roosevelt, telegram to Norman Thomas, March 13, 1936, both in OF 1650, FDR Library.
38. *The Sharecroppers Voice*, February, 1936.
39. *The Sharecroppers Voice*, March, 1936.
40. Gardner Jackson to Henry A. Wallace, February 14, 1936; Jackson to H. L. Mitchell, April 6, 1936; Howard Kester to Mitchell, n.d. [March, 1936]; Mitchell to Sidney Hertzberg and Aron Gilmartin, August 30, 1936; Mitchell to Jackson, September 3, 1936; Jackson to Mitchell, September 12, 1936, all in STFU Papers; *The Sharecroppers Voice*, May, 1936; William T. Ham to H. R. Tolley, Memorandum on Labor—Sharecroppers Conference, March 30, 1936, L-TS, RG 145, N Arch.

# FARM WORKERS — COTTON CHOPPERS DAY LABORERS

# DEMAND

## $1.50 per 10 hour day . . .

### Tractor Drivers, $2.50 per 10 hour day

Refuse to work for starvation wages now being paid by the owners, stay out the fields until your demands are met,

**CENTRAL WAGE COMMITTEE
SOUTHERN TENANT FARMERS' UNION**

## *This Call is Effective Today*

All members of the Southern Tenant Farmers' Union, who work for wages, and all other workers now employed as day laborers will stay out of the fields until the union wage is paid.

HONEST WORKERS WON'T SCAB, await orders to return to work by your local committees.

*Fifteen cents an hour: a goal to fight for in 1936*

when weeds must be hoed out of the young cotton plants—
Mitchell again turned from publicity to "real union" action.
With farm workers across the Delta receiving only 75 cents a
day, he was confident that a strike at the peak of the chopping
season might push wages as high as $1 or $1.25. Unfortunately,
the strike vote was taken almost three months in advance, and
the results inevitably leaked out, giving the planters abundant
time to plan counter-measures.[41] Possibly union leaders had forgotten that the picking strike had succeeded largely because it
took the power structure by surprise.

Despite Governor Futrell's disapproval of the STFU, he had
no immediate plans to break the strike. Believing the planters'
claim that it was ineffective rather than the STFU claim that
three thousand men were idle, he declared that the strike was
"nothing to worry about. If it so arises to require my attention
it will be taken."[42] But, responding to planter demands, a local
sheriff, J. M. Campbell, requested the governor to send in the
National Guard. "Things look pretty bad just now," the sheriff
said. "We arrested two Negro strikers late today and found
high-powered rifles and dum-dum bullets in their homes." No
proof of this accusation was given and no further mention of it
was made. Local planters and lawmen admitted that there was
no apparent threat of violence—their fears "were for tomorrow,"
they said. The American Civil Liberties Union promptly urged
the governor *not* to send any troops.[43] Governor Futrell sent a
contingent of twenty-five National Guardsmen and some state

41. Memphis *Press-Scimitar*, May 27, 1936; *Arkansas Gazette*, May 30,
1936; Oral History MS, pp. 52–54; H. L. Mitchell to Gardner Jackson,
May 6, 1936, STFU Papers.
42. *Jonesboro Daily Tribune*, May 21, 1936.
43. *New York Times*, June 1, 1936, p. 10; *Arkansas Gazette*, May 31,
1936; Memphis *Press-Scimitar*, June 1, 1936; ACLU, telegram quoted in
the [St. Paul] *Minnesota Leader*, June 20, 1936. To help assess the prob-
able effect of their telegram on Governor Futrell, the ACLU asked W. E.
Green, a former official of the Arkansas Department of Labor, to tell
them what Futrell was like. Replied Green: "I found him a man without
knowledge of law, with no interest in any measure that might not suit his
'sponsors' in Greene County, mentally and physically lazy—and superim-
posed on these, a vicious but cautious hatred of all who incurred his
enmity; I found him wholly irresponsible—his word or pledge meant
nothing, if it did not suit him to make good." W. E. Green to the ACLU,
June 7, 1936, STFU Papers.

rangers to the strike area anyway, "following reports that striking cotton choppers would march on Eastern Arkansas plantations to try to persuade all workers to quit the fields." Captain
John Dillon, commanding officer of the detachment, said that
his orders "were to guarantee protection against interference to
any man who wanted to work." Captain Dillon and Lieutenant
Dennis Horton set up machine guns at key crossroads and
visited their families' plantations to make sure everyone was
safe. Then they "dispersed" some workers who were ready "to
stage a picket march on plantations," jailed union members C.
K. Hamlin, Will Johnson, Bud Veasey, and Alex Washington for
"interfering with labor," and, concluding their day's work,
mounted a large machine gun and trained it on two Negroes
who were "a little impudent."[44]

Hamlin, Johnson, Veasey, and Washington were promptly
brought to trial and fined from $100 (Johnson) to $700 (Washington)—except for Hamlin, who repudiated the STFU and was
freed. The three others were sent to a prison farm to work off
their sentences at 75 cents a day.[45] Such legalized slavery quickly became a standard response to the strike, often without for-
malities such as judges, juries, warrants, or attorneys adding red
tape to the process. In one case, thirteen Negroes were thrown
in the Crittenden County jail without trial, charge, or sentence
other than the Governor of Arkansas's offhand remark that he
would decide when they had been "sufficiently punished."[46]

Although the freedom of black men was entirely nominal to
Arkansas authorities, the culprits they most wanted to punish
were, of course, the "outside agitators." One, Dave Benson, was
driving slowly along behind a column of strikers when his District of Columbia license plate caught the eye of a National
Guard officer who stopped him, seized his papers, was horrified
to read attacks on capitalism—Benson was a Socialist—and threw
him in jail. He was quickly fined $500 for "interfering with
labor," $500 for "rioting," $50 for having left his driver's license

44. Memphis *Press-Scimitar*, June 1, 1936; *Jonesboro Daily Tribune*,
June 1, 1936. See also Oral History MS, pp. 55–56.

45. *Arkansas Democrat*, June 2, 1936; *Arkansas Gazette*, June 3, 1936.

46. *Jonesboro Daily Tribune*, June 6, June 8, 1936. See also Lula Bron-
son, signed affidavit, n.d., and Floyd Thompson, signed affidavit, June 6,
1936, both in STFU Papers; Memphis *Press-Scimitar*, June 1, 1936.

in Memphis, and $10 for having an out-of-state auto license "while apparently working in Arkansas." As Benson was being tried, STFU organizer Clay East narrowly escaped lynching by a mob outside the courthouse.[47] At the same time, lawmen of the same county—named for St. Francis—arrested Pulitzer Prize winner Josephine Johnson and two associates, holding them until the St. Louis *Post-Dispatch* negotiated their release. As Miss Johnson left the jail, an irate deputy yelled "Go where you want to. See what you want to. You're welcome. *But don't talk to niggers!*"[48]

The "niggers" found ways to get word of their plight to the outside. Months after the strike, the following message, written on the back of a gaily colored movie advertising poster, reached STFU headquarters: "Statement of Will Harrell . . . he says that Tommie Tompson and Tommie Sellers Beat him with a ax handle on the 8th of June 1936 and that he was confined to the Bed for 1 month and was not treated by any Doctor and has not had the use of his Right arm he was hit two times on his head and 2 times on his arm." In other cases, union members just disappeared; Will Bailey, for example, was last seen running from a mob of planters and deputies.[49]

Two particularly noteworthy cases were those of Josh Turner and Nathaniel Smith, and Sam Bennett. According to the STFU, Turner and Smith were picked up the day after the strike began, imprisoned in planter Henry Craft's commissary, and beaten all day with guns and clubs in an effort to make them reveal the whereabouts of a local strike leader. They refused to do so. Two weeks later, Crittenden County Sheriff Howard Curlin announced that they had been arrested "after firing several shots

47. *Arkansas Gazette*, June 3, June 6, June 7, 1936; Memphis *Press-Scimitar*, June 5–7, 1936; Oral History MS, pp. 55–56; J. F. Hynds to the STFU, June 13, 1936, STFU Papers. See also Dave Benson to H. L. Mitchell, March 3, 1936, STFU Papers, for a sample of the language that horrified the National Guardsman.

48. *Jonesboro Daily Tribune*, June 5, 1936; Josephine Johnson, clipping in *New Masses*, n.d. [June, 1936], STFU scrapbook, STFU Papers; STFU press release, June 5, 1936.

49. Will Harrell, statement, n.d., and Annie Bailey, statement, January 25, 1937; A[aron] L[evenstein], "Case of Will Bailey," n.d.; Frank Weems, signed affidavit, May 5, 1937; and C. J. Spradling to the STFU, September 15, 1936, all in STFU Papers.

into a crowd of 25 or 30 other negroes." Their guns were confiscated, said Curlin, and they had signed a confession.[50] They
were charged with assault with intent to kill and held under
$2,500 bond. Mitchell asked the American Civil Liberties Union
to come to their defense, but the ACLU reluctantly declined because it seemed that they might actually be guilty.[51] Trying to
defend them anyway, Mitchell sent out an investigator who
promptly reported that "this is the most pathetic case of injustice and inhumane treatment of innocent people that I have
been connected with."[52] Every time a lawyer came to see them,
Turner and Smith had to remain silent because the jailer refused
to leave them alone with anyone. Three months after they were
first imprisoned, they finally managed to smuggle a letter out of
the jail; the truth, they said, was that they didn't even have
guns when arrested—deputies had taken the weapons from
their homes. Turner had been chopping corn and Smith had
been fencing his cow pasture when the alleged shooting had occurred, and as for their confession—"Here is the thing we are
Gaying to say an it true," they wrote, "we did nat do the Shoting
But they told Us if We diding say we did so thy was gaying to
Kill Us." (They had protested their innocence when first arrested, they continued, but the deputies told them they were
lying and that "we would tell a diffen thing when we get to
Marion Jail.")[53] STFU attorney C. A. Stanfield, armed with
the truth about the incident, forced the previously adamant authorities to compromise; first the two prisoners pleaded guilty,
to eliminate any possible future charges of false arrest, then,
after almost four months in jail, they were freed.[54]

Sam Bennett barely escaped a fate more severe. When the

50. STFU, press release, June 2, 1936, STFU Papers; *Arkansas Democrat*, June 17, 1936.
51. H. L. Mitchell to Roger Baldwin, June 30, 1936; Mitchell to Sidney
Hertzberg and Aron Gilmartin, August 30, 1936; J. C. Brookfield to J. R.
Butler, July 23, 1936, all in STFU Papers.
52. K. T. Sutton to Newell Fowler, July 15, 1936, STFU Papers.
53. Josh Turner and Nathaniel Smith to H. L. Mitchell, September 9,
1936; J. C. Brookfield to J. R. Butler, July 23, 1936; A. B. Pittman to Gardner Jackson, July 20, 1936; all in STFU Papers.
54. H. L. Mitchell to Josh Turner and Nathaniel Smith, October 10,
1936; Evelyn Smith to Aron Gilmartin, September 28, 1936, both in STFU
Papers.

strike began, he decided to stay at home for a few days, and his landlord came after him with a gun. Now, Sam Bennett was black and solid and muscular; he was over six feet tall and he weighed more than 250 pounds. When planter J. H. Shaffer got to Bennett's cabin, he saw him in the doorway, silently holding a shotgun. Shaffer turned and ran for help. Bennett picked up what few belongings he could carry with him and left his home forever. With a posse looking for him and a $50 reward on his head, he hid in the woods by day and walked northward by night; he knew that when Negroes who threatened their landlords were found, they were often "killed while trying to escape." A mob from St. Francis County, looking for him, drove into Wynne shortly after 2 A.M. on Saturday morning, June 8, blocked the streets of the Negro section with their cars, caught a boy they found awake and beat him until he told them where Bennett's brother, a minister, lived. Then they broke into the preacher's home and kicked him around until satisfied he knew nothing of his brother's whereabouts.[55] Riding the rails and hitch-hiking, Bennett finally reached Chicago. As soon as his presence there became known, Governor Futrell demanded his extradition to face Arkansas justice. But, responding to protests by the ACLU and other interested organizations, Illinois Governor Henry Horner, a Lincoln scholar, refused to send Bennett back.[56] He was a free man.

In the midst of the terrorism that raged for a fortnight after the strike began, President Franklin Roosevelt found himself in an embarrassing position. He was scheduled to come to Arkansas to praise the state and its favorite son, Senate Majority Leader Joseph T. Robinson, on the occasion of the Arkansas Centennial celebration, but with Robinson's friends in the Delta busy beating sharecroppers, the situation was delicate, to say the least. Consequently, before leaving on the trip, FDR asked Secretary of Labor Frances Perkins to draw up a memo on the

55. *Memphis Commercial Appeal,* June 8, 1936; see also *Jonesboro Daily Tribune,* May 21, 1936; STFU, press release, n.d. [June, 1936], STFU Papers; *Arkansas Gazette,* June 17, 1936.
56. Memphis *Press-Scimitar,* June 17, 1936; *Arkansas Gazette,* June 17, 1936; J. R. Butler and Donald Kobler to Governor Henry Horner, August 5, 1936; and Hy Fish, telegram to H. L. Mitchell, August 29, 1936, both in STFU Papers; *The Sharecroppers Voice,* September, 1936.

Arkansas sharecropper situation for him. She replied that the Department already had an investigator looking into the terrorism—which was true, but as of that time still entirely confidential.[57]

STFU leaders knew only that the president was going ahead with the trip as scheduled, without a word of protest as Senator Robinson kept announcing that the violence was "promoted, stimulated, and exaggerated by outside agitators." At the urging of Norman Thomas and Gardner Jackson, the union drew up a statement on the strike and the terrorism and prepared to send a delegation to present it to the president at Little Rock. But Roosevelt's secretary, Marvin McIntyre, expressing regret that the presidential schedule was full, declined to receive the delegation and offered to handle the STFU petition himself. He promised to present it to Roosevelt at the first opportunity.[58] Union leaders, disgusted with the whole episode, complained that they "never got within 100 ft. of President Roosevelt or Secretary McIntyre. President Roosevelt made his speech in which he told about what a wonderful state Arkansas was and how it took 100 years for it to get as good as it was, and what a wonderful Senator 'Greasy Joe' [Robinson] was, but he forgot to say anything about the wonderful conditions of the sharecroppers."[59] Could this be the president who was claiming to lead a bold New Deal for the Forgotten Man seventy-three years after the Emancipation Proclamation?

57. Frances Perkins to Franklin D. Roosevelt, June 8, 1936, OF 407–B, FDR Library.
58. Gardner Jackson to H. L. Mitchell, June 5, 1936, STFU Papers; Memo on H. L. Mitchell–M. H. McIntyre correspondence, June 7–10, 1936, in OF 1650, FDR Library; M. H. McIntyre, telegram to H. L. Mitchell, June 10, 1936, STFU Papers; *American Guardian* [Oklahoma City], June 19, 1936, clipping in STFU scrapbook, STFU Papers; *New York Times*, June 11, 1936, p. 12.
59. *The Sharecroppers Voice*, July, 1936. Gardner Jackson objected to calling Senator Robinson "Greasy Joe." He wrote, "No campaign of which I've ever heard has been aided by calling people names," but Butler replied that the nickname "is only a mild expression of Mitchell's feelings toward him. I may say we all feel about the same. However the expression of feeling may, as you suggested, have been the wrong tactic." Jackson to Butler and Mitchell, July 28, 1936; Butler to Jackson, July 31, 1936, both in STFU Papers.

# In Arkansas—The Wonder State

"This is the first chance I have had to enjoy the generosity, the kindness and the courtesy of true Arkansas hospitality."——Franklin D. Roosevelt.

*Roosevelt and Southern "Democrats": the sharecropper's view, 1936*

*H. L. Mitchell, Norman Thomas, and Howard Kester . . .*

*. . . were among those who led the people in their struggle.*

E. B. McKinney,
vice-president of
the Southern
Tenant Farmers' Union

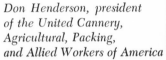

Don Henderson, president
of the United Cannery,
Agricultural, Packing,
and Allied Workers of America

Deputy Paul Peacher,
twentieth-century slaveholder

Gardner (Pat) Jackson,
the Southern tenant farmer's
voice in Washington

*The Reverend Claude Williams, radical ("Thy will be done on earth. . . .")*

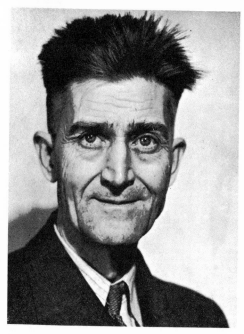

*J. R. Butler, president of the Southern Tenant Farmers' Union*

*H. L. Mitchell, founder and executive secretary of the Southern Tenant Farmers' Union*

# 6.

# The Rediscovery
# of Slavery

$A$s President Roosevelt praised Arkansas on that June day in 1936, sharecroppers were being assaulted and jailed illegally by friends of his chief lieutenant in the United States Senate. Roosevelt's dilemma—how sharecroppers could be protected without losing the support of their landlords—was about to be solved for him: the powerful people of the Delta, nettled by the STFU strike, were ready to lash out, not any more violently, but so unwisely and carelessly that the nation's growing sympathy for the sharecropper would reach its peak simultaneously with that of the 1936 election campaign.

It all began with the "marches," a picketing technique introduced by white tenants who, to create an exaggerated impression of their numbers, would march in a long single file, maintaining a regular six to eight foot interval between men, calling out to workers to leave their fields. White strikers were seldom molested as they marched, but whenever a predominantly Negro group attempted the tactic its members ran great risks. In one such case, a man named Frank Weems, having heard that his picket march was to be attacked, was hurrying down a dirt road to warn other members when suddenly five cars overtook him. Out leaped Boss Dulaney, Jerome Hood, Tom Thomas, Percy Magnus, Clifford Throgmorton, and several others who proceeded to smash Weems with baseball bats while a character known only as "Old Man Bam" held a gun on the proceedings to make sure the fight came out right. Friends of Weems hastened to pick up his unconscious body, but he was nowhere to be found. Word rapidly spread that he had been killed, and the national wire services, which had been carrying news of the strike increasingly as violence mounted, now reported that a sharecropper had been murdered.[1]

The excitement over Weems's disappearance and presumed death angered Sheriff Howard Curlin, who charged that "the backers of the sharecroppers' disturbance are using his disappearance to obtain funds for their own private uses." Curlin promised to find Weems within the next forty-eight hours, and then failed to. Governor Futrell supported the sheriff anyway; Weems's unexplained exit was "deliberately planned by H. L. Mitchell . . . and his confederates as propaganda," said the governor.[2]

With Weems's supposed murder already making the nation's front pages, Mitchell determined to capitalize on the event still further. A funeral service to commemorate the missing man would be highly appropriate; it would attract additional publicity and yet, because of its religious nature, would probably be immune from attack. Mitchell knew just the man to preach the funeral sermon. The charismatic Reverend Claude Williams, one of the most dedicated and controversial clergymen the modern South has produced, had been an organizer of the union since early 1935 and a close friend of its leaders before

1. Transcript of H. L. Mitchell's recorded interview for the Columbia University Oral History Collection, STFU Papers and elsewhere (referred to hereafter as Oral History MS), pp. 54–55; Frank Weems, signed affidavit, May 5, 1937, STFU Papers. A more dramatized, less accurate account is given by John Handcox in John Greenway, *American Folksongs of Protest* (Philadelphia: University of Pennsylvania Press, 1953), pp. 220–21.

2. *Arkansas Democrat*, June 17, 1936; *Jonesboro Daily Tribune*, June 18, 1936; Howard Curlin is also quoted in *Time* page proofs, July 6, 1936, pp. 8–9, STFU scrapbook, STFU Papers. Actually, Futrell and Curlin were right, though they could not prove it. Weems, after recovering consciousness, hid in the woods and escaped to the North, like Sam Bennett. But there is no evidence that the union planned the episode for publicity. Frank Weems, signed affidavit, May 5, 1937, STFU Papers; *The Sharecroppers Voice*, June, 1937.

that.[3] He was born in West Tennessee in 1895, the son of a part-Cherokee tenant farmer; his mother gave him a fundamentalist upbringing, but after he enrolled at Vanderbilt University's Divinity School, where he encountered Dr. Alva Taylor's Social Gospel and became a friend of radical young ministers like Howard Kester, Don West, and Ward Rodgers, where he read Jeans, Eddington, Millikan, and books like Harry Emerson Fosdick's *The Modern Use of the Bible* and Rabbi Hillel Silver's *Religion in a Changing World,* he began to feel the hypocrisy of preaching the old certainties to his congregation. He decided to take a new charge in the coal mining area around Paris, Arkansas, where he could abandon conformity to fight for the suffering miners. "The choice," Williams felt, "was between being decent and being respectable."[4]

In 1935, sponsored by Willard Uphaus's Religion and Labor Foundation, he established a workers' school in Little Rock which he called the New Era School. As its director, he had become national vice-president of the American Federation of Teachers and had established numerous contacts with liberal educators at the time Mitchell asked him to arrange Weems's funeral.[5]

Just before leaving for the Earle area, Williams stopped by the STFU office for final instructions. A visitor there, Miss Willie

3. On Williams's first STFU connections and Mitchell's request for him to preach the funeral sermon, see Mitchell, telegram to Williams, June 12, 1936; Mitchell and W. H. Stultz, STFU organizer's commission for Williams, March 15, 1935; Mitchell and J. R. Butler, STFU organizer's commission for Williams, May 28, 1936; all in Claude Williams Papers. On Williams's personal magnetism, see Lee Hays to the author, n.d. [September, 1962]; Harry Koger, tape recorded conversation with Williams, n.d. [January 16, 1963], Reel 1, Claude Williams Papers. The author, having met Williams, can also testify to this.

4. Interview with Claude Williams, August 18, 1962; Cedric Belfrage, *South of God* (New York: Modern Age Books, 1941), pp. 3–36, 52–81. Belfrage's book (and its later revised version, *A Faith to Free the People*) is a factually accurate, though highly partisan and emotionally colored, biography of Williams.

5. Belfrage, *South of God,* pp. 155–62, 178–284; *Economic Justice,* III (February, 1935), p. 1; "Champions of Sharecroppers . . . ," *Philadelphia Record,* March 8, 1935, CCP, Reel 1; *Columbus* (Ohio) *Labor Tribune,* June 19, 1936, clipping in STFU scrapbook, STFU Papers; *The Sharecroppers Voice,* September, 1935; Oral History MS, pp. 69–70.

Sue Blagden, Socialist daughter of a prominent and allegedly erratic Memphis family, decided she would just love to go along for the ride. Williams agreed to take her, perhaps reluctantly— he probably knew that Clarence Senior considered her "an unbalanced, irresponsible child" and that Mitchell thought "going off at a tangent is quite characteristic of her. . . . [The] queer quirk in her make up that makes her unreliable . . . is probably an inherited trait, as I am told that her mother is a religious fanatic and her brother a damn fool of the worst sort."[6]

She and Williams were sitting in an Earle drugstore later that afternoon when six men—"five of them dressed nicely in summer whites and looked like fine men," said Willie Sue— came in and ordered them both outside. They made them get into Williams's car, got in with them, and told them to drive out into the country. Night had fallen before Williams was ordered to stop beside a field and to get out and strip off his coat and shirt. The "fine men" flogged him brutally with harness straps. Then they remembered Willie Sue. "Now it's your turn," they laughed. She giggled. They gallantly raised the barbed wire strands for her as she stepped under a fence into the field, and then they parted the bushes so she wouldn't tear her dress as they led her down to a river bank. "Swim across," they joked, and she laughed again. Then they teased her about kissing "niggers" and asked her what she was doing taking a ride with a married man. Finally one of them told her to lie down. He was attractive, she noticed. She tremulously complied, and he whacked her bottom a few times. But he put too much muscle behind it, leaving a welt which was apparently not intended. After they all got back to Earle, they put Willie Sue on a bus to Memphis, while telling Williams to drive back to Little Rock. Two of the gang followed Williams several miles, until he managed to shake them off.[7]

6. Clarence Senior, circular letter, October 21, 1934, SP Arch, Duke; H. L. Mitchell to Gardner Jackson, August 21, 1936, STFU Papers; Memphis *Press-Scimitar*, June 17, 1936; *Arkansas Gazette*, June 17, 1936; W. L. Blackstone [to Claude Williams], n.d., Claude Williams Papers.

7. Memphis *Press-Scimitar*, June 17, June 18, 1936; St. Louis *Post-Dispatch*, June 17, June 18, 1936; *Arkansas Gazette*, June 17, June 18, 1936; *Time* page proofs, July 6, 1936, STFU scrapbook, STFU Papers; Oral History MS, p. 54; interview with Claude Williams, August 18, 1962;

The furor that erupted the next day was unparalleled in the STFU's history. Throughout the South, Negro men, women, and children had been bludgeoned for years; their liberty was fictitious whenever their labor was needed; thousands had been railroaded to prison and hundreds had been lynched and legally murdered. Few whites outside of civil rights organizations had been concerned. But now the planters had made the mistake of beating a minister and smacking a white woman's posterior. Suddenly the public was horrified, and even Southern newspapers, cherishing chivalry, published reproving editorials. More than any other single event, the beating made the nation demand action on behalf of sharecroppers; little more than six weeks elapsed between the bruising of Miss Blagden's bottom and the appointment by President Roosevelt of a special commission on farm tenancy, and the proximity in time was not coincidental.[8]

In order to convert national indignation into constructive action, the STFU leaders first leaped down one blind alley, that of direct legal attack upon the planters responsible for the violence. The same hoodlums who were accused of the Williams-Blagden beating were also responsible, according to sworn affidavits, for vastly more vicious attacks upon Mrs. Eliza Nolden, a Negro, and Jim Reese, a white man. Williams declined to sue because his injuries were insignificant compared to those of Reese and Mrs. Nolden. Their suits, however, never came to trial: Reese's beating was so savage that he fell into insanity, while Mrs. Nolden died of her injuries in a Memphis hospital. This left only Willie Sue, whose suit had to be dropped when

---

Willie Sue Blagden, "Arkansas Flogging," *New Republic*, July 1, 1936, pp. 236–37.

8. After a doctor described Miss Blagden's injuries for the wire services —"a severe bruise five inches wide across the back of the entire thigh, another severe bruise five inches wide entirely across the left buttock and on to the right buttock"—newspapers everywhere published the story, in some cases with a photo of Miss Blagden lifting her skirt to reveal the extent of damage. "Your correspondent takes for granted that every reader of The Christian Century already knows of the recent flogging . . . ," said John Petrie in that journal (July 22, 1936, p. 1021); and to enlighten those who might have missed some of the details, Miss Blagden told her story in *New Republic*, July 1, 1936, pp. 236–37. Another popular account was "Woman Flogged," *Literary Digest*, June 27, 1936, p. 29.

she decided that it was too much trouble and she'd rather travel.[9]

Adding to H. L. Mitchell's problems, as he and Jackson and Kester sought to keep Arkansas slavery in the national eye, were attacks from his friends as well as his enemies. At Commonwealth College and among the hard-hit black union members in the most violent counties, he was personally blamed for the failure of the strike; Negro leaders like E. B. McKinney threatened "a parting of the ways" because "the Negro is the Goat of the S.T.F.U.," while at Commonwealth he was so bitterly reproached for insufficient cooperation with the Communists that a susceptible student tried to murder him. Vainly did Gardner Jackson try to encourage Mitchell.[10] Only one thing could cheer the young union leader: positive action to rescue Southern tenants and sharecroppers from violence and legalized slavery, and such action still seemed remote.

Nevertheless, at the end of June, 1936, when Williams and Willie Sue were flogged, one slim hope still remained. A month before, Dr. Sherwood Eddy, a nationally known YMCA official, had gone out to visit a prison farm operated by the notorious Deputy Paul D. Peacher, the man who had been involved with Deputy Everett Hood in the arrest of Jim Bass and subsequent murder of Willie Hurst. The guards were indifferent and Peacher was out to lunch, so Eddy walked in and began talking to the thirteen Negro prisoners. Without exception, each one told Eddy he had been sent to the farm for "vagrancy"—though some of them were property owners and all were known to be long-time residents of the general area. None had been represented by an attorney, and not one could explain what the charge meant: "It's just something they lock you up for when they don't

9. Complaints at Law, District Court of the United States for the Jonesboro Division of the Eastern District of Arkansas, Eliza Nolden *vs.* Boss Dulaney *et al.*, Jim Reese *vs.* Boss Dulaney *et al.*, and Willie Sue Blagden *vs.* Boss Dulaney *et al.*, n.d., copies in STFU Papers; J. R Butler and H. L. Mitchell to Willie Sue Blagden, n.d. [1936], and C. A. Stanfield to Butler, September 30, 1938, both in STFU Papers.

10. *The Sharecroppers Voice*, July, 1936; E. B. McKinney to H. L. Mitchell, May 2, 1936, July 11, 1936; Steve Turner and Lee Wright to the STFU, July 15, 1936; Lee Dora Bryson to Mitchell, July 20, 1936; Gardner Jackson to Mitchell, April 6, 1936, June 5, 1936, October 21, 1936; fragment of letter [Edwin "Little Boy" Mitchell to H. L. Mitchell], n.d. [April, 1936], all in STFU Papers; Oral History MS, pp. 60–61; Mitchell to the author, July 17, 1961.

like what you're doing," was the general consensus. Eddy spent the afternoon getting corroborating statements, arrived back in the lobby of Memphis's Peabody Hotel late at night and burst out to Howard Kester, who had been anxiously awaiting his return, "Howard, take a telegram." As Eddy proceeded to dictate a message to Attorney General Homer Cummings, who had been his classmate at Yale, he explained to Kester that he and Cummings had sat side by side in a history class and learned that slavery had been abolished in 1863; now, he said, he was going to tell Cummings that it simply wasn't true.[11]

Kester might have been wryly amused by Eddy's towering indignation over the Peacher case, because union leaders knew that such practices were common. They had just publicly charged planters L. L. Barham and A. L. Lancaster with working men at gunpoint, and two other planters with kidnapping.[12] No denials were forthcoming. In addition, legalized private prison farms operated all over Arkansas.

Eddy's complaints first came before the regional United States District Attorney, Fred Isgrig, a prominent member of Little Rock's conservative Planters' Club. Isgrig's replies were moderate in tone, but he assured the STFU that the laborers in question had all been sentenced to pay fines and had been unable to do so. Sending them off to prison farms as a consequence, said Isgrig, "is not peonage." Eddy and Gardner Jackson thereupon demanded that the Justice Department take the matter out of Isgrig's hands and entrust it to someone more unbiased.[13]

Attorney General Cummings did replace Isgrig—with one Sam E. Whitaker, who also was unsympathetic to sharecropper complaints. As soon as he arrived in Arkansas he sought out Governor Futrell's state rangers and conducted his entire "in-

11. STFU, mimeographed press release, May 28, 1936; Dr. Sherwood Eddy, telegram to Homer Cummings, as quoted in STFU press release, n.d. [May, 1936], STFU Papers; Eddy to Cummings, May 29, 1936, in STFU folder, L-TS, RG 145, N Arch; "Striking Croppers," *Literary Digest,* June 13, 1936, p. 7; Eddy, "Lawless Arkansas," May, 1936, copies in STFU Papers and in STFU folder, L-TS, RG 145, N Arch.

12. STFU, mimeographed press releases, May 20, 1936, June 5, 1936, copies in STFU Papers.

13. Fred Isgrig to H. L. Mitchell, May 25, 1936, STFU Papers; *Arkansas Gazette,* June 3, 1936; Sherwood Eddy to Homer S. Cummings, May 29, 1936, in STFU folder, L-TS, RG 145, N Arch.

vestigation" in their tow. While he was in Arkansas, the American Civil Liberties Union announced its offer of a $1,000 reward for conviction of STFU attackers, but the ACLU was told not to expect that any immediate claim to the reward would result from Whitaker's brief escorted tour. And the *Nation* editorially predicted he would find no peonage because of the fact that private prison farms were legal in Arkansas.[14] Joining the controversy, Governor Futrell told the *Nation* and the ACLU that although "the greater part" of what they heard was "untrue," he would act immediately if any wrongs were disclosed. So, once again, this time in an open letter submitted to the newspapers, the STFU named those it accused of holding sharecroppers by force and working them as slaves: in addition to Peacher, Lancaster, and Barham, Henry Craft, H. D. Torrance, and Charlie Dabbs were accused.[15] Governor Futrell did nothing.

"Investigator" Sam Whitaker did very little more. But, as he was concluding his tour and writing his placid report, the Rev. Williams and Miss Blagden were—most embarrassingly for him —beaten. Whitaker hastily appended a few paragraphs deploring the action but reminding the Justice Department that assault and battery was, alas, no Federal offense. The report arrived, via the Attorney General, at the White House about the same time as the nationwide publicity over Miss Blagden's bottom. President Roosevelt immediately prodded Governor Futrell: "I feel certain you will wish to be fully informed. Two citizens on an apparently peaceful mission were subjected to cruel and inhuman treatment within the boundaries of the State of Arkansas."[16] Roosevelt said nothing about the treatment black union members had received, undoubtedly because Whitaker had reported nothing about it. When union leaders had asked him to investigate the prison farm captives, Whitaker's only reply had been a bored "They're all Negroes, aren't they?"[17]

14. "No Peonage," *Nation*, June 24, 1936, p. 794; W. E. Green to the ACLU, June 7, 1936, STFU Papers; *Arkansas Gazette*, June 7, 1936.
15. *Arkansas Gazette*, June 7, 1936; H. L. Mitchell, "An Open Letter to the Governor of Arkansas," June 8, 1936, copy in STFU Papers.
16. Sam E. Whitaker to Brien McMahon, June 19, 1936; Homer Cummings to Stephen Early, June 20, 1936; Franklin Delano Roosevelt to Norman Thomas, n.d. [July 6, 1936]; Roosevelt to J. Marion Futrell, n.d. [July 6, 1936], all in OF 407–B, FDR Library.
17. Clay East, signed affidavit, n.d.; NAACP Press Release, June 26,

What was vastly more important than Roosevelt's temporary inadequacy of information was his permanent change in attitude. The Department of Agriculture, which had been supremely uninterested in sharecroppers since the AAA purge, now began discreet contact with the Federal Bureau of Investigation. Complaints about illegal treatment of sharecroppers had previously been sent to Agriculture, which did nothing but acknowledge receiving them; now Roosevelt saw to it that such complaints went to the Department of Justice instead.[18] Slowly Attorney General Cummings's men built up dossiers on the Arkansas situation, while the plight of the sharecropper loomed larger and larger as an election year issue. In the middle of August, Cummings announced at a press conference that "conflicting evidence" regarding peonage—legalized slavery—had been found, and would be placed before a Federal Grand Jury. The effect was electrifying: "conflicting" could only mean that evidence confirming, as well as denying, the charge had reached Washington. The surprised STFU leaders were still further amazed by the choice of a big, tough-looking liberal attorney from Minnesota, George P. Jones, to direct the Grand Jury investigation.[19]

About a month later, the day after the Crittenden County Grand July solemnly declared that no peonage existed there, the Federal Grand Jury indicted Paul D. Peacher, Deputy Sheriff of Crittenden County, for "aiding and abetting in holding in slavery." Liberals across the nation were so elated that fundraising for the STFU suddenly became effortless; typical was the response of columnist Drew Pearson, a friend of Pat Jackson's, who sent $300 to the union.[20] At the end of November

[1936]; Brien McMahon to Walter White, July 9, 1936; White to Howard Kester, July 15, 1936; White to McMahon, July 15, 1936, all in STFU Papers.

18. Leonard O. Carson to [?] Bowyer, July 8, 1936, Solicitor's File, RG 16, N Arch; Marvin McIntyre, various memos to the Department of Justice, June 17–19, 1936, and other correspondence, OF 1650, FDR Library.

19. *Arkansas Gazette*, August 13, 1936; Memphis *Press-Scimitar*, August 13, 1936; Gardner Jackson to H. L. Mitchell, August 18, 1936; Jackson to Willie Sue Blagden, August 19, 1936, both in STFU Papers.

20. Memphis *Press-Scimitar*, September 24, 25, 1936; *New York Post*, September 25, 1936; Workers' Defense League, press release, October 28,

Peacher was brought to trial, despite the assertion of his defense lawyer, N. S. Lamb, that the proceeding had been instigated by "Northern union agitators" in order to build support for Roosevelt against Landon: "I thought when the election was over, this lawsuit would be allowed to die out," Lamb declared. Regarding the merits of the case, Lamb implied that black men had to be forced to work because "you can't expect negroes in a short time among civilized people to rise to the level of good citizens." The jury of Jonesboro white men was so reluctant to convict Peacher that Judge John Martineau all but directed the inevitable guilty verdict. Peacher's penalty, a $3,500 fine, was quickly met by Arkansas planters who saw him as a scapegoat, knowing that thousands of Southern whites had been freely doing exactly the same thing ever since Reconstruction.[21]

The Peacher case was salutary not only indirectly, in the money and publicity it brought to the sharecropper cause, but directly, in that it so discredited the practice of peonage that private prison farms began to disappear everywhere. Before World War II began, Arkansas, for example, outlawed such farms altogether. [22]

Moreover, there was an even more immediate reaction to Cummings's bombshell announcement of "conflicting evidence" in mid-August. Arkansas's Governor Futrell had done nothing publicly when Roosevelt, through Senator Robinson, had warned him against violence the preceding spring (though the violence had duly ended); nor had Futrell reacted immediately to Roosevelt's message of disgust over the Williams-Blagden beatings. But, the day after Cummings announced that a Federal Grand Jury investigation was coming to Arkansas, Governor Futrell proclaimed that he was going to appoint a commission to study tenancy and recommend action to remedy its ills. The

1936, and Gardner Jackson to Homer Cummings, October 31, 1936, both in STFU Papers.

21. Memphis *Press-Scimitar*, November 25–27, 1936; St. Louis *Post-Dispatch*, November 26, 27, 1936; *New York Times*, November 29, 1936, p. IV–6; "Slavery in Arkansas," *Time*, December 7, 1936, p. 17; " 'Slaves,' " *Newsweek*, December 5, 1936, p. 19; Oral History MS, p. 59.

22. *Arkansas Gazette*, September 13, 18, 1938; "Arkansas Kills Private Prison Farms," *The* (Commonwealth College) *Commoner*, March, 1939, CCP, Reel 3.

governor's past record revealed scant sympathy for the under-privileged. Indeed, he had been re-elected in 1934 after empha-sizing that he had reduced the "cost" of state government by 50 per cent, mainly by abolishing "useless offices and commis-sions."[23] When this same man abruptly turned about face and *created* a "useless commission," many cynical individuals at-tributed the singular occurrence to the governor's desire to head off Federal prosecution of anti-union criminals rather than to any sudden humanitarian impulse.[24] This, of course, was not the stance Futrell presented to the press. "Retiring from office in January," he let it be known, "the Governor has decided to de-vote the rest of his term to the sharecropper problem." Specifi-cally, his decision "was the result of conferences with State leaders starting last Spring when a cotton croppers' strike was called in Eastern Arkansas by the Southern Tenant Farmers Union."[25]

Futrell's admission that the commission was inspired by the STFU did not, however, impel him to name any tenants or union members to the new body. Instead, he picked seven businessmen, six government officials, five planters, five lawyers, five educators, four publishers, three clubwomen, two ministers, and a student. Named as chairman was Clyde E. Palmer, the ultra-conservative editor of a chain of small Texas and Arkansas newspapers. True, Attorney C. T. Carpenter was picked for the commission,[26] but Carpenter had not represented the STFU for more than a year. Futrell explained that he wanted to name a sharecropper representative to the commission but had diffi-culty finding any "with common sense . . . no member of any organized group will be selected."[27] Futrell's attitude reinforced

23. Political advertisement for Futrell, *Arkansas Gazette*, August 5, 1934.

24. For expressions of this cynicism about the governor's motives, see *New York Post*, September 17, 1936; Memphis *Press-Scimitar*, August 15, 1936; Norman Thomas, "Arkansas' Shame," copy of speech at Memphis, September 17, 1936, STFU Papers; "Tenant Farmers," *Literary Digest*, August 29, 1936, p. 9.

25. *New York Times*, August 16, 1936, p. II–2.

26. *Southwest American* (Fort Smith, Ark.), August 27, 1936; Mem-phis *Press-Scimitar*, August 27, 1936; *Memphis Commercial Appeal*, August 28, 1936; *New York Post*, September 17, 1936.

27. J. Marion Futrell to J. R. Butler, August 21, 1936, STFU Papers.

the conviction of STFU leaders that his commission was no more than an attempt to avoid Federal investigation of Arkansas terrorism. Mitchell and Butler were ready to denounce it as such publicly, and Norman Thomas called it "pure hypocrisy." At least one Southern newspaper, the Dallas *News*, took a look at Futrell's record and agreed with Thomas.[28]

But Gardner Jackson knew that blasting Futrell could only harm the union. Instead, Jackson successfully urged Mitchell to contain his anger, to issue a simple statement pointing out that Futrell could demonstrate wisdom, statesmanship, and good faith by acting vigorously against anti-union terrorists, by producing the missing Frank Weems, and, above all, by naming an STFU representative to the commission.[29]

August became September, cotton bolls began to burst, children returned to school, and still Futrell refused to name any union representative to his commission. On Monday, September 21, 1936, the dignitaries appointed by Governor Futrell assembled in Hot Springs for the first meeting of the Governor's Commission on Farm Tenancy. Outside the commission's headquarters hotel, a few trucks drove up, full of tenants in dusty overalls, and out of the trucks' cabins jumped STFU President Butler and the now-famous radical preacher, Claude Williams. They strode briskly into the hotel just as the commission members were rising to introduce themselves to each other. At the proper time, Butler and Williams also stood up, stated that they were happy to be present as visitors, but added that they had been denied representation on the commission despite the fact that they represented the nation's largest organization of farm tenants. As reporters crowded around them and flashbulbs popped, the weatherbeaten little white-thatched governor was whispering to his friends, "I won't be pressured! I won't be pressured!"[30]

28. Dallas *News*, August 22, 1936, clipping in STFU scrapbook, STFU Papers; *Memphis Commercial Appeal*, August 17, 1936; J. R. Butler and H. L. Mitchell, typed memo to Norman Thomas, Gardner Jackson, and William R. Amberson, n.d. [August, 1936], STFU Papers.

29. Gardner Jackson, telegram to H. L. Mitchell and J. R. Butler, August 16, 1936; Jackson to Mitchell, August 24, 1936; Mitchell to Jackson, August 26, 1936, all in STFU Papers.

30. *Arkansas Gazette*, September 22, 1936; interview with J. R. Butler, July 22, 1962; *Arkansas Democrat*, September 22, 1936. The *Gazette* story

As soon as he finished telling people he wouldn't be pressured, he huddled with his aides and emerged with an invitation to the STFU spokesmen to consider themselves members of the commission. Two weeks later Chairman Clyde Palmer notified Butler and white tenant farmer W. L. Blackstone of Wynne that their names had been officially added to the list of members.[31]

Well before it gained representation on the commission, the STFU had prepared a statement on the causes and cures of tenancy's evils. The document, written by Howard Kester, begged the commission to "face facts . . . in the name of truth and justice." Many of the effects ascribed to tenancy, the statement maintained, were traceable to the South's willingness "to withhold economic, civil, and political privileges from white men because we wished to deny them to colored men." The evils blamed on tenancy arose partially because cultural isolation of the South precluded acceptance of new ideas and partially because the landlord-tenant relationship stifled ambition. To attack these evils, a variety of actions was recommended. Aimed directly at the plantation system were such suggestions as the abolition or regulation of plantation commissaries, enforcement of the legal 8 per cent interest rate, enforcement of child labor laws and eviction laws, and compensation to tenants for improvements made on the land. Going beyond these recommendations were demands for the enactment, abolition, or enforcement of specific laws: the union called for abolition of the poll tax, private prison farms and other forms of peonage, and for enforcement of the workers' lien law and of workers' rights of free speech and assemblage. The STFU also advocated enactment of a minimum wage law applicable to agriculture and called for the establishment and encouragement of cooperative farms to replace large plantations.[32]

---

is a little garbled, claiming that "a delegation purporting to represent the Southern Farm Tenants Union, led by C. T. Carpenter, the Memphis lawyer"—five errors there—was what entered the ballroom and demanded representation.

31. Clyde E. Palmer to J. R. Butler, October 8, 1936; Palmer to W. L. Blackstone, October 8, 1936, both in STFU Papers; *Arkansas Democrat*, September 22, 1936; Hot Springs *New Era*, September 22, 1936; Oral History MS, pp. 93–94.

32. STFU, Statement to the Governor's Commission on Farm Tenancy,

After two days of discussing the STFU program and a few less ambitious recommendations, mainly suggestions that "better" tenants be helped to buy their own farms, the Arkansas commission adjourned. Before its members left Hot Springs, Governor Futrell told them to forward their ideas to a 19-man subcommittee which would draw up the commission's final report. "Stay with this thing until we work something out," the governor admonished them. He warned them, however, to recommend only changes of a "constitutional nature" and told them there was no way they could hope to make a landlord pay standard wages or "keep him from removing a tenant with or without cause. These legal rights of the property owner must be kept in mind."[33]

Around Thanksgiving, the governor's commission issued its final report. While none of the recommendations were breathtakingly novel, the document was a far cry from the evasive "whitewash job" union leaders had expected. To some extent, this might be attributed to the presence of Butler and Blackstone on the commission. The two men must have been wryly amused when Chairman Palmer, transmitting the report to Governor Futrell, stated that enactment of the commission's program would "end all dangers from Socialist and Communist activities in rural sections."[34] Palmer never thought to mention that the "Socialist and Communist activities" had brought about establishment of the commission to begin with.

---

n.d. [August, 1936]; STFU, Supplement to the Statement on Farm Tenancy, October 10, 1936; *New York Post*, September 19, September 20, 1936; *Arkansas Democrat*, September 19, September 20, 1936. The union did what it could to aid its members in the absence of the Federal action it called for: it established its own cooperative plantation, Hillhouse, near Clarksdale, Mississippi; it tried to educate many of its members, first at Commonwealth College, later with its own adult education program, and always through the pages of its newspaper, *The Sharecroppers Voice*; it sent some women and children to summer camps; it encouraged challenges to voting discrimination in the Delta, and made plans to meet the challenge of agricultural mechanization and more widespread union organization in the South. See the author's "The Southern Tenant Farmers' Union and The New Deal" (Ph.D. dissertation, University of Florida, 1963), pp. 478–90.

33. Memphis *Press-Scimitar*, September 23, 1936; *Arkansas Gazette*, September 21–23, October 3, 1936.

34. *Arkansas Democrat*, December 13, 1936.

Tenancy, the commission's report declared, "has become a serious menace to American institutions." Its causes were cash-crop monoculture, speculation, inability of small farmers to purchase and market efficiently, the expense of farm credit, "energy-sapping diseases," and "cultural and recreational deficiencies in rural life causing people to move into the cities." No mention was made of the heritage of slavery and the influence of Jim Crow.

The cure recommended by the commission, when compared to the causes it had listed, was a non sequitur. The goal of public policy, the commission decided, should be to enable "those who cultivate the soil to own their own farm homes and . . . so improve living conditions on the farm as to prevent a repetition . . . of present conditions." To this end, the Federal government should purchase state lands and sell them, in parcels large enough to furnish a family "a comfortable living," to tenants "upon terms which may be met by any reasonably good and industrious farmer." The tenancy commission did not recognize that this, by itself, would do little to overcome the small farmer's marketing and purchasing disabilities, the evils of concentration on cotton, and many of the other tenancy causes the commission named. Land speculation, however, the commission was determined to attack. In doing so, as one contemporary commentator pointed out,[35] it made its greatest departure from American orthodoxy. For the commission proposed an unprecedented interference with freedom of contract: Federal restriction of all lands sold to tenants "for all time as homesteads, and not subject to encumbrance." Specifically, the commission recommended that Congress pass laws "so that no common law trust or corporation can hereafter purchase land for farming purposes." The commission also called for cheap government credit "to avoid the evils of the furnish system" and recommended additional public health and education measures. Tenants should have standard written contracts with their landlords and the right to prompt, impartial arbitration of landlord-tenant disputes.[36] Even the Arkansas Extension Service, following

35. Alva Taylor, "Tenancy Report Scores System," *Christian Century,* December 23, 1936, p. 1730.
36. Arkansas Farm Tenancy Commission, "Findings and Recommendations," Hot Springs, November 24, 1936.

up the commission report with similar recommendations of its own, agreed that some form of arbitration should be guaranteed to tenants.[37]

The commission did not end with the submission of its report. Carl Bailey, who succeeded Futrell as governor, reorganized it in 1937 and reappointed it in 1939. Many original members remained on the commission, but Bailey, more liberal than Futrell, named such figures as Brooks Hays and Labor Commissioner E. I. McKinley to the body. He began appointing state legislators to the commission, thus smoothing the way to state legislation such as the Land Policy Act of 1939.[38]

Governor Futrell, for his part, wanted his commission to serve as the model for a nationwide conference on farm tenancy. Fully a month before the commission met to debate its final report, Futrell invited the forty-seven other state governors to join him in Little Rock to discuss the tenancy problem. The most noteworthy response to Futrell's invitation came from Governor Hugh White of Mississippi: "There is no tenant farm problem in Mississippi," said he.[39]

On the other side of Arkansas, oil magnate Ernest Whitworth Marland, the governor of Oklahoma, responded to Futrell's invitation in exactly the opposite fashion. Not to be outdone by Futrell's fifty-man commission, Governor Marland named nearly a hundred state leaders to a similar assembly of his own, which was to meet at Oklahoma City toward the end of October. Oklahoma STFU leader Odis Sweeden was named to this unwieldy congress at the beginning, with no unusual pressure on his part, and Butler was invited to address it—another assignment subsidized by Gardner Jackson. In Oklahoma as in Arkansas, the first tenancy conference produced extensive results. At the next session of the Oklahoma legislature, in 1937, a tenancy act was passed, and the state Extension Service es-

37. J. A. Baker and J. G. McNeely, "Land Tenure in Arkansas: I. The Farm Tenancy Situation," Arkansas Agricultural Experiment Station Bulletin No. 384 (Fayetteville, 1940), pp. 59–60.

38. "C. E. Palmer Again Heads Tenancy Board," Arkansas Gazette, November 19, 1939.

39. Memphis Press-Scimitar, October 24, October 29, 1936; Southwest American (Fort Smith, Ark.), October 29, 1936; New York Post, September 17, 1936; Alva Taylor, "Cotton Tenants Held in Peonage," Christian Century, October 7, 1936, p. 1341.

tablished a Landlord-Tenant Relationship Department in the fall of that year. In the summer of 1938 the first statewide Landlord-Tenant Day was held, a festive occasion which attracted some 3,500 persons from every county in the state.[40] Clearly, anything Oklahoma's tenancy program might lack in success it would make up in spectacle.

Oklahomans and Arkansans, close as they were to the scenes of STFU activity, were not the only Americans who considered tenancy a serious problem by the latter part of 1936. Largely because of the headlines, newsreels, and radio broadcasts stimulated by the STFU's struggles in the Arkansas Delta, the problem of farm tenancy had become a leading topic of discussion across the country. It was unanimously agreed that there was a problem, but few knew the nature of it; it was widely held that something must be done, but proposed solutions were inspired far more by emotion than study. However, thanks to the frequency with which they were bombarded with tenancy statistics, many people must have known that over four out of ten of the nation's farms were operated by tenants. To be exact, there were 2,664,365 tenant farmers in 1930 and 2,865,155 in 1935—a numerical increase which, because of the greater increase in the total number of the nation's farms, amounted to a slight reduction in the *percentage* of tenant-operated farms. This small decline from 1930 to 1935, the first in half a century, gave doubtful evidence that the trend had finally been reversed, because the only reason for the fall-off between 1930 and 1935 was the tremendous reduction in the number of Southern tenants—outside the South, only one state could boast a tenancy decline during that period. Tenancy in the South remained above the 50 per cent level, and about two out of every five Southern tenants were sharecroppers. Of the 769 counties which contained the nation's most disadvantaged rural population, 87 per cent were in thirteen Southern states.[41]

40. "Proceedings of Oklahoma Farm Land Tenantry Conference," Oklahoma City, October 22, 1936; Oral History MS, p. 94; Memphis *Press-Scimitar*, October 24, 1936; J. R. Butler to Gardner Jackson, October 20, 1936, STFU Paper; "Getting at the Bottom of Oklahoma's Landlord-Tenant Problem," *Extension Service Review*, IX (November, 1938), 162, 170.

41. U. S. Department of Commerce, Bureau of the Census, *United*

And yet it was precisely where the problem was most acute that its importance was minimized most often. Tenancy was shrugged off for exactly the same reason that it was so grave a problem: as a result of slavery and "the systems of labor utilization and control which replaced the slavery economy"—to use Louis C. Gray's nice euphemism for sharecropping—tenants were regarded as shiftless and improvident, were treated as such, and commonly responded from generation to generation by being such.[42] The *Memphis Commercial Appeal* probably spoke for most of the planters of the Mid-South when it declared that the "steady, hard working" tenant must be differentiated from the "shiftless, disinterested variety . . . that has brought about the unrest and caused the agitation that farm tenants have been 'mistreated.' "[43] "There isn't anything you can do for a certain type of fellow," declared the *Commercial Appeal's* chief editorial writer.[44]

Journalists holding these opinions often found their sentiments shared by supposed authorities. A North Carolina agricultural economist wrote that black sharecroppers could not "be given on an extensive scale, the status of owner. . . . The Negro is for a number of reasons an indifferent individual. He cannot be characterized as an ambitious person."[45] Governor Futrell told his tenancy commission that "worthless people cannot be helped" and that although the average tenant "has fared as well and usually better than his landlord," he "has the mentality of a 12-year-old child" and should be subject to compulsory birth control or sterilization.[46] Asked whether a good farm

*States Census of Agriculture: 1935*, Vol. III (Washington: Government Printing Office, 1937), pp. 105, 107–8; Carl W. Taylor and Helen W. Wheeler, "Disadvantaged Classes in American Agriculture," *Agricultural Situation*, XXII (November, 1938), 17–18.

42. Louis C. Gray, "Disadvantaged Rural Classes," *Journal of Farm Economics*, XX (February, 1938), 76.

43. H. J. Adair, "Convention Now Uppermost," *Memphis Commercial Appeal*, September 13, 1936.

44. *Memphis Commercial Appeal*, June 25, 1936; see also *Arkansas Democrat*, September 22, September 27, 1936.

45. G. W. Forster, "Progress and Problems . . . ," *Journal of Farm Economics*, XVIII (February, 1936), 91.

46. *Arkansas Gazette*, September 21, 1936; Memphis *Press-Scimitar*, September 21, 1936; New York *World Telegram*, September 22, 1936.

tenancy program should help "the thrifty tenant" or, on the other hand, "those who cannot get credit elsewhere," genial Senator Tom Connally of Texas boomed his reply: "If you want to make it a success, you would not select the inefficient, the man who had not made a success at anything, would you?"[47] And even Secretary of Agriculture Henry Wallace, in a speech at—of all places—Tuskegee Institute, said he doubted "whether the government should do more, in the beginning at least, than enable tenants who can manage their own affairs to buy land on reasonable terms."[48]

Judging from such statements as these, America's disadvantaged and disinherited farmers could expect little help from their country's leaders; nevertheless, by appealing to their good will and their horror of tenancy conditions, one could convince almost all of them that at least a token gesture must be made. And the tenancy controversy furnished an opportunity for good-hearted people to defend Home almost as touchingly as God and Country. Almost everyone who made a public speech on the subject eagerly welcomed the chance to advocate universal home ownership. Toward the end of 1936, the year in which the STFU most often publicized the evils of tenancy, one of Dr. George Gallup's polls revealed that 83 per cent of the nation's voters favored government loans "to enable farm tenants to buy the farms they now rent." Gallup sent Secretary Wallace the poll and told him, "I hope, for your own sake, that you become well identified with the movement to mitigate the problem of farm tenancy." Wallace was so impressed that he asked Gallup to meet with him and bring a complete regional analysis of the poll.[49]

47. U. S. Congress, House, Committee on Agriculture, *Hearings, Farm Tenancy,* 75th Cong., 1st Sess., 1937, pp. 278–79 (hereinafter cited as Farm Tenancy Hearings).

48. Henry Wallace, "Common Aims in Agriculture," speech at Tuskegee, Ala., September 10, 1936, in "Speeches of the Secretary (1936)" file, RG 16, N Arch; Memphis *Press-Scimitar,* September 10, 1936. Wallace told one reporter that cooperative agriculture, unlike individual ownership, was economically unsound and "too much like the Russian system." (Wayne Gard, "The American Peasant," *Current History,* XLVI (April, 1937), 52.) Wallace's ideas did not remain at this level, however.

49. Institute of Public Opinion poll, December 13, 1936; George Gallup

The widespread sentiment that Gallup and Wallace noted continued the American tradition of agrarian individualism that ran back through Bryan to Jefferson and beyond. The Great Commoner and the great Virginian could hardly have defended the farmer's life more glowingly than the Arkansas Farm Tenancy Commission, which, after hearing from Governor Futrell that farm home ownership "will give our country more real protection against foreign invasion and conquest than the expenditure of millions on our armies and navies," responded: "Farming is a special pursuit fundamentally different from all others . . . a way of life all its own. . . . Farm-home ownership is definitely related to character and patriotism. It is conducive to high character and good citizenship . . . America will not be a great nation by the end of the century unless she preserves a healthy rural life."[50]

Few authorities supported farm ownership simply for the benefit of the prospective home owner. Far from it: they saw home ownership as a good American manner of meeting a problem that might otherwise be solved in very unsettling and un-American ways. They feared, for example, that if sharecroppers could not buy homes they might join the Southern Tenant Farmers' Union. Columnist Herbert Agar wrote that he had "defended unionization . . . in big-scale industry" but that the STFU could only cause "a dangerous and fundamentally hostile tug-of-war. . . . The alternative to sharecroppers unions, and industrial war thruout the land, is the restoration of genuine property in small farms."[51] Southern economist Wilson Gee charged that "Communist agitators are at work today among the tenant farmers' unions in . . . Arkansas and Alabama" and

to Henry Wallace, December 9, 1936; Wallace to Gallup, December 14, 1936, all in "Tenancy (1936)" folder, RG 16, N Arch.

50. *Memphis Commercial Appeal*, September 21, 1936; *Arkansas Gazette*, September 21, 1936; Arkansas Farm Tenancy Commission, "Findings and Recommendations," Hot Springs, November 24, 1936. For similar statements, see Wilson Gee, "Reversing the Tide Toward Tenancy," *Southern Economic Journal*, II (April, 1936), 7; Representative Otha D. Wearin of Iowa in *Congressional Record*, Vol. 81, Pt. 4, 75th Cong., 1st Sess., 1937, p. 3827.

51. Herbert Agar, "Answer to Sharecropper Evil Is Land Ownership," Memphis *Press-Scimitar*, September 28, 1936.

said that the best way to thwart their evil designs would be to encourage farm home ownership.[52]

More specifically, it was believed that no property owner could possibly become a Communist. "You know, farmers are equity owners. In a way they are capitalists," a Farm Bureau spokesman pointed out, explaining why his organization could not think of cooperating with labor leaders.[53] The Farm Bureau's elementary lesson was taken to heart by those who wished to protect the countryside from labor unions, Communists, and other radical influences. Secretary Wallace declared on several occasions that "the present conditions, especially in the South, provide fertile soil for Communist and Socialist agitators. . . . The cure is . . . to give these dispossessed people a stake in the social system."[54] Wallace's belief was enthusiastically shared in the halls of Congress, where the property-not-communism oratory of Senators Tom Connally of Texas, Kenneth McKellar of Tennessee, and Representative Reuben Wood of Missouri paled only slightly before that of Oklahoma's Senator Josh Lee. "If you want people to say 'This is mine, my native land,' " Lee advised, "let them own some of it. If you want them to sing 'My country, 'tis of thee, I love thy rocks and rills,' let them own some of those rocks and rills. . . . A man cannot lean up against the forks of his own apple tree and plan the destruction of his own government."[55]

Advocates of individual home ownership advanced two principal arguments. In the first place, many tenants were considered redeemable because, as Speaker of the House William B.

52. Wilson Gee, "Reversing the Tide," pp. 2–3, 9; see also R. B. Snowden, interview in Memphis *Press-Scimitar*, February 14, 1935.

53. Chester H. Gray to Luke W. Duffey, April 2, 1937, in "Labor (1937)" folder, RG 16, N Arch.

54. Wallace's remark appears in Farm Tenancy Hearings, p. 360, and in his statement, "The Problem of Farm Tenancy," March 5, 1935, folder 466–B, Solicitor's File, RG 16, N Arch. See also the statement of Dr. Clarence Poe, editor of *The Progressive Farmer*, in Farm Tenancy Hearings, p. 353.

55. On Connally, McKellar, and Wood, respectively, see *Congressional Digest*, XVI (February, 1937), 51; *Congressional Record*, Vol. 81, Pt. 6, 75th Cong., 1st Sess., 1937, p. 6671; *Congressional Record*, Vol. 80, Pt. 7, 74th Cong., 2nd Sess., 1936, p. 7727; for Lee's remark, see *Congressional Digest*, XVI (February, 1937), 52.

Bankhead put it, "some of these poor tenant farmers, by descent, are of the best blood of this Republic, sons of the Cavaliers and of the Huguenots." Writers on the subject agreed that "many of the white tenants represent the country's purest strains of Anglo-Saxon blood" and that they were "largely of the old native stock."[56] Even liberals who should have known better fell into this racial hocus-pocus on rare occasions: Virginius Dabney said the average tenant "comes of sturdy Anglo-Saxon yeoman stock" and STFU sponsor Dr. William Amberson remarked, "These people can rise again. The racial stocks are basically sound."[57] This racism, by implication, condemned black tenants to a secondary position. Arthur Raper noted that land ownership was the Southern badge of distinction and predicted that any tenants-to-owners program would be gravely handicapped by anti-Negro prejudice.[58]

Second, it was felt that a home ownership program could succeed because similar undertakings had worked in Ireland and Denmark. The same Congressmen who warned against the socialistic innovations of the decadent Old World now shifted ground to praise the self-reliant Danish and Irish yeomen and the program of their farsighted governments. "Some of the most prosperous farmers in the world live in south Ireland," Senator Connally misinformed his colleagues. Those students of tenancy who warned that the Irish solution was completely unadapted to the United States and that Danish agriculture was entirely unlike that of the South were merely voices crying in a home-loving wilderness.[59]

56. *Congressional Record*, Vol. 81, Pt. 6, 75th Cong., 1st Sess., 1937, p. 6452. For admiring repetitions of Speaker Bankhead's racial observations, see *Ibid.*, p. 6473 and elsewhere. See also Wayne Gard, "The American Peasant," *Current History*, XLVI (April, 1937), 51; Arthur Krock, "In Washington," *New York Times*, April 6, 1937, p. 22.

57. Virginius Dabney, *Below the Potomac* (New York: Appleton-Century, 1942), p. 4; William R. Amberson, "Forty Acres and a Mule," *Nation*, March 6, 1937, p. 266.

58. Arthur F. Raper, *Preface to Peasantry* (Chapel Hill: The University of North Carolina Press, 1936), pp. 151–52.

59. On Connally, see *Congressional Record*, Vol. 81, Pt. 6, 75th Cong., 1st Sess., 1937, p. 6679. For a good outline of the Irish program, see Farm Tenancy Hearings, pp. 243–46; for praise of it and the Danish program, see *Congressional Record*, Vol. 81, Pt. 4, 75th Cong., 1st Sess., 1937, pp. 3828–29; *Congressional Record*, Vol. 81, Pt. 6, pp. 6558, 6562; Wilson

It was not merely the racism, emotionalism, and misapplication of precedent indulged in by home ownership advocates that convinced STFU leaders their arguments were unsound. It was what proponents of the small family farm failed to consider, as well: that the small farm owner had almost no competitive chance in an area dominated by large farms and plantations. Even if one could assume that most tenants had the knowledge and experience to manage their own farms—a highly questionable assumption—one had to admit that they faced almost insuperable buying and marketing disadvantages vis-a-vis the large plantation. STFU leaders foresaw that bigness was to become (in the plantation country, to *remain*) as dominant in agriculture as in industry. But they had no way of knowing that a second World War and a consumers' boom afterward would take thousands of people out of the South and put them into Northern and Western cities. They were faced, as they saw it, with an uncertain future for the national economy, a countryside swollen with a population surplus, and an agriculture permanently committed to large-scale enterprise.[60]

Cooperative agricultural communities, the union's leaders decided, were the answer. Only if millions of tenants and small farmers could form such cooperatives would the problems associated with farm tenancy be solved; only in this way could many rather than few farmers benefit from the economies of large-scale production. As the tenancy debate reached a peak in 1936 and 1937, Howard Kester, Dr. William Amberson, Norman Thomas, and Gardner Jackson took every opportunity to publicize the advantages of such cooperatives. They emphasized that mechanization could be undertaken to an extent no single small farmer could afford; the result would be a higher

---

Gee, "Reversing the Tide," pp. 4–7. For criticism of the applicability of the foreign solutions to this country and particularly the South, see STFU, Statement to the Governor's Commission on Farm Tenancy, n.d. [August, 1936]; STFU, Supplement to the Statement on Farm Tenancy, October 10, 1936; Norman Thomas, speech at Memphis, September 17, 1936, copy in STFU Papers; Peter Nelson, "Is Farm Tenancy Inherently An Evil?" Oklahoma *Current Farm Economics* series, Vol. 10, No. 2 (April, 1937), pp. 29–34.

60. STFU, Supplement to the Statement on Farm Tenancy, October 10, 1936, pp. 17–18, and *passim*.

standard of living and more leisure for all the cooperative members, not riches for a plantation owner and poverty for the workers displaced by his machinery. Also crop diversification could be better undertaken: experts could be hired to plan crop rotation and soil conservation, and the large tracts at the cooperative's disposal would enable all crops to be grown in profitable amounts. Furthermore, union leaders noted, there were a host of other advantages. Division and specialization of labor would be possible; village life would replace rural isolation; group buying and selling would be economical; pride of possession would not be stifled but would be raised to a new level, encompassing the vast extent of the entire cooperative; greatly improved medical and educational facilities could be secured; individual incentives could be maintained by income differentials and by private ownership of homes and gardens. To Howard Kester, who was always something of a mystic, there was another advantage. The new experience of conducting economic enterprise for social well-being rather than individual aggrandizement, he felt, would be so revolutionary to members of the cooperative that it would be tantamount to a "new birth." "Reorientation plus New Birth equals New Society," Kester kept telling his associates.[61] In a very real sense, he saw the institution of cooperative agricultural communities as the first step toward the Kingdom of God on earth, and he worked toward his objective with appropriate fervor.

The glow in Kester's dark eyes notwithstanding, cooperatives were thought eminently practical by many students of the nation's rural ills. As a pragmatic solution to rural overpopulation, cooperative subsistence homesteads had been set up early in the New Deal by various governmental agencies and were continued by the Resettlement Administration. After the STFU attained national prominence, its leaders' support for cooperatives became widely known; numerous liberals endorsed the

61. Howard Kester to H. L. Mitchell and Dr. William Amberson, March 13, 1936, STFU Papers. This letter also contains a long discussion of cooperatives as the STFU envisioned them; on this topic, see also STFU, Supplement to the Statement on Farm Tenancy, October 10, 1936; Kester, speech to the American Economics Association, Chicago, December 29, 1936, copy in STFU Papers; Amberson, "Forty Acres and a Mule," *Nation*, March 6, 1937, pp. 264–66.

idea, and both the *Nation* and *New Republic* editorially approved it.[62] Eventually people all the way up to the Secretary of Agriculture accepted it. Wallace had originally believed in small-farm ownership as thoroughly as the most politically shrewd Congressman, but on Thursday morning, February 18, 1937, he appeared before the conservative House Committee on Agriculture to testify that small farms were not a sufficient answer to tenancy. "In some areas," said the Secretary, "it is desirable to create holdings of a size and character to permit systems of farming predominantly commercial." He recommended "cooperative ownership of the more expensive types of farm machinery and breeding stock, and . . . cooperative buying, processing, and marketing." Wallace even recommended that Congress encourage less experienced tenants to form cooperatives, the better to be supervised and educated in techniques of farm management.[63] But Wallace's suggestions fell on deaf ears. Members of the House Committee on Agriculture were entirely too orthodox to favor anything more "collectivistic" than marketing cooperatives for well-established producers.

It was terribly easy, of course, to write off the cooperative idea as "socialistic" and "collectivist." And there was, to some extent, an ideological basis for the STFU's support of the co-

62. "A Program for Farm Tenancy," *Nation*, March 6, 1937, p. 257; "Tenancy—A Way Out?" *New Republic*, February 24, 1937, pp. 61–62.

63. Farm Tenancy Hearings, pp. 221–22. It should be admitted that the ideas of Rexford Tugwell and other leaders of the Resettlement Administration were probably more effective in modifying Wallace's beliefs than were the ideas of the STFU, but there was considerable intellectual interplay between STFU leaders and Resettlement leaders, via Gardner Jackson. By 1939 Wallace had departed far enough from his previous convictions to state that if the United States learned to depend more on cooperatives "we will build here, in these United States, as good a democracy as they have in Norway, Sweden, and Finland. . . . I think they have done a better job than we have here. I think they are out in front of the United States, though I think we are next to them." On another occasion that same year, he spoke of farm cooperatives as creating "a stronger bridge between democracy and capitalism" and going far toward solving "our problem of combining democracy and capitalism."—"The Cooperative Movement and the American Way," speech at the University of Chicago, August 7, 1939, and "Farm Cooperatives on the Business Front," speech at Peoria, Illinois, October 18, 1939, both in "Speeches of the Secretary (1939)" folder, RG 16, N Arch. Not the least interesting thing about these remarks is the question whether a cabinet officer could express such sentiments today and remain in office.

operative idea; Mitchell had agreed with Clarence Senior that the union's solution to rural ills should be distinctively Socialist, not one which could be taken over by the major parties.[64] At the same time, it was the STFU, not the Socialist party, which emphasized the applicability of cooperatives to tenancy problems. The STFU was backing cooperatives when the party was still calling for a farm ownership program; and Sam Romer, editor of the *Socialist Call*, publicly apologized for accidentally giving the Party rather than the union credit for the promotion of the cooperative idea. Norman Thomas stressed the protection of civil rights rather than cooperative communities as the best answer to tenants' problems; Amberson and Kester were the leading proponents of cooperatives. And the fact that their motives were more practical than ideological—even, perhaps, in Kester's case—was demonstrated by their willingness to experiment with many different types of cooperative organization, some of them quite limited and conventional, in an effort to discover what would best answer union members' needs.[65]

In other words, the controversy was not primarily between "socialists" and "individualists," but between those who did, and those who did not, perceive that the trend toward large-scale agriculture was as irreversible as the trend toward large-scale industry. The only question was whether the many or the few would benefit from the factory farms and agri-businesses of the future; whether tomorrow's countryside would be a land of economic democracy or a region of riches and poverty.

64. H. L. Mitchell to Clarence Senior, November 22, 1935; Senior to Mitchell, November 26, 1935, both in SP Arch, Duke. Both Senior and Mitchell were quite interested in Lázaro Cárdenas's Laguna cooperative project in Mexico; see Senior to Mitchell, December 9, 1936, Mitchell to Senior, December 11, 1936, Mitchell to J. Isabel Garcia, December 21, 1936, Mitchell to Hubert Herring, March 19, 1938, and others, all in STFU Papers.

65. Clarence Senior to H. L. Mitchell, January 15, 1936, SP Arch, Duke; interviews with Robert W. (Pete) Hudgens, June 24, 1961, and with Mitchell, December 3, 1961; Norman Thomas, "What Next for the Sharecropper?" speech over CBS radio network, February 10, 1937, copy in STFU Papers; H. L. Mitchell to Douglas Cobb, November 20, 1936; Mitchell to all locals, December 11, 1936; Fred R. Lown to the STFU, February 9, 1937; J. R. Butler to Lown, February 17, 1937; Harriet Young to Mitchell, June 2, 1938; Mitchell to Young, June 6, 1938, all in STFU Papers; Mitchell to the author, November 26, 1968.

Two observations—parenthetical and superficial, but perhaps suggestive—may be made. First, our attitudes toward rural inequality at home in the 1930's may furnish clues to our attitudes toward rural inequality overseas in the 1970's. Second, perhaps we can find three Reconstructions, three attempts to eliminate slavery, in our history. It is commonplace to refer to today's black freedom revolution as the Second Reconstruction; it could be considered the third. The second would comprise the discovery in 1936 that Southern tenancy was slavery slightly altered, the Farm Security Administration's attack on this version of slavery, and the eventual defeat of the FSA in World War II. One can argue that the failure of the first two reconstructions may be traced ultimately to certain features of the private property shibboleth; perhaps the present Third Reconstruction may crumble under the same pressure. We may be sure that the black people of America will not accept a third denial.

In 1936 the Second Reconstruction was beginning. That summer, election year awareness of sharecropping made some governmental attack on tenancy evils inevitable. But how superficial or fundamental, how permanent or ephemeral the attack would be, remained to be discovered.

# 7.

# The Coming
## of Farm Security

Gardner Jackson was always a believer in direct approaches. With the 1936 election campaign furnishing a favorable climate for his straightforwardness, he began discussing sharecropper grievances with Senate Majority Leader Joseph T. Robinson of Arkansas even before the Democratic National Convention met. Although STFU leaders despised Robinson for his service to prominent Delta planters, Jackson found the Senate leader surprisingly amenable to suggestions that action be taken to remedy tenancy ills. Robinson agreed to meet formally with H. L. Mitchell, Jackson, and others during the Party convention at Philadelphia in June.[1]

Mitchell was glad the meeting had been arranged, but doubtful that it would produce tangible results. He wondered how news of the meeting would be received by some of the Arkansas delegates to the convention: Sheriff Howard Curlin; Mrs. Alex East, wife of the manager of the Norcross plantation; J. O. E. Beck, the largest planter in Crittenden County; other planters from Blytheville and Osceola; and, of course, Junius Marion Futrell. Knowing that New York friends of the STFU intended to picket the convention in protest against Arkansas terror, Mitchell decided not to veto their plans unless his meeting with Robinson should actually prove fruitful.

1. Interview with Gardner Jackson, August 14, 1961.

Jackson, Negro leader John P. Davis, and Mitchell met with Robinson and Assistant Secretary of Labor Edward McGrady, both of whom represented the convention's Resolutions Committee, and attempted to convince them they should push through the committee a resolution calling for, in effect, extension of the Wagner Act to agricultural labor. Amazingly, Robinson agreed, said he would fight for inclusion of such a plank in the Democratic platform, and promised to support Federal investigation of civil rights violations in the Delta. It was McGrady, a union organizer before he entered the Department of Labor, who flatly refused to back the resolution: he feared it would be misinterpreted as a threat to the nation's farmers.[2]

So Philadelphia's Bellevue-Stratford Hotel, convention headquarters, was picketed by STFU sympathizers despite Robinson's apparent change of heart. Perhaps the Arkansas Senator had not really changed his mind since declaiming that STFU organizers had convinced sharecroppers "they should resort to violence" and that "there is little doubt, from the literature circulated among the tenants by some of the organizers, that the agitation is communistic."[3] From the day President Roosevelt, through Tugwell, directed Robinson to see that Governor Futrell clamped down on violence against sharecroppers, such oratory sprang from Robinson's lips no longer. Once it became

2. The most reliable account of the meeting is probably Gardner Jackson's "Memorandum to John L. Lewis, John Brophy, Ralph Hetzel, and Donald Henderson," October 1, 1937, copy in STFU Papers; see also *Jonesboro Daily Tribune*, June 24, 1936; *The Sharecroppers Voice*, July, 1936; Transcript of H. L. Mitchell's recorded interview for the Columbia University Oral History Collection, STFU Papers and elsewhere (hereafter cited as Oral History MS), pp. 72–73. McGrady was willing to back a milder, more general resolution.

3. *Congressional Record*, Vol. 79, Pt. 6, 74th Cong., 1st Sess., 1935, pp. 5927–8. See also the criticism of Robinson's STFU stand in an otherwise favorable article, "The Senator from Arkansas," *Fortune*, XV (January, 1937), 107; Nevin E. Neal, "A Biography of Joseph T. Robinson" (Ph.D. dissertation, University of Oklahoma, 1958), p. 395. Neal out-Robinsons Robinson on the subject of the STFU: "Many outsiders, including Mrs. J. B. Mitchison, English Labor Party member; Norman Thomas, leader of American socialism; and Sherwood Eddy of New York encouraged tenants to attack landlords. The local landlords with the support of city and county police units effectively dispersed the tenants, and little violence resulted."

clear that the leader of the Democratic party was going to help farm tenants, Joseph T. Robinson was going to help farm tenants. Everybody who has ever written about Robinson, from conservative biographer Nevin Neal ("As a loyal Democrat, he demanded party regularity above personal convictions") to iconoclastic H. L. Mencken ("He was a party hack, and no more"), emphasizes that the Democratic party's public positions automatically became the Senator's public positions.[4]

And there could no longer be any doubt that Robinson's chief intended to move against farm tenancy. The Republicans showed considerable interest in using AAA sharecropper displacement against the President, but Landon, despite his criticisms of the AAA, was unable to say more in support of "farm home ownership" than Roosevelt did.[5] FDR had felt deep personal sympathy for impoverished tenants as long as Gardner Jackson or Norman Thomas had known him; by early 1935, Jackson had the impression that he was "seriously concerned."[6] But in 1934 and 1935 he felt that political pressures precluded any public stand on behalf of tenants. In order to pass his major "second New Deal" legislation—banking, labor relations, social security, relief—the support of high Southern officials and Congressmen was absolutely necessary.[7] "We must wait for a new generation of Southern leaders," he told Norman Thomas.[8]

4. Neal, "Robinson," pp. 2–3, 390; H. L. Mencken, "Semper Fidelis," *American Mercury*, XLII (December, 1937), 436–39; see also the unanimous testimony to Robinson's "party regularity" contained in Rexford Guy Tugwell, *The Democratic Roosevelt* (Garden City, N.Y.: Doubleday, 1957), p. 401; "Robinson Will Not Do!" *Nation*, May 29, 1937, pp. 607–8; "The Senator from Arkansas." *Fortune*, XV (January, 1937), 107–8. See also Wilbur J. Cash, *The Mind of the South* (New York: A. A. Knopf, 1941), pp. 365–68, which shows that Robinson's attitude was typical in the South.

5. Gardner Jackson, "Memorandum to John L. Lewis, John Brophy, Ralph Hetzel, and Donald Henderson"; Tugwell, *Democratic Roosevelt*, pp. 420–25; "Share-Cropper Hope," *Literary Digest*, October 3, 1936, p. 9; Mastin G. White, "'Memorandum for the Files," July 23, 1936, folder 467, Solicitor's File, RG 16, N Arch.

6. Interviews with Gardner Jackson, August 14, 1961, June 30, 1962.

7. Sidney Baldwin, *Poverty and Politics: The Rise and Decline of the Farm Security Administration* (Chapel Hill: University of North Carolina Press, 1968), pp. 150–53.

8. Interview with Norman Thomas, July 5, 1962, confirmed in later conversations.

But if Roosevelt respected the political power of the South's rulers, he respected equally the advice of well-informed liberal friends who assured him that tenant conditions must be remedied. Early in 1935 he was discussing the subject at occasional private meetings with Will Alexander, Frank Tannenbaum, and Edwin Embree of the Rosenwald Fund.[9] He often saw liberal Congresswoman Caroline O'Day of New York, who was on the best of terms with the Gardner Jacksons and with Marguerite ("Missy")LeHand, the presidential secretary. Roosevelt once urged Representative O'Day to speak to Senator Robinson about protection for STFU members.[10] Professor Broadus Mitchell, a native Southern economist then at Johns Hopkins, appealed to the President to furnish moral support to the STFU by receiving its leaders at the White House. Roosevelt was afraid of the political consequences of such a meeting, but after conferring with Harry Hopkins he told Mitchell that "I am sure" the STFU would be consulted about any action taken by the administration.[11] The President made similar promises to Gardner Jackson, who conferred with him from time to time. An even more frequent White House visitor was "my good friend Norman Thomas," as Roosevelt sincerely called him despite their differences.[12]

Roosevelt was convinced by early 1936 that, to a limited extent, he could afford to support congressional action against tenancy. He was still unready to make anti-tenancy action openly an administration objective, but he held frequent strategy

9. Baldwin, *Poverty and Politics*, pp. 127–31; George Foster Peabody, telegram to Marvin McIntyre, January 10, 1935, OF 1650, FDR Library.

10. H. L. Mitchell, telegram to Mrs. Caroline O'Day, February 28, 1936; Mrs. O'Day to "Missy" LeHand, February 29, 1936; Franklin D. Roosevelt memo, March 3, 1936, all in OF 1650, FDR Library.

11. Broadus Mitchell to Franklin D. Roosevelt, April 1, 1935; Marvin McIntyre, confidential memo to Harry Hopkins, April 23, 1935; Roosevelt to Mitchell, April 26, 1935, all in OF 1650, FDR Library.

12. See, for example, Franklin D. Roosevelt to Oswald Garrison Villard, June 8, 1932, in Elliott Roosevelt (ed.), *F.D.R.: His Personal Letters, 1928–1945*, Vol. I (New York: Duell, Sloan, and Pierce, 1950), p. 283; Marvin McIntyre, telegram to Norman Thomas, April 27, 1935, OF 1650, FDR Library. For evidence of Roosevelt's growing understanding of rural poverty, see also Floyd Murray to Franklin D. Roosevelt, March 19, 1937; Marvin McIntyre to Murray, March 24, 1937, both in OF 1650, FDR Library; Franklin D. Roosevelt to Fred I. Kent, February 11, 1938, in E. Roosevelt (ed.), *F.D.R.: His Personal Letters*, II, 758–759.

conferences with Tugwell, Will Alexander, Henry Wallace, members of the National Resources Committee and other Federal planning boards, and of course with congressional leaders like Senator John Bankhead of Alabama and Representative Marvin Jones of Texas, who were leading the home-ownership attack on tenancy.[13] Gardner Jackson, who was kept informed about these conferences, reported to H. L. Mitchell that Roosevelt wanted the Bankhead-Jones tenancy bill "hurried through" Congress because of "the need for it in the South, politically as well as socially." Jackson heard that "Will Alexander is playing close to Wallace and will be the real master of the new show if it goes through."[14]

Not until September 21, 1936, however, did Roosevelt publicly endorse even the limited Bankhead bill.[15] Then, in the middle of October, he was approached by management engineer Morris L. Cooke, a Pennsylvania Republican who was serving as head of the Rural Electrification Administration. New information would spur Congress to move more strongly against tenancy, Cooke suggested, and consequently a special fact-finding commission should be appointed. Similar suggestions had been made to Secretary Wallace by members of the National Resources Committee, a Federal conservation planning board on which Cooke had once served.[16]

13. On Tugwell, see, for example, Marvin McIntyre, memo, January 28, 1936, OF 1650, FDR Library. A friend's ideas on tenancy problems, which Tugwell evidently accepted, are in J. G. Evans to Tugwell, June 2, 1934, in "Tenancy (1934)" folder, RG 16, N Arch. On the National Resources Committee, see M. L. Wilson to Dr. H. C. Taylor, January 20, 1936, in "Tenancy (1936)" folder, RG 16, N Arch. For the ideas of Edwin Embree, another of Roosevelt's consultants, see his "Southern Farm Tenancy, The Way Out of Its Evils," *Survey Graphic*, XXV (March, 1936), 153.
14. Gardner Jackson to H. L. Mitchell, January 15, 1936, STFU Papers; much of Jackson's report is corroborated by Senator John H. Bankhead to Henry Wallace, December 14, 1936, in "Tenancy (1936)" folder, RG 16, N Arch.
15. Franklin D. Roosevelt to Senator John Bankhead, September 21, 1936, and to Representative Marvin Jones, September 21, 1936, OF 1650, FDR Library.
16. On the suggestions by Cooke and the National Resources Committee, see Morris L. Cooke to Franklin D. Roosevelt, October 13, 1936; Roosevelt, memo to Henry Wallace and Rexford Tugwell, October 19, 1936; Wallace to Roosevelt, November 5, 1936; Roosevelt to Wallace, November 10, 1936; mimeographed memorandum on the Special Com-

On November 16, two months after Roosevelt's letter to Bankhead and Jones revealed that he thought the tenancy problem
was primarily a matter of non-ownership of real estate, he directed Wallace to form a special Committee on Farm Tenancy,
its deliberations to be under the auspices of the liberal National
Resources Committee. Though the President made reference to
"the traditional American ideal of owner-operated farms," it
was significant that he did not, as in the Bankhead-Jones letter,
recommend individual ownership as a panacea. Instead, Roosevelt was now concerned with "the great group of present and
prospective farm tenants,"[17] while eight weeks before he had
been content to recommend help only for those "who have
demonstrated their ability to manage"—a phrase which ex-
cluded the millions of Southern croppers and tenants who never
had any opportunity to develop management ability, let alone
to demonstrate it.

Significant also was the fact that Roosevelt and Wallace entrusted guidance of the Tenancy Committee to liberals like
Louis C. Gray and Will Alexander, who, with a few associates,
controlled the Committee from the beginning. Calling themselves the full committee's "Technical Committee on Farm
Tenancy," these insiders assumed the entire task of preparing
the committee's final report. Members of the Technical Committee, in addition to Alexander, were Dr. Arthur G. Black of
the Bureau of Agricultural Economics, Dr. Charles S. Johnson
of Fisk University, Utah farm sociologist Lowry Nelson, Dr.
John D. Black of Harvard, Edwin G. Nourse of the Brookings
Institution, and M. W. (Bill) Thatcher of the Farmers' Union.[18]

Formally and informally, directly and indirectly, the thought
of Roosevelt, Wallace, and the Technical Committee was af-
fected by the STFU and the STFU-inspired Arkansas tenancy

mittee on Farm Tenancy, n.d. [November, 1936]; all the above in OF
1650, FDR Library.

17. Franklin D. Roosevelt to Henry Wallace, November 16, 1936, in
OF 1650, FDR Library.

18. Henry Wallace to Rexford Tugwell, December 2, 1936, in "Ten-
ancy (1936)" folder, RG 16, N Arch; Frederic A. Delano to Harold Ickes,
February 1, 1937, OF 1650, FDR Library; "The President's Committee at
Work," *Congressional Digest*, XVI (February, 1937), 41; interview with
Gardner Jackson, June 30, 1962.

commission. Roosevelt's promise to Broadus Mitchell that the STFU would have a voice in any Federal program began to be carried out when W. L. Blackstone, a minor union official, was belatedly named to the full committee. Much more important was the receptivity of the highest Federal executives to Arkansas recommendations. The President's secretary, Marvin McIntyre, personally turned over copies of the Arkansas Commission's report to Secretary Wallace; Brooks Hays sent copies of the Arkansas Policy Committee's broader report, a document sympathetic to STFU demands, to both Wallace and M. L. Wilson. The Secretary was quite impressed by the latter report and told Hays to send copies to all members of the President's Committee—especially to Chairman Gray.[19] Moreover, at regional hearings held in Dallas and Montgomery, the Arkansas Commission and the STFU were well represented. Both at the hearings and in a long "Open Letter" to Roosevelt, the STFU advocated long-term leases, written contracts, enforcement of fair plantation practices through Federal control of AAA contracts, and, of course, Federal aid to cooperative communities for large-scale production.[20] Gardner Jackson saw to it that the right to organize was also stressed; Henry Wallace had just made a stirring speech in Pasadena advocating more and more organization for farmers, but, as most farm spokesmen were prone to do, he left out any mention of organization for farm tenants and laborers. In addition, Jackson demanded that the Department of Labor rather than that of Agriculture be given jurisdiction over farm workers for the same reasons that Labor rather than Commerce had jurisdiction over industrial workers.[21] But Jackson's petition went unheeded; to the day of this

19. Marvin H. McIntyre to Henry Wallace, December 14, 1936; J. D. LeCron to Brooks Hays, December 15, 1936; M. L. Wilson to Brooks Hays, December 15, 1936, all in "Tenancy (1936)" folder, RG 16, N Arch.

20. Louis C. Gray to J. R. Butler, December 24, 1936; H. L. Mitchell to Gray, December 31, 1936; Howard Kester to Mitchell, December 25, 1936, all in STFU Papers; *The Sharecroppers Voice*, November, 1936, January, 1937; Kester, testimony to the President's Committee on Farm Tenancy, Montgomery, Ala., January 6, 1937, copy in STFU Papers.

21. Henry A. Wallace, "Agricultural Security," speech at Pasadena, California, December 9, 1936, as quoted in Edwin G. Nourse *et al.*, *Three Years of the Agricultural Adjustment Administration* (Washington: The Brookings Institution, 1937), p. 563; Gardner Jackson, telegram to Howard Kester, January 5, 1937, STFU Papers.

writing, farm workers remain the only ones whose interests are "protected" in the cabinet and in congressional committees by representatives of their employers.

The short shrift given to some STFU proposals led Lawrence Westbrook, a high official of the Resettlement Administration, to declare in a national magazine that "the Southern Tenant Farmers' Union . . . cannot in reason or justice be continuously ignored."[22] But Westbrook may not have known that the union did have a considerable indirect influence on the committee. STFU material was in the hands of most committee liberals and many of its friends in Congress; Senator Rush Holt of West Virginia was one of those who asked the union to send him all its available information.[23] Dr. Charles Johnson of Fisk University, co-author of *The Collapse of Cotton Tenancy* and one of the most influential members of the Technical Committee, praised the STFU's "most excellent and forceful statement" and said he would see that the union's ideas were given much weight in the Committee's deliberations.[24] With noted Southern scholars Rupert Vance, Arthur Raper, and H. C. Nixon serving as his colleagues on the Southern Policy Association's tenancy subcommittee, Johnson placed before the President's Committee recommendations which included the encouragement of STFU-style cooperatives.[25]

Still more significant than the impact of specific STFU proposals on specific persons, however, was the role the union played in creating the climate of opinion in which the United States' only significant assault on rural poverty could be undertaken. After all, Rexford Tugwell, Alexander, and their associates had been influential in the New Deal's agricultural wing for three years; why did the President suddenly constitute them a tenancy commission and present their conclusions to Congress during the fall and winter of 1936–37? Political motives might

22. Lawrence Westbrook, "Farm Tenancy: A Program," *Nation*, January 9, 1937, p. 39.

23. Senator Rush Holt to the STFU, November 28, 1936, STFU Papers.

24. Dr. Charles S. Johnson to H. L. Mitchell, December 14, 1936, STFU Papers.

25. Southern Policy Association, "Recommendations Regarding Tenancy Legislation . . . ," December 14, 1936, in "Tenancy (1936)" folder, RG 16, N Arch.

explain Roosevelt's adoption of the popular home-ownership approach during the campaign, but certainly not his decision, only two months later, to direct a group of reform-minded scholars to seek new facts under the auspices of the liberal National Resources Committee. In the space of a few months, both Roosevelt and Wallace changed from advocacy of a few home-ownership loans to support of an all-out attack on rural poverty. That this change occurred precisely during the few months that STFU agitation reached a climax was hardly coincidental; as H. L. Mitchell said of Roosevelt the politician, "Being the kind of man he was, he only functioned on issues where there was a demand and we created the demand."[26] This "demand" was brought to bear on Roosevelt quite directly, as we have seen, through Gardner Jackson and Norman Thomas. Mrs. Roosevelt met Howard Kester after he wrote a report for Walter White concerning a brutal Florida lynching; she remained on good terms with him thereafter. Kester felt that she communicated her sympathies to the President and influenced him inestimably.[27] But of all the STFU leaders, it was Jackson who was most responsible for producing action from the White House. The well-informed Drew Pearson contended that "Jackson . . . probably more than any other one individual was the indefatigable and belligerent instigator" of the President's decisions on tenancy.[28] Jackson told the author that his influence through sympathetic Congressmen was probably more important than any direct pressure. But, he wryly noted, only three Southern Congressmen ever lent him any support: Alabamans Hugo Black, John Sparkman, and very rarely Lister Hill.[29] Nevertheless, after 1935 even conservative Congressmen had to deal with large numbers of constituents demanding action against sharecropper problems. Most journalists recognized the Arkansas

26. Oral History MS, pp. 63–64.
27. Interview with Howard Kester, July 17, 1961.
28. As quoted by H. L. Mitchell in Oral History MS, pp. 76–77. Pearson's opinion is upheld by Jackson's old colleague Sam Bledsoe, who told the author that as a publicist for the AAA he was impressed by the fact that incidents involving the STFU had an impact far out of proportion to the union's numbers and geographical extent. "Gardner Jackson was mainly responsible for this," continued Bledsoe. "He hit at conditions everybody knew were bad." Interview with Bledsoe, July 10, 1962.
29. Interview with Gardner Jackson, August 14, 1961.

source of this public concern.[30] Scholars, too, even when they had no idea of the STFU's connections in Washington, saw a direct link between the union, public concern, and presidential action.[31]

Perhaps the influence of the STFU was demonstrated most convincingly by its impact on popular opinion and literature. Prior to the formation of the STFU, only the most well informed knew what a sharecropper was. Howard Odum, Rupert Vance, and Arthur Raper had examined tenancy, but attention was given them mainly by other scholars. Erskine Caldwell had published *Tobacco Road* in 1932 and *God's Little Acre* in 1933, but many of the millions who read them probably considered them more pornographic than sociological, more fictional than real. Stories of plantation life still emphasized the graciousness of Southern womanhood and the gallantry of Ole Massa rather than the evils of sharecropping.

Then in 1934 the STFU was founded, Norman Thomas published *The Plight of the Share-Cropper*, and the flood gates were open. *The Collapse of Cotton Tenancy*, which failed to mention the STFU only because its scope was restricted to the Deep South, appeared in 1935 and Howard Kester's impassioned *Revolt Among the Sharecroppers* came out a year later.[32] In 1936 and 1937 sharecropper stories written mainly by the worst of the "proletarian" authors became a distinct genre and poured

30. Arthur Krock, "In Washington," *New York Times,* April 6, 1937, p. 22; M. C. Blackman, "Tenancy in Arkansas," *Arkansas Gazette Magazine,* April 4, 1937, p. 7; "The Nation-wide Problem of Farm Tenancy," *Congressional Digest,* XVI (February, 1937), 37–38. See also the comment on "all the Southern stir" in *Newsweek,* June 13, 1936, p. 8.

31. Donald Crichton Alexander, *The Arkansas Plantation, 1920–1942* (New Haven: Yale University Press, 1943), p. 70; J. A. Baker, "Farm Tenancy: Report of the Arkansas State Policy Committee," *Journal of Land and Public Utility Economics,* XIII (February, 1937), 90; Karl Brandt, "Farm Tenancy in the United States," *Social Research,* IV (May, 1937), 150; Edwin R. Embree, "Southern Farm Tenancy, The Way Out of Its Evils," *Survey Graphic,* XXV (March, 1936), 149.

32. Kester's book was, perhaps, overdone, but not as much as one columnist, Herbert Agar, claimed. Agar, supposedly liberal, said it was "over-sentimentalized," "unfair to the landlords," and "bitterly unfair to Mr. Wallace and his plans for abolishing tenancy." (Wallace, at that time, favored home ownership for the deserving few.) Agar, "Time and Tide: How to Make Communists," Louisville *Courier-Journal,* March 30, 1936, clipping in STFU scrapbook, STFU Papers.

off the presses by the dozens. In a single 1937 issue of *New Masses*, James Agee reviewed two of them: one told of a white cropper in need of money who became a bootlegger and was ostracized; the other was about a Negro cropper who returned from college (!!?) to organize tenants, murder the white "owner" of his sweetheart, and finally join a jazz band.[33] Some of the tenant tales copied the history of the STFU so slavishly that Mitchell, Kester, and Butler should have demanded royalties.[34]

After the STFU was formed, Southern travel accounts usually had to include the Arkansas Delta, and most of the literary tourists were sympathetic to the union.[35] One of the visitors was the noted American artist Thomas Hart Benton, whose paintings of rural poverty include many scenes of tenant life in the South. The more radical Rockwell Kent also portrayed sharecropper misery in many of his paintings, etchings, and woodcuts. Photography, more than any other art, captured the suffering of the South's rural poor. After the STFU helped bring about establishment of the Farm Security Administration in 1937, FSA photographers traveled throughout the South to record the bit-

33. James Agee, "Sharecropper Novels," *New Masses*, June 8, 1937, p. 23. A less ideological cropper story was Harry Kroll's *I Was A Share-Cropper* (Indianapolis: Bobbs-Merrill, 1937).

34. Mrs. Charlie May Simon, for example, who specialized in children's stories, tried her hand at a sharecropper novel in which a young tenant's landlord cheats him out of AAA benefits and then keeps him from getting relief. A friendly lawyer, after helping the tenant start a union, begins writing stories for national magazines and becomes the target of planters who oppose the "Reds"—but instead of getting his porch light shot out, he only gets a brick through the transom of his office. After the lawyer insists that the union be interracial, the young hero is evicted. He moves into an old church with a Negro friend; he gets horsewhipped and the friend gets killed. Thereupon his union (which has its offices in Memphis and has called a strike about this time) tries to preach a funeral for the dead man. Union members, arrested on vagrancy charges, are put to work chopping cotton. The book is called *The Share-Cropper* (New York: E. P. Dutton & Co., 1937); pp. 127–79, 190–247 are almost 100 per cent Southern Tenant Farmers' Union history. No acknowledgement to the STFU is made.

35. Some of the travel accounts that featured trips to the STFU area were Jonathan Daniels's *A Southerner Discovers the South* (New York: Macmillan, 1938), Thomas Hart Benton's *An Artist in America* (New York: Halcyon House, 1939), and Nathan Asch's *The Road: In Search of America* (New York: W. W. Norton & Co., 1937).

terness of a type of existence their agency was pledged to destroy. Four persons used a combination of prose and photography to produce modern masterpieces: Erskine Caldwell and Margaret Bourke-White created *You Have Seen Their Faces* in 1937; four years later the lyric yet masculine prose of James Agee and the camera artistry of Walker Evans were combined in *Let Us Now Praise Famous Men.* Academic works on tenancy, moreover, became more thorough and more common after 1934.

Of course, to thousands of STFU members, the most important consequences their union could produce would be political, not literary. Their attention was riveted on Washington, where, on January 5, 1937, the 75th Congress of the United States convened. Conspicuous among the first measures introduced was the Bankhead-Jones tenant home ownership bill, which President Roosevelt endorsed in his opening message. "The prevalence of an un-American type of tenant farming," Roosevelt warned Congress, was one of the "far-reaching problems still with us for which democracy must find a solution if it is to consider itself successful."[36] Over a month later, the report of the President's Committee on Farm Tenancy was also presented to Congress. The document was composed of findings, recommendations for action, and a series of supplements—photographic, statistical, and technical—demonstrating the condition not only of tenants but of impoverished owners. The Committee ascribed their condition to abuses attending the nation's disposal of its public domain, the institution of fee-simple ownership, and other factors encouraging acquisition of land by speculators and corporations. Furthermore, the Committee asserted, the Southern plantation system, the effect of recurring depressions, and inadequate farm credit had also increased tenancy and rural poverty.

To attack these evils—to move "toward farm security," as the Committee put it—the Resettlement Administration should become the nucleus of a "Farm Security Administration." This agency should buy land, lease it to tenants during a probation-

36. *New York Times*, January 5, 1937, p. 15; January 6, 1937, p. 2; January 7, 1937, p. 2.

ary period of training and supervision, and finally sell it to them as they developed the ability to manage. In some areas, cooperative communities of the STFU type "may well be aided," the Committee added. It also called for continuation of the Resettlement Administration's land retirement, farm labor, and rehabilitation loan programs, and for state action to improve leasing practices, make land taxation equitable, and protect civil liberties.[37]

But the Congress which received the report seemed likely to consider nothing more than a home ownership loan program. Though the Bankhead-Jones bill was designed primarily for such limited purposes, it still allowed the government to acquire land for tenants and to provide them with the education and supervision needed to make them independent farm owner-managers. Largely because of these provisions, Congressman Jones had an impossible task getting his bill out of the House Agriculture Committee, even though he was its chairman. On the last day of March the committee's thirteen conservatives formally voted to knock out of the bill all provisions allowing the government to buy land or even hold it long enough to educate ex-tenant lessees and enforce conservation practices. The *New York Times* called the thirteen to eleven vote the "sharpest rebuff received by the President from any Congressional committee on farm legislation since he came into office."[38] Bitterly disappointed, but determined to get some kind of legislative foundation for an attack on rural poverty, Roosevelt, Jones, Alexander, and Wallace conferred at the White House and agreed to accept a proposal allowing loans only—no government ownership—provided restrictions on resale of the land were kept in the bill. This "takes the government out of the picture," pleaded Chairman Jones, but the inflexible thirteen refused to listen. After a fortnight Jones gave up and reported a completely emasculated substitute bill out of committee. Per-

37. President's Committee on Farm Tenancy, *Farm Tenancy, Report of the President's Committee* (Washington: Government Printing Office, 1937), pp. 5–6, 11–20, 39–46. See also *New York Times*, February 12, 1937, p. 1.

38. *New York Times*, April 1, 1937, pp. 1, 40; Baldwin, *Poverty and Politics*, pp. 180–82.

mitting no restrictions on land resale, it gave speculators carte blanche to buy up the ex-tenants' land. It allowed no government ownership, leasing, or supervision; loans, available in less than half the nation's counties, would go only to the handful of tenants who could make a down payment or who possessed livestock; and local committees—principally white planters in the South—would have final authority. The great majority of tenants and sharecroppers were thus left out of the measure entirely. President Roosevelt announced that he was highly dissatisfied with the House bill and that he hoped to get a good bill through the Senate and then have it accepted by the House.[39]

During the long struggle in the House Committee, it became obvious that administration supporters were relying on three major arguments which the majority of Congressmen simply could not understand or accept. In the first place, they refused to believe that the need was to make tenure secure and attack poverty rather than merely to encourage home ownership. (For that matter, at the rate the conservatives were willing to appropriate money for farm homes, it would have taken 1,500 years for every tenant to get one.)

Second, the conservatives believed it was un-American to forbid a tenant to resell his newly acquired land to speculators or corporations. None of them claimed to *want* speculators to acquire the land; it was just a matter of principle with them, of course.

Finally, they failed to see any reason for government supervision and education of the tenants; they held almost unanimously that loans should go only to tenants who already knew how to manage, and the fact that this philosophy consigned millions to landless poverty did not seem to bother them.

The tenacity with which conservatives clung to these convictions becomes more understandable when it is realized that most administration liberals had only recently abandoned them. It was not until the end of 1936 that one typical farm economist, C. A. Wiley, could decide that the problem was "not how to change the statistical position of farmers in the census returns,

39. *New York Times*, April 7, 1937, p. 10; April 15, 1937, p. 13.

but how to improve their economic status."[40] About the same time, as we have seen, President Roosevelt and Secretary Wallace were first being led to similar conclusions.

In changing the attitude of such men, perhaps the most influential role was played by Rexford Tugwell, who wrote that "the simple process of making debt-ridden owners by the thousand would create more problems than were solved," and argued that the goal of public policy should be "security of possession with a more adequate family living" rather than mere ownership.[41] To guarantee this "security of possession," administration liberals—who remembered that huge tracts of the public domain intended for settlers under the Homestead Act and its successors had actually passed to railroads, insurance firms, mining concerns, and other corporations—insisted that the Federal government should retain title to all land conveyed to tenants. If this were done, the Tugwell-Wallace group argued, not only would land remain in the hands of those for whom it was intended, but also conservation practices could be carried out on a large scale. This position was one of the Southern Tenant Farmers' Union had long advocated. Indeed, the STFU may have strongly influenced Wallace, at least, according to Gardner Jackson's report in the fall of 1936:

I had an hour and a half session yesterday morning with Secretary Wallace at his solicitation in the course of which we hashed the Bankhead proposition over very thoroughly. I quoted Justice Brandeis to him (and this is strictly confidential, please, for yours and Mitch's and Buck's and Amberson's information only) as strongly endorsing our stand that the government should retain title to whatever land it buys and should not try to sell but should lease on an occupancy lease basis if possible or at most a nominal lease rate. This is a reversal of the Justice's position after many sessions with

40. C. A. Wiley, "Tenure Problems . . . ," *Journal of Farm Economics*, XIX (February, 1937), 129.
41. Rexford Tugwell, "Behind the Farm Problem," *New York Times Magazine*, January 10, 1937, pp. 4–5, 22; for echoes of Tugwell, see the editorial "Tenant Farm Problem," *New York Times*, February 14, 1937, p. IV–8; Peter Nelson, "Land Tenure Problems . . . ," Oklahoma *Current Farm Economics* series, Vol. 10, No. 4 (August, 1937), p. 83; T. W. Schultz, "A Comment on the Report of the President's Committee . . . ," *Journal of Land and Public Utility Economics*, XIII (May, 1937), 207–8; Karl Brandt, "Farm Tenancy in the United States," *Social Research*, IV (May, 1937), 145; Farm Tenancy Hearings, pp. 179–82, 193–94.

him. Wallace concurred fairly completely. He and the Justice also
are agreed that cooperative projects are essential.[42]

Even after congressional conservatives defeated the idea of
government ownership and training, many still opposed what
remained of the Bankhead-Jones bill. They were sure that no
farm problem could remain if higher prices were achieved, and
they were equally certain that any tenancy problem would cost
too much.

Regarding farm commodity prices, only recently had even
liberal scholars and Department of Agriculture officials begun
to realize that, while price was basic, there were a whole host
of problems—soil conservation, production efficiency, marketing, distribution, to name only a very few—that would remain
troublesome even at optimum prices.[43] But this was understood
by only a handful of Congressmen and farm spokesmen; many
leading supporters of the Bankhead bill failed to grasp it. As
late as October, 1936, in his farm speech at Omaha, President
Roosevelt had been certain that "lower interest rates and better
prices" would bring "the ultimate objective of every farm family owning its own land."[44] Senator Bankhead himself explained,
"I'm not trying to up anybody's standard of living. I'm trying to
raise the price of cotton."[45] And Representative Jones, opening
his committee's tenancy hearings, declared, "Tenancy is not the
problem. It is but an outcropping of the problem. Behind the
tenant question is the problem of price and income."[46] With even

42. See the long-term lease provisions in the STFU's proposed "New
Homestead Bill," as given in Proceedings of the Second Annual Convention, pp. 13–16. The quotation is from Gardner Jackson to J. R. Butler,
September 29, 1936, STFU Papers.
43. See Grant McConnell, *The Decline of Agrarian Democracy* (Berkeley: University of California Press, 1953), pp. 84–85; Gardner Jackson in
Farm Tenancy Hearings, p. 196; C. A. Wiley, "Tenure Problems . . . ,"
*Journal of Farm Economics*, XIX (February, 1937), 130; Arthur G.
Black, "Discussion," *Journal of Farm Economics*, XX (February, 1938),
161.
44. As quoted in *Congressional Record*, Vol. 81, Pt. 6, 75th Cong., 1st
Sess., 1937, p. 6476.
45. Interview with R. W. (Pete) Hudgens, June 24, 1961.
46. For this and similar statements by Jones, see Farm Tenancy Hearings, pp. 10, 252–53, 291. See also the price-is-the-problem argument of
Representative Wright Patman of Texas, another fairly liberal Bankhead
bill proponent, in *Congressional Record*, Vol. 81, Pt. 6, 75th Cong., 1st
Sess., 1937, pp. 6439–43.

liberal Congressmen making such statements, it goes without saying that most conservatives were content to think commodity price was the only real issue.[47] Believing this, it is understandable that they would discount the admonitions of the President's Committee and wonder instead when Congress would return to discussing fundamentals. Significantly, after the conservatives had emasculated the Bankhead bill, all that was left was a mild farm credit bill, credit being the only agricultural concern other than price that they considered legitimate.

Conservatives were also sensitive about the cost of a tenancy program. They would consider appropriating only funds for lending, and then only if possible recipients were limited to credit risks as impeccable as Farm Credit Administration clients. "While we cannot help all [tenants] . . . we ought to do what we can to help the most deserving," said Representative Clifford Hope of Kansas.[48] To make sure that only the "deserving" were helped, several Congressmen wanted to limit aid to those who could plunk down, in hard cash, 5 to 10 per cent of the purchase price of the farm they wished to buy.[49]

The conservatives' sharp-eyed scrutiny of cost posed an interesting dilemma for proponents of the Bankhead bill. If they tried to appropriate enough money to buy most tenants a home, the sum would be too astronomical for any self-respecting conservative to consider. (Wallace pointed out that $160 million per year, an amount far too large to request from Congress, would buy farms for only the annual *increase* in the ranks of tenant farmers.)[50] If, on the other hand, administration spokesmen re-

47. For price-is-the-problem statements by conservatives, see Farm Tenancy Hearings, pp. 272, 311; *New York Times*, January 4, 1937, p. 14; *Congressional Record*, Vol. 81, Pt. 6, 75th Cong., 1st Sess., 1937, pp. 6434, 6471, 6474–75.

48. *Congressional Record*, Vol. 81, Pt. 6, 75th Cong., 1st Sess., 1937, p. 6459. See also *Ibid.*, p. 6456, and B. K. Rankin, statement in *Congressional Digest*, XVI (February, 1937), 55.

49. *Congressional Record*, Vol. 81, Pt. 6, 75th Cong., 1st Sess., 1937, pp. 6457, 6459, 6470–71, 6476, 6481. H. L. Mitchell had discovered long before that the Farm Credit Administration would loan to tenants prosperous enough to make a down payment; he must have been ready to tear out his hair upon hearing that some Congressmen wanted to make the tenancy bill into a duplication of what the FCA was doing already. See Alice R. Griffith to H. L. Mitchell, April 30, 1936, STFU Papers.

50. Farm Tenancy Hearings, pp. 242–43; see also pp. 199–202, 246–

quested only the small amount they could get from Congress, the bill's inadequacy would be ridiculous. The latter course was chosen; to pacify conservative spending fears, the billion dollar outlay of the original Bankhead bill was sliced to $10 million for the program's first year, $25 million the second, and $50 million thereafter. At the first year's rate, it would have taken 1,500 years to buy the nation's three million tenants small $5,000 farms, but at the third year's rate it would have taken only three centuries.

Conservatives had a field day heaping sarcasm on the inadequacy of the bill. Just a moment after blasting $10 million as "a heavy drain upon the Treasury," Representative Joe Martin criticized it as inadequate: "The average tenant farmer has as much chance of getting aid as the average purchaser of a ticket to win the English [Irish?] Sweepstakes."[51] Wealthy New York Congressman Hamilton Fish, arch-enemy of the entire Roosevelt clan, declared that the very idea of a tenancy bill was ridiculous—"half-baked legislation"—because it was impossible to appropriate enough money and appropriating a fiscally sensible amount was farcical. Consequently, Fish reasoned, nothing should be done at all.[52]

On Monday, June 28, 1937, the House of Representatives formed a Committee of the Whole for final discussion of the Bankhead bill. Incongruously, a consistent Arkansas landlord spokesman, Representative William J. Driver of Osceola, became chairman of the session. Edwin Markham's poem "The Man With the Hoe" was recited and Congress was called the tenant's "only temple of refuge"; nothing significant was said. The next day the bill was passed 308–25, but with 99 abstentions—mainly conservatives who hardly wanted to record them-

---

49, 271; for other estimates of the cost of an adequate program, see *New York Times*, February 12, 1937, p. 1; Arthur Skreberg, "The Bankhead Bill," *Commonwealth College Fortnightly*, November 15, 1936, CCP, Reel 3; Peter Nelson, "Land Tenure Problems . . . ," Oklahoma *Current Farm Economics* Series, Vol. 10, No. 4 (1937), p. 81; Howard Kester, statement to the President's Committee on Farm Tenancy, Montgomery, January 6, 1937, copy in STFU Papers.

51. *Congressional Record*, Vol. 81, Pt. 6, 75th Cong., 1st Sess., 1937, p. 6433.

52. *Ibid.*, p. 6435–36. See also similar remarks on pp. 6464, 6470.

selves against such a popular idea as home ownership.[53] The
Senate, in view of its approval of the stronger Bankhead bill
two years before, passed its own version of the bill almost without debate. Unlike the House bill, the Senate measure provided
for a continuing program, allowed the government to buy and
hold land for tenants, and provided for education and supervision. (Congressmen Lucas and Charles Tobey warned that it
would lead to "socialization of the land.") Both houses of Congress named conferees to meet and iron out the differences between the bills, but the House conferees were told that unless
the Senators eliminated government land ownership, the compromise bill would have to be brought before the entire House
once more—in other words, would probably not be accepted.[54]

The warning was unnecessary. The Senate's attention was
captured almost entirely by the climax of the Supreme Court
"packing" battle, and it was in no mood to quibble over a tenancy bill. It conceded almost every point of contention to the
House, retaining only a provision which forbade ex-tenants
from selling their land within five years and required them to
follow certain soil conservation practices for that period. Even
this small gesture alarmed some Congressmen. Georgia's Stephen Pace called it "the first step by Congress to put the farmers
of this Nation into irons," and Earl C. Michener of Michigan
agreed that "we will . . . be giving the Secretary of Agriculture
absolute control to regiment over 42 percent of the farmers in
the country." More accurate was the reactionary Representative
Lucas, who beamed, "I want to pay a tribute to the House conferees for standing by their guns."[55]

Routinely, both House and Senate approved the conference
version of the bill. It was almost exactly the tenancy "cure" that
Southern planters and the established, upper-middle-class-

53. *Ibid.*, pp. 6450–51, 6582–83; *New York Times*, June 29, 1937, p. 1;
June 30, 1937, p. 7.
54. *Congressional Record*, Vol. 81, Pt. 6, 75th Cong., 1st Sess., 1937,
pp. 6762, 6815–16, 6853; *New York Times*, July 3, 1937, p. 4, July 7, 1937,
p. 9.
55. *Congressional Record*, Vol. 81, Pt. 6, 75th Cong., 1st Sess., 1937,
p. 7138; for the conference report and discussion of it, see pp. 7133–38;
*New York Times*, July 14, 1937, p. 2.

dominated farm organizations had been advocating. Since there were no restrictions on resale other than the mild one added by the Senate conferees, the comment of Representative Biermann regarding the House version was still apropos: "We are not making owner-operators, we are making land speculators."[56] The government was allowed to buy submarginal land from large-scale operators, to retire it, but was specifically forbidden to buy land for resale to tenants. Instead, tenants had to find farms for sale on their own; local committees of prosperous farmers could then veto any transaction if they disapproved the farm, the price, or the tenant—whose "character, ability, and experience" had to satisfy them. (One might safely assume that in the South few black men, and no unionized radicals of any color, need have applied.) Preference was to be given tenants who could make a handsome down payment—which, in view of the extremely limited nature of the program, meant that it would be necessarily restricted to such tenants. The Senate-imposed resale provision did not prevent an ex-tenant from paying his entire debt and receiving full title at any time he cared to do so, thus allowing speculators and corporations to pay his balance and acquire his land. The bill appropriated no funds for anything other than home ownership loans; any other tenant programs had to be paid for out of leftover Federal relief appropriations.[57]

Resettlement chief Will Alexander discussed the disappointing measure at length with Department of Agriculture officials M. L. Wilson, Milo Perkins, and Paul Appleby. Finally they decided to ask Wallace to recommend that President Roosevelt sign the measure, because a veto would be extremely embarrassing to Congress and to Bankhead and Jones in particular.[58] But

56. Representative Fred Biermann, "Minority Views," in House Committee on Agriculture, *Farm Security Act of 1937*, House Reports 586, 1065, 75th Cong., 1st Sess., 1937. Though the Act as passed was referred to no longer as a "Farm Security Act," but simply as the "Farm-Tenant Act," these reports will be referred to hereinafter as Farm Security Act Reports, as their title has it.

57. Farm Security Act Reports; "Farm Tenancy," *Congressional Digest*, XVI (August–September, 1937), 194.

58. P. H. A[ppleby] to Henry [Wallace], July 19, 1937, in "Tenancy (1937)" folder, RG 16, N Arch.

they probably felt much like Representative Henry Teigan, a farmer-labor progressive from Minnesota, who complained, "The farm-tenant bill as finally enacted is almost useless."[59]

Nevertheless, Roosevelt signed the bill into law on July 23; reporting the action, the *New York Times* somewhat perplexedly described the measure as "a sort of experiment in eliminating farm tenancy."[60] The sad episode was not yet over. Three weeks later the House Appropriations Committee tried to kill the Act by cutting off the money required for it, explaining that the sum appropriated was too small to do any good. Representative Charles L. South of Texas inquired sarcastically, "I wonder if that committee would have approved an amount greater than this." The next day, sitting as a Committee of the Whole, the House restored the funds.[61]

Examination of the Act makes it hard to understand why Rexford Tugwell could call it, years later, one of Roosevelt's "only two considerable accomplishments" during 1937.[62] The reason—which also explains Roosevelt's willingness to settle for anything he could get out of Congress—is that the Bankhead Act was significant, not in itself, but as a legislative foundation for the broadening of the Resettlement Administration. Naturally the President had attempted to secure as strong a bill as possible; Representative Tobey claimed that a conservative colleague had declared that White House pressure on behalf of the bill "surpassed anything he had ever known in his public life."[63]

59. *Congressional Record*, Vol. 81, Pt. 10, 75th Cong., 1st Sess., 1937, p. 2521; see also Baldwin, *Poverty and Politics*, pp. 187–92.

60. *New York Times*, July 24, 1937, p. 4.

61. *Congressional Record*, Vol. 81, Pt. 8, 75th Cong., 1st Sess., 1937, pp. 9120–21; *New York Times*, August 17, 1937, p. 10; August 18, 1937, p. 1.

62. Tugwell, *Democratic Roosevelt*, p. 435.

63. *Congressional Record*, Vol. 81, Pt. 4, 75th Cong., 1st Sess., 1937, pp. 3873–74. Elaborating, Tobey said the President had promised administration support of one congressman's "pet bill" in exchange for his vote on the Bankhead bill; allegedly, another congressman was threatened with presidential opposition to his re-election unless he voted for the administration version of the bill; if he did so, however, the president would aid his re-election campaign. Roosevelt was trying "to overcome men's honest convictions and to thwart the will and judgement of a House committee," complained Tobey.

In the end, one of the few things left in the measure the President signed was authorization for him to set up a Farm Security Administration, and that was all he really needed. The meaningful attack on rural poverty, the program the President's Committee had recommended and Congress had refused to enact, could be largely carried out through administrative rulings of the new FSA. As early as March, in full confidence that some kind of farm security bureau would be authorized, Roosevelt met with Gardner Jackson, H. L. Mitchell, STFU attorney Newell Fowler, and STFU organizer Dave Griffin to discuss ways in which the FSA-to-be could be of service to the STFU's membership.[64]

On the first day of September, 1937, a little over a month after Roosevelt signed the Bankhead-Jones Tenant Act, Secretary of Agriculture Wallace transformed the Resettlement Administration into the Farm Security Administration and entrusted it with control over all the old Resettlement programs plus the new ownership program established by the Bankhead Act. The top officials of the new FSA included a number of liberals from the President's Committee; Will Alexander, who had been head of Resettlement, continued as chief of FSA, with Dr. Louis C. Gray as his chief assistant and Dr. Arthur G. Black as one of the leading directors of the Farmers Home Corporation set up under FSA to administer the home ownership program.[65]

Only the home loan program was new; most of FSA's other responsibilities were inherited from earlier New Deal enterprises. The "new" agency was essentially a revivified Resettlement Administration with the congressional home loan program tacked on. Its real fathers were not Bankhead and Jones but Gray, Wallace, Alexander, and the President's Committee on Farm Tenancy. Radical Southern reformism, such as that of the Southern Tenant Farmers' Union which had helped bring the President's Committee into existence, continued to be reflected in the FSA. Its administrator, Will Alexander, and a disproportionate number of its officials were liberal Southerners; about 40

64. Gardner Jackson, telegram to Marvin H. McIntyre, March 5, 1937, and attached memos, OF 1650, FDR Library.

65. *New York Times*, September 2, 1937, p. 6; October 10, 1937, p. 2.

per cent of its clients lived in the South. Negroes participated in the FSA programs almost in proportion to their percentage of the population. Negroes and union members were invited not only to vote for but to serve on local FSA committees, a practice which horrified most Southern and farm bloc Congressmen.[66] The least effective FSA program was the congressional one. So limited were the funds allotted that it operated in less than 20 per cent of the nation's counties; and in each of the few hundred where it did operate, only ten farm home loans were allowed. In Arkansas, these loans were available in only four of the counties where the STFU had locals; elsewhere, in Craighead, Poinsett, St. Francis, Jefferson, or Lonoke counties, among many others, tenants were simply out of luck. Since the chance of receiving a loan was almost nonexistent, FSA tried to discourage applications, but there was still an average of about thirty applicants for every loan.[67]

To the STFU, the token home loans were far less important than the success of FSA's cooperative farms. At the most famous of these, the Dyess Co-operative in Mississippi County, the STFU had a strong local encouraged by the FSA,[68] but the union's leaders were inclined to favor a greater degree of collective ownership than that which prevailed at Dyess: "They've used enough lumber in giving every colony member his own individual barn to build a barn big enough to take care of half

66. Virginius Dabney, *Below the Potomac* (N.Y.: Appleton-Century, 1942), pp. 66–68; McConnell, *Decline of Agrarian Democracy*, pp. 94–95; H. L. Mitchell, draft of telegram to Henry A. Wallace, October 12, 1937, and R. W. Evans to Mitchell, October 29, 1937, both in STFU Papers.
67. *Memphis Commercial Appeal*, December 1, 1937, has the Arkansas figures. On the program as a whole, see *New York Times*, August 9, 1937, p. 24; October 7, 1937, p. 45; October 10, 1937, p. 2; James G. Maddox, "Suggestions for a National Program of Rural Rehabilitation and Relief," *Journal of Farm Economics*, XXI (November, 1939), 892; C. B. Baldwin, "Helping Tenants Become Owners," *Agricultural Situation*, XXII (September, 1938), 11–12; Paul V. Maris, "From Tenant to Owner," *Extension Service Review*, IX (October, 1938), 154; Maris, "Farm Tenancy," *U. S. Yearbook of Agriculture, 1940* (Washington: Government Printing Office, 1940), p. 899. For dozens of pitiful letters asking for land, see the "Tenancy" folders for various years, 1935–39, RG 16, N Arch.
68. H. L. Mitchell to Lawrence Westbrook, October 11, 1937, STFU Papers.

of Arkansas," newspaperman Jonathan Daniels agreed.[69] The STFU so persuasively called for cooperative plantations with individually owned houses and gardens but collectively owned cotton lands, gins, stores, and equipment that the FSA established several STFU-style cooperatives in Arkansas alone: the Twist Plantation in Poinsett County, the Lake View project in Phillips County, and the Plum Bayou and Lake Dick cooperatives in Jefferson County were the best known. STFU leaders felt quietly gratified—and no little vindicated—when former enemies such as Senator Hattie Caraway, T. Roy Reid, and E. B. Whitaker proudly appeared and offered praise at the first public inspection of the Lake Dick cooperative.[70]

Although there was wide appreciation of the projects, particularly among persons who realized they were intended for demonstration and experimentation, the opposition was far more powerful. Its headquarters were the offices of American Farm Bureau Federation leaders, men dedicated to the defeat not only of the projects but of the entire agency. Before the outbreak of World War II, their attacks resulted only in minor victories such as the reduction of FSA appropriations and the resignation, under pressure, of key FSA personnel. And even these small triumphs were unwittingly aided by well-intentioned Secretary of Agriculture Claude Wickard, who, pressed from the right by the Farm Bureau and from the left by FSA's radicals, simply vacillated—and weakened the agency by his indecision.[71]

In 1942, with the establishment of the Byrd Committee, a

69. Daniels, *Southerner Discovers the South*, pp. 130–31; see also pp. 142–48. On the Dyess Colony, see M. C. Blackman, "Uncle Sam Waves a Wand," *Arkansas Gazette Magazine*, September 22, 1935; *The Share-croppers Voice*, February 1, 1936; Memphis *Press-Scimitar*, November 20, 1936; Lawrence Westbrook, "Farm Tenancy: A Program," *Nation*, January 9, 1937, p. 39; Elizabeth C. Wherry, "A Chance for the Share-Cropper," *Wallace's Farmer*, May 7, 1938, pp. 333, 344.
70. *Arkansas Gazette*, September 14, 1938. On the "collective" cooperatives and others in Arkansas, see M. C. Blackman, "Arkansas's Largest Landlord," *Arkansas Gazette Magazine*, October 13, 1935; Earl Clement Blake, "Tenancy in Arkansas" (Seminar) thesis, University of Arkansas, College of Business Administration, 1939), pp. 109–13; Oral History MS, pp. 97–98; McConnell, *Decline of Agrarian Democracy*, pp. 91–92.
71. Baldwin, *Poverty and Politics*, pp. 367–77.

joint congressional committee on reduction of "non-essential" government expenditures for the better prosecution of the war effort, Farm Bureau President Edward O'Neal saw the key to the FSA's abolition before him. Now whole articles blasting the agency began appearing in *Nation's Agriculture*, the Farm Bureau magazine. One of the more ridiculous of these charged that FSA clients on cooperative projects made "about 1 cent an hour, and they borrow money at 5% interest from the Government to pay themselves this wage."[72] Other "facts" like these were "discovered" by a special investigator O'Neal sent South to seek ammunition which could be used before the Byrd Committee. There, however, most of the charges were refuted by FSA spokesmen, so the Farm Bureau repeated them to the House Committee on Appropriations, the Senate Committee on Appropriations, and to friendly individual Congressmen. After FSA tried to establish a minimum wage for cotton picking, the cotton lobby joined the Farm Bureau, and together they succeeded in establishing within the House Agriculture Committee a subcommittee which for more than a year provided an open forum for all charges against the FSA, including those previously discredited. The cooperatives were declared copies of Soviet kolkhozy, and the FSA regional director for the Southwest was called "communistic" on the grounds that he was married to a Mexican woman. As a result of the subcommittee's hearings, FSA appropriations for 1944 were withheld, and two years later the prostrate agency was killed by transformation into a weak "Farmers' Home Administration." Thus ended what one writer has called "the greatest innovation in agricultural policy since the passage of the Homestead Act" and "the greatest attempt to cope with the problem of rural poverty—perhaps the only significant attempt—in the nation's history."[73]

72. William G. Carr, "The Return of the Carpetbagger!" *Nation's Agriculture*, XVII (April, 1942), 7–10; see also Horace Cate, "Rehabilitation in Arkansas," *Nation's Agriculture*, XVII (June, 1942), 7–9; J. Gilbert Hill, "Land Ownership Won't Make Smart Farmers," *Nation's Business*, XXVI (March, 1938), 28–30, 98.

73. McConnell, *Decline of Agrarian Democracy*, pp. 96, 112. This account is based mainly on McConnell, pp. 97–111, and Baldwin, *Poverty and Politics*, pp. 325–404. See also Leif Dahl, "Agricultural Labor and Social Legislation," *American Federationist*, XLIII (February, 1937), 145. R. W. (Pete) Hudgens, former Southern administrator of FSA, pointed

The Farmers' Home Administration limped impotently onward throughout the fifteen Truman and Eisenhower years. Then, under Kennedy and Johnson, it became a beneficiary of the "New Frontier" and the so-called War on Poverty. From 1961 through 1966 it pumped more than $4 billion into rural America for home improvement loans, swimming pools, tennis courts, and similar benefits for those whose poverty was not too horrible to keep them from being good credit risks. The people whose haunted faces FSA photographers had once recorded remained, for the most part, in rural shacks—or in the more soul-destroying urban ghettoes.[74] Truly the old Farm Security Administration was long dead.

---

out to the author during an interview on June 24, 1961, that the New Deal had two agricultural objectives—to remove the economic disparity between agriculture and industry and to remove the disparity between income extremes within agriculture—and that big farmers helped the New Deal achieve the first goal, then used the political power gained thereby to defeat the second. Hudgens also observed, relative to the demise of FSA, that "Farm Security borrowers never organized in their own interest. Once they got their own farm they forgot about everybody else." Of the cotton lobby-Farm Bureau attack on FSA, he remarked that his agency "wasn't killed, it was starved to death."

74. Baldwin, *Poverty and Politics*, pp. 401–3, 414–18.

# 8.

# Into the CIO
# and Disaster

When the Seventy-fifth Congress convened in early 1937, Franklin Roosevelt had just won the greatest electoral landslide in history; he had done so partially on the basis of his pledge to aid the "forgotten men" of rural America with tenancy legislation, just as he had assisted the "forgotten men" of industrial America two years previously with the Wagner Act.

And how greatly that Act was remaking the nation! After its passage in 1935, local industrial unions—"federal unions," as the AFL called them—sprang up across the country, and when William Green and his cohorts refused to sponsor industrial unions in the mass production industries, John L. Lewis's forces formed the Committee for Industrial Organization. By the time Congress was well into its deliberations over the Bankhead tenancy bill, the CIO drive to organize automobile and steel workers was at full throttle. With figurative horns blowing and cymbals crashing, the greatest bandwagon in the history of the American labor movement was rolling onward—and leaders of the Southern Tenant Farmers' Union wanted to jump aboard so badly that their legs hurt. But when to leap, and in response to whose call: here indeed was a dilemma. Donald Henderson and his Communist comrades were irrevocably in command of the nationwide farm workers organizing drive, and the CIO was prepared to accept this. Yet, on the other hand, the CIO itself was led equally authoritatively by Lewis and his United Mine Workers hierarchy, many of whom had spent their lives fighting "radicals" and were now prepared to cooperate with the Left to the smallest extent necessary. In Lewis's metaphor, he would work with militant leftists as the hunter uses his bird dogs.[1]

To stand with the hunter, or to stand with the bird dogs—the question rode along with each STFU official as he drove the snowy road to Muskogee, Oklahoma, in the second freezing week of January, 1937. By the time he arrived at the drafty, leaky old hall where his union's third annual convention was beginning, he had made his decision. To Claude Williams, his popularity enhanced by the beating he had taken, it was absolutely necessary to support the Communist position that workers had to be organized by tenure: small farmers in one organization, tenants and croppers in another. Moreover, union democracy required that schools like Commonwealth College must educate workers in militant class consciousness. Leon Turner, a courageous young black protege of Williams, was ready to run against H. L. Mitchell himself as the STFU's chief executive, while his supporters, most of them more in the Commonwealth orbit than the STFU's, fought quite openly for Communist party positions.[2]

To Gardner Jackson, receiving telegrams of support for the STFU at his headquarters in the Huber Hotel in downtown Muskogee, it was all-important to avoid any public airing of hunter vs. bird dog problems. To Howard Kester and H. L. Mitchell, growing antipathy toward Commonwealth College's noisy, disruptive factionalism—as they saw it—was now coupled with a desire to please the hunters, the top CIO leadership, at all costs.[3] And John L. Lewis's man in Muskogee was a hard-

1. Arthur Meier Schlesinger, Jr., *The Coming of the New Deal* (Boston: Houghton Mifflin, 1958), p. 419.

2. Transcript of H. L. Mitchell's recorded interview for the Columbia University Oral History Collection, STFU Papers and elsewhere (referred to hereafter as Oral History MS), pp. 74–79; Aaron Levenstein, unpublished typed MS, n.d. [1937]; Levenstein, confidential report to Sidney Hertzberg and Norman Thomas, n.d. [1937], all in STFU Papers; interview with Claude Williams, August 18, 1962; Leon Turner to Claude Williams, December 26, 1936, Claude Williams Papers.

3. Levenstein report; Levenstein typed MS; Howard Kester to Roger Baldwin, January 28, 1937; Levenstein to the editors of the *Socialist Call*, January 29, 1937, all in STFU Papers.

nosed, allegedly racketeering UMW bureaucrat named Dave Fowler, who had detested Claude Williams ever since Williams had helped miners around Fort Smith fight against Fowler's autocratic control of their union. Jackson, Mitchell, and Kester lacked any love for Fowler themselves, but when he ordered public disavowal of Commonwealth as the price of discussing CIO affiliation, the STFU leaders obeyed. The popular Williams, denied even a seat on the tenant union's executive council, remained furious for weeks despite Kester's attempts to placate him. "As a result of our patching things up with Fowler," Mitchell explained, "a telegram was later received from John L. Lewis greeting the convention." Williams's reaction: "So what!"[4]

During the rest of the winter of 1937, Williams's contemptuous view of the value of making overtures to John L. Lewis seemed to be bolstered by the facts. Frustratingly, the CIO leadership brushed aside all hints from their Memphis suitors, while Don Henderson and his associates were too busy elsewhere to worry about winning over the STFU. Congress, deliberating on the Bankhead bill, was taking a tragically limited view of the problem of rural poverty, and even nature seemed to be malignant: the St. Francis and other tributaries of the Mississippi, swollen with winter rain and melting snow, flooded thousands out of their homes.[5] And at STFU headquarters in Memphis, all was disrupted by Mitchell's newest love affair; this time the wife of one of his closest associates was involved, making Kester and Evelyn Smith, the STFU's unofficial moral guardians, considerably more exasperated at him than usual. Though Kester was a clergyman, he claimed that his concern

4. Howard Kester to Roger Baldwin, January 28, 1937, and Claude Williams to Gardner Jackson, January 23, 1937, both in STFU Papers; Williams to Maynard Kreuger, January 20, 1937, and H. L. Mitchell MS on the Muskogee Convention, with Williams's marginal comments, n.d. [1937], both in Claude Williams Papers.
5. *Chicago Daily Tribune*, February 14, 1937; Los Angeles *United Progressive News*, February 2, February 22, 1937, and other labor news clippings, STFU scrapbook, STFU Papers; H. L. Mitchell to Gardner Jackson, January 25, 1937, J. R. Butler to Tom Powers, January 29, 1937, and Aaron Levenstein to Walter White, February 18, 1937, all in STFU Papers.

arose primarily out of a desire to avoid unfavorable publicity. "With some men it was alcohol; with Mitch it was women," sighed Kester.[6]

Of all the union's leaders, the least distracted by these problems was probably President J. R. Butler, and it was he who finally secured a promise from CIO spokesman Dave Fowler that the STFU, in one manner or another, would be allowed to affiliate. But in June, Fowler's words were superseded by John L. Lewis's action. Only after the fact did Lewis tell Gardner Jackson what had happened: Henderson had enlisted his ideological brother, San Francisco longshoremen's leader Harry Bridges, in the campaign for a farm and cannery laborers international union; and Bridges "sold Lewis on the idea that he could deliver the California and other Pacific Coast ag. workers unions to him $3,600 a month per capita tax taken away from [AFL President] Bill Green if he gets them. Don immediately came down and followed up on Bridges' persuasion. Now, Mitch, you and Howard Kester know what I think of Don. . . . However I think we must play ball on this thing if Lewis goes thru."[7]

6. Interview with Howard Kester, July 18, 1961; Aaron Levenstein to J. R. Butler, March 10, 1937, and H. L. Mitchell to Gardner Jackson, April 17, 1937, both in STFU Papers; John Handcox to Claude Williams, March 8, 1937, and March 13, 1937, both in Claude Williams Papers. On July 25, 1961, Mitchell wrote the author, "To hear those three [Kester, Butler, and Miss Smith] talk one would think every girl or woman who came by to visit us was in love with me. It just wasn't true, I was just interested in people. There was an incident . . . that lasted for a couple of weeks . . . . Then there was another [woman] who was severely handicapped, but very brilliant, who formed an attachment for me, and once told Buck [Kester] she wanted him to marry us. That friendship has lasted for all of the years . . . . I am loyal to my friends and they are to me. I was first married when I was 19 years old. My wife came from a large farm family in a higher economic and social stratum. I was immature but a rebel against accepted things. She raised the family while I took care of the world I thought I was saving. She was interested in a home, church, and social acceptance none of which appealed to me. We drifted apart, without sharing things. So my only romance came late in life when I met [my present wife] Dorothy in 1940 when we were both working for NYA."

7. Gardner Jackson to H. L. Mitchell, June 5, 1937, and Frank Trager to Mitchell, August 25, 1937, both in STFU Papers; interview with Gardner Jackson, August 14, 1961. See also Frank Trager to J. R. Butler, June

The Bridges-Henderson idea, as applied to California and other areas where food processing and shipping were important, was an excellent one: use year-round cannery employees as the nucleus of industrial unions which automatically, through union shop or hiring hall arrangements, would enlist seasonal employees each year. To implement their idea, the disciplined Henderson forces met in Denver during the second week of July, 1937, to form a new CIO International—the United Cannery, Agricultural, Packing, and Allied Workers of America (UCAPAWA). Numerous unions other than those in the Henderson camp were invited, chief among them the STFU, but Henderson was in absolute control of the convention. As his chief aide remembered, "at Denver we were all mainly interested in the situation back home";[8] few had great knowledge of agricultural labor problems in areas other than their own. Henderson, tenaciously clinging to his idea that the STFU was "neither fish nor fowl" because farm workers belonged in one class and farm tenants in another, still could not be persuaded that in the Cotton Belt tenure legalisms meant little. He and John Bosch, the midwestern radical who represented the Department of Agriculture at the convention, misunderstood even the name of the STFU.[9] Full of misgivings, the tenant leaders insisted that Henderson promise them autonomy within UCAPAWA, and, for further effect, publicized the agreement despite Gardner Jackson's customary anxiety that no hint of factional disagreement appear in print. The strength of the "autonomy" promise seemed ominously undercut by Henderson's statement that UCAPAWA "will be centralized and coordinated so that we can build a union that will have the prestige and power that it ought to have." Autonomy would be allowed, said Henderson,

17, 1937, STFU Papers; Oral History MS, pp. 84–85; "Southern Tenant Farmers Union and United Cannery, Agricultural, Packing and Allied Workers," outline of correspondence, n.d. [1938?], STFU Papers.

8. Interview with Leif Dahl, July 12, 1962; Ward Rogers to H. L. Mitchell, June 16, 1936, and Rodgers's report to Norman Thomas, Frank Trager, Mitchell, and J. R. Butler, n.d. [June, 1937], both in STFU Papers; John H. Bosch to Paul Appleby, July 16, 1937, "Labor (1937)" folder, RG 16, N Arch.

9. Oral History MS, pp. 84–85; John Brophy et al., *The CIO and the Farmers* (Denver: July 10, 1937), pp. 5–6, 16, copy in STFU Papers.

"on administrative and organizational questions."[10] Reassuring STFU spokesmen seemed much less important to UCAPAWA's leaders than reassuring the nation's "working farmers," through James Patton of the Farmers' Union, that the new union was formed to struggle beside rather than against them.[11]

Knowing as little about UCAPAWA as UCAPAWA knew about them, STFU members saw only that CIO affiliation was within their grasp; all they had to do was meet officially to accept it. Mitchell and Kester, increasingly doubtful about UCAPAWA, urged Pat Jackson to cajole John L. Lewis into allowing direct STFU affiliation with the CIO. Not until September 24, 1937, as STFU delegates assembled in Memphis to vote on affiliation, could Jackson telephone Mitchell that Lewis, most reluctantly, had stated that the tenant union could affiliate directly with the CIO only if it insisted on spurning UCAPAWA. The delegates heard Lewis's promise as unenthusiastically as he had made it; their constituents wanted action now, not more promises for later. The idea of direct affiliation faded still further when Henderson again promised autonomy and certain, not doubtful, CIO affiliation through UCAPAWA. But the man who decided the issue was the Rev. Claude Williams, who brought delegates to their feet crying and cheering for his vision of a great international people's movement led by the CIO:

10. Don Henderson, speech in Brophy, *C.I.O. and Farmers*, p. 18; interview with Howard Kester, July 17, 1961. On the origin of the STFU autonomy question, see also Gardner Jackson's telegrams to H. L. Mitchell, June 24, 1937, and July 2, 1937; Henderson to J. R. Butler, June 27, 1937; Mitchell to Henderson, June 29, 1937, all in STFU Papers. Fearing that Henderson would be much more autocratic than his aide Leif Dahl—also a Communist but more flexible than Henderson—Gardner Jackson tried secretly to replace Henderson with Dahl, who, however, refused to cooperate. Interviews with Jackson, August 14, 1961, and Dahl, July 12, 1962.

11. Don Henderson and James Patton, speeches in Brophy, *C.I.O. and Farmers*, pp. 13–18, 20; John H. Bosch to Paul Appleby, July 16, 1937, "Labor (1937)" folder, RG 16, N Arch. The STFU, bringing the largest number of members into the UCAPAWA, could not be totally ignored, so J. R. Butler, whose position in the STFU was of less importance than his title of "President" would indicate, was given the ceremonial post of vice-president of the new International. Henderson had excellent reason to believe Butler would be more manageable than Mitchell. Enclosure, Henderson to Mitchell, October 9, 1937; "An Open Letter to Friends of the Southern Tenant Farmers' Union," October 1, 1939, both in STFU Papers; Oral History MS, pp. 86–87; (New York) *Daily Worker*, July 13, 1937.

"The Lord spake unto the children of Moses: Go Forward! He that putteth his hands to the plow and looketh backward is not fit for the Kingdom of God. Go forward, FORWARD INTO THE CIO!"[12]

And verily, into UCAPAWA and the CIO the STFU went. The problems began immediately. Mitchell and Williams were now each convinced that the other was a political opportunist of the worst kind; moreover, the affiliation convention had demonstrated that Williams's charisma might be far more effective than Mitchell's administrative ability. Mitchell therefore decided to isolate his rival from STFU activity as much as Williams's popularity would permit, and asked Henderson to discourage Williams's "divisiveness."

Henderson cooperated;[13] but on the issue of dues payment to UCAPAWA, another issue which, of course, arose immediately, his lack of understanding was almost total. Cotton workers hardly even saw money except at "settling time" in the fall, and yet Henderson expected each of the thirty to thirty-five thousand STFU members to pay dues of fifty cents a month. It may as well have been fifty dollars. Previously, the realistic STFU leaders had asked for a dime a month, had received this irregularly from about a sixth of the members, but had kept all the others in the organization as well.[14] Under the new dispensation, little such leniency could be permitted. "Brookins and Henretta McGhee has ruined our Local, he has got the peoples money and they all has just about quit the Local," complained a former member of the STFU's executive council, "and now he

12. Interview with Claude Williams, August 18, 1962. When Williams re-enacted the climax of the speech for the author, he was surprised to find himself as moved as the delegates had been. Only if one equates demagoguery with effectiveness rather than insincerity could one consider Williams a demagogue. See also Gardner Jackson, "Memorandum to John L. Lewis, John Brophy, Ralph Hetzel, and Donald Henderson," October 1, 1937; H. L. Mitchell to Jackson, July 9, 1937, both in STFU Papers; Oral History MS, pp. 88–89; "Tenant Union Parley Votes to Join Lewis . . . ," *Arkansas Gazette*, September 25, 1937.
13. Gardner Jackson, "Memorandum . . . ," October 1, 1937; H. L. Mitchell to Jackson, July 9, 1937; Mitchell to Donald Henderson, September 30, 1937, and October 6, 1937, all in STFU Papers.
14. Gardner Jackson, "Memorandum . . . ," October 1, 1937; H. L. Mitchell to Jackson, July 9, 1937; Mitchell to all locals of the STFU, September 29, 1937, all in STFU Papers.

and Mrs McGhee are getting new people and he is always talk-ing about money and pay. . . . I will not serve under no body like him, its no good and right in him and such people will never let nothing be successful."[15]

Quickly—one might almost say "eagerly"—officers of the So-cialist party attempted to convince their comrades in the STFU that all difficulties were traceable to the Communist nature of UCAPAWA's leadership.[16] On the contrary, in addition to Don Henderson's unfamiliarity with sharecroppers, there was the simple fact that John L. Lewis, more interested in building power than subsidizing the poor, was squeezing UCAPAWA financially and thus forcing it, in turn, to tighten the screws on the STFU.[17] Responding to these problems, the STFU's leaders only compounded them: they sent UCAPAWA documents to about 170 locals that seemed most able to pay, while the more impoverished locals—also about 170, but with fewer members—were left with only their STFU membership, insofar as the official record was concerned. Although the UCAPAWA-STFU locals had almost 20,000 members, the STFU was able to pay per capita tax—UCAPAWA's share of their dues—on only 7,389 of them as of February, 1938.[18] In addition to confusion over dues, members were confounded by the complex reporting forms and membership books which UCAPAWA sent them.

15. Marie Pierce to H. L. Mitchell, January 27, 1938, STFU Papers.
16. Arthur G. McDowell (National Labor Secretary of the Socialist Party) to Paul Preisler (a Socialist, Vice-President of the American Fed-eration of Teachers), September 22, 1937, STFU Papers. See also various letters from Frank Trager, McDowell's predecessor as Socialist Party Labor Secretary, in the STFU Papers and S.P. Archives, Duke University.
17. Interview with Gardner Jackson, August 14, 1961; Jackson to H. L. Mitchell, June 5, 1937, and Donald Henderson to all members of the UCAPAWA International Executive Board, January 18, 1938, and other reports to UCAPAWA's I.E.B., all in STFU Papers. In the January, 1938, report, Henderson stated that the CIO had just dropped support for all but two of UCAPAWA's twenty-eight organizers at the very time the farm union was trying to publish a periodical and begin educational, legal, and legislative work—with not enough money coming in from members to even cover the cost of services to them. History records John L. Lewis's vast success in pursuing power rather than philanthropy, but history should record what happened to the millions of rural poor as well as the thou-sands of steel and auto workers.
18. H. L. Mitchell, "The Southern Tenant Farmers' Union in 1937," official report, n.d. [February, 1938], p. 9, copy in STFU Papers.

Moreover, in spite of "STFU autonomy," it was difficult to understand why problems should still be addressed to the Memphis STFU headquarters rather than the Washington UCA-PAWA headquarters, especially when the latter represented the legendary CIO and increasingly contacted the STFU locals directly.[19] The taproot of the tangle was everyone's insistence that the American labor union system held hope for people too poor to pay dues, too uneducated to handle paperwork, and too helpless to bargain collectively. Nevertheless, "we have got to do a job of educating the unions as to the importance of organizing the southern workers in agriculture," Mitchell was still convinced. "Our support has got to come from Labor—depending on liberal, religious etc. groups can't last."[20]

In such a frustrating atmosphere, insignificant details became symbols of cosmic importance. In the early months of 1938, Mitchell and Henderson became ever more bitterly estranged over such colossal issues as whether local charters and membership books would have only the STFU name, or the name, seal, and excerpts from the STFU Constitution. Another issue, limitation of the STFU's geographical area to Arkansas, Missouri, and Oklahoma, was far less important than it seemed; the STFU leaders had no funds to expand outside the area UCAPAWA was willing to grant them, making the question largely moot.[21]

19. Almost all of the STFU Papers, from the time of the union with UCAPAWA until the break with it, document this confusion over dues and paperwork. For the period under consideration above, see especially STFU press release, September 30, 1937; H. L. Mitchell to Donald Henderson, October 6, 1937; Henderson to Mitchell, October 8, 1937, October 9, 1937; Mitchell to Henderson, October 11, 1937; Mitchell to Phillip Ham, October 29, 1937, and similar letters to other local secretaries; Evelyn Smith to Ida Dailes, November 5, 1937; Mitchell to Henderson, November 27, 1937; Dailes to Smith, November 30, 1937, and Smith to Dailes, December 7, 1937, all in STFU Papers.
20. H. L. Mitchell to Gordon McIntyre, September 8, 1937, STFU Papers.
21. Proceedings of UCAPAWA International Executive Board meeting, April 28, 1938; Don Henderson to all STFU locals, May 23, 1938; Henderson to H. L. Mitchell, June 4, 1938; Mitchell and J. R. Butler to Henderson, June 6, 1938; Butler and Mitchell to all locals, June 27, 1938; Henderson to Butler, July 29, 1938; outline of STFU-UCAPAWA correspondence, n.d. [October, 1938?], all in STFU Papers. Of the geographical areas which, for administrative reasons, UCAPAWA wished to

Increasingly, the UCAPAWA-STFU relationship was seen as a contest rather than a marriage, even one of convenience; partisan suspicions and personality clashes were pushing more significant matters into the wings. When, for example, Mitchell and Butler were actually granted audience with Lewis himself, who promised no more than reconsideration of their complaints after they had gone through UCAPAWA channels, they were nevertheless far more impressed with him "than people who come from entirely different backgrounds. With his past history and the fact that he came up from the mines," he was a kindred spirit, unlike a certain former Columbia Communist.[22] Henderson, for his part, was too cold, autocratic, and tactless to dismantle walls easily. He insisted on sending *The CIO News* directly to all paid-up STFU members rather than handling it through Memphis; he mailed only his side of controversies out to STFU locals; he gave late replies to urgent questions; his written confirmations of oral agreements often left out important details.[23]

Whatever twists in Don Henderson's psyche may have made him difficult to deal with, his loyalty to the Communist party apparently composed only a small part of the pattern; it made him imagine a great class gulf between cotton tenants and wage workers when none, in fact, existed, but this ideological banner was one which he ceased to wave in the STFU's face as soon as the tenant union had joined his organization. The real difficulties between UCAPAWA and the STFU—dues, with a mountain of misunderstandings piled on—can hardly be shown

---

place off limits to the STFU, the tenant union had strength only in one: a portion of East Texas near Austin, where Negro organizer J. E. Clayton was moderately successful. And Mitchell encouraged continued STFU affiliation there despite UCAPAWA's wishes. Mitchell to secretaries of all Texas locals, June 27, 1938, STFU Papers.
22. H. L. Mitchell to Gardner Jackson, May 18, 1938; see also Mitchell and J. R. Butler, telegram to Evelyn Smith, April 15, 1938; Mitchell to Powers Hapgood, May 16, 1938, all in STFU Papers.
23. Outline of STFU-UCAPAWA correspondence, n.d. [October, 1938?]; Don Henderson to H. L. Mitchell, March 31, 1938; Henderson to all locals of the STFU, May 23, 1938; Mitchell to Henderson, May 30, 1938; Mitchell to Elinor Henderson, October 30, 1938, all in STFU Papers; J. R. Butler to Claude Williams, June 8, 1938, Claude Williams Papers.

to derive from Henderson's political beliefs. Max Kampelman, castigating CIO Communists, found "very little evidence to prove that the goal of the Communists in the trade union movement is to achieve economic revolution. . . .There is, however, overwhelming evidence to prove that the goal of Communists in the trade union movement is support of Soviet strategy in foreign affairs."[24] UCAPAWA and the STFU discussed foreign affairs about as often as *Little Women*. Mitchell lost no sleep over the Soviet purge trials, but Walter Moskop's attempt to "purge" him at Commonwealth College in 1936 remained fresh in his mind. Though his former Socialist partisanship had faded, he was increasingly inclined to heed the Cassandras among his comrades: Socialist officials like Jack Herling and Arthur Mc-Dowell, CIO anti-Communists like Barney Egan and Dave Fowler.[25] With their enthusiastic agreement, every Henderson directive, every rumor that one had to join the Communist party to get ahead in UCAPAWA, every Communist organizer who breezily equated STFU goals with party goals, was seen—sometimes only in retrospect—as part of a Communist takeover plot.[26] In other CIO unions, Communists, non-Communists, and anti-Communists were all using the same Machiavellian techniques to gain and hold control; but Mitchell's Henderson happened to be a Communist, and, by the summer of 1938, he wanted to tell the world about it. "We would like to know just what attitude John L. Lewis will take in case we withdraw and

24. Max Kampelman, *The Communist Party vs. the C.I.O.* (New York: Frederick Praeger, 1957), p. 255. Regardless of the intent implied in his title, Kampelman's study fails to show that Communists were any more autocratic, high-handed, secretive, or devoted to a "rule-or-ruin" philosophy than Socialists, Democrats, or the bureaucratic in-groups that controlled, say, the Carpenters, Teamsters, or John L. Lewis's United Mine Workers and CIO.
25. John ("Jack") Herling to H. L. Mitchell, April 20, 1936; M. E. Bendelari to Mitchell, September 14, 1937; Arthur McDowell to Paul Preisler, September 22, 1937; Barney Egan to Mitchell, June 9, 1938; Mitchell to Ernest Morgan, July 25, 1938, all in STFU Papers.
26. H. L. Mitchell to Powers Hapgood, May 16, 1938; Mitchell to Stanley High, July 10, 1938; High to Mitchell, September 14, 1938; J. R. Butler to Fred Matthews, December 27, 1938; [Mitchell?], "Notes on UCAPAWA in San Antonio, Texas, and Florida," n.d. [1939?]; untitled memorandum on STFU-UCAPAWA relations, n.d. [1939?]; Mitchell and Butler, bill for injunction, n.d. [April, 1939], all in STFU Papers.

state very plainly the real reasons," Mitchell asked Pat Jackson. "He did not give his attitude toward us starting a fight in the C.I.O. to rid it of CP. influence. As we see this move of ours it could well be used as a beginning to clean house all down the line."[27]

Once more it was necessary for Jackson to order his friends not to wash dirty linen in public, but even Jackson's pocketbook, personality, and influence could hardly keep "Communist take-over tactics" out of the newspapers when such tactics reached into the STFU's own ruling body, its executive council. The enormously attractive Claude Williams, with allies particularly among the STFU's Negro leaders, had been named to the council in the summer of 1937, soon after his appointment as head of Commonwealth College. Mitchell, Butler, and Kester still had misgivings over Williams's endorsement of the Com-munist divide-by-tenure policy and over Commonwealth's sus-picion of Socialist partisanship among STFU leaders, but they felt that Williams's socio-religious vision was broad enough to transcend any political affiliation he might have.[28]

Then, on August 22, 1938, J. R. Butler noticed a coat that Wil-

27. H. L. Mitchell to Gardner Jackson, May 18, 1938; see also Mitchell to Powers Hapgood, May 16, 1938. Throughout, J. R. Butler was a little more cautious: "I am not sure that we can show John L. Lewis any con-nection between this thing [dues payment] and the leadership of the UCAPAWA," he remarked. Butler to Mitchell, August 27, 1938, all above in STFU Papers.

28. *Commonwealth College Fortnightly*, August 15, 1937, February 15, 1938; *The* (Commonwealth) *Commoner*, July, August, September, 1938, all in CCP, Reel 3; Claude Williams to H. L. Mitchell, November 19, 1936, and Howard Kester to Roger Baldwin, January 8, 1937, both in STFU Papers; J. R. Butler to Williams, June 8, 1938, Williams Papers; Lee Hays to the author, n.d. [September, 1962]. To Williams, nothing mattered but teaching all workers that by uniting they could gain higher wages in the short run and ownership of productive facilities in the long run. Convinced that the Communist party was working more effectively toward that end than anyone else, he joined under the name "Galey" for a short while, but let his membership lapse when he took the helm of Commonwealth, having promised to keep the college nonpartisan. Everyone who knew Williams recognized that, for him, program was everything and party was nothing; therefore, any concern with a man's party affiliation was contemptible "red-baiting," the cheapest and most emotionalized form of attacking labor unity. Interviews with Williams, August 18–20, 1962, and H. L. Mitchell, December 3, 1961; Oral History MS, pp. 87–88.

liams had left in his home while visiting several days before; he picked it up, a piece of yellow paper fell from a pocket, and on the paper such phrases as ". . . an extraordinary opportunity to move into the most important organization in the agricultural South" and "if this program could be carried out we believe it would place us in a position to capture the union for our line at the next convention" leaped to his attention. Butler was shocked; the man he had repeatedly defended had been planning to move Communists into the STFU and convert it to the party line. Coldly furious, Butler took the document to the Memphis *Press-Scimitar*, then demanded Williams's resignation. When the persuasive clergyman begged Butler for time to explain, his old friend withdrew the resignation request, only to have Kester step in and call officially for Williams's expulsion.[29]

Before the STFU's executive council on September 16 and 17, with several Commonwealth witnesses supporting him, Williams tried desperately to save himself with the only portion of the truth he felt able to reveal: numerous Commonwealth students had drafted papers appealing to various groups for money; and although Williams had disapproved of the "takeover" aspects of Ralph Fields's appeal to the Communist party, he had left it in his pocket until it could be rewritten. The executive council refused to believe in Fields's unaided authorship, primarily because nobody but Williams could possibly have known all the STFU details mentioned in the paper. Williams was unable to confess that he had indeed given the facts not only to Fields but to his friend Cedric Belfrage—whose name, if revealed, would implicate writers in Hollywood and elsewhere, many of them totally innocent of any Communist aims. Belfrage, Fields and others had then written their rough draft in Williams's absence.[30] The executive council members, agreeing

29. [Ralph Fields, Cedric Belfrage and Claude Williams?], untitled plan to take over the STFU, n.d. [August, 1938], STFU Papers; interviews with Howard Kester, July 17, 1961, and Claude Williams, August 18, 1962; Oral History MS, pp. 106–8; Memphis *Press-Scimitar*, August 23, 1938.

30. Interviews and discussions with Claude Williams, August 18–20, 1962, completed and explained the written records: STFU, National Executive Council, minutes of meeting, September 16–17, 1938; "Complete Proceedings, Trial of Claude C. Williams by the Executive Council, Southern Tenant Farmers' Union," September 16–17, 1938, both in STFU

that they were condemning not Williams's political beliefs but rather his apparent attempt to subvert the STFU with them, unanimously expelled him from the council and formally broke all ties with Commonwealth College.[31]

Some reactions were predictable: Gardner Jackson and Commonwealth, for somewhat different reasons, were angry about the publicity. But many who shared Jackson's unity-above-all approach to reform nevertheless agreed with the executive council's action. "It looks like we always manage to fight among ourselves to the good of the common enemy. I expect we would be unable to manage the country if it were voluntarily turned over to the radicals without specifying which ones," lamented the STFU's chief attorney.[32] Though the Memphis leaders were happy that so many applauded their action, they had no way of knowing that two of their supporters, Jay Lovestone and Martin Dies,[33] would build two of the next generation's strongest bastions of Cold War anti-communism: George Meany's labor establishment (ideology by Lovestone) and the House Un-American Activities Committee (foundation by Dies).

The most disastrous response to Williams's expulsion was his own. Convinced that the struggle was only beginning, that even half a union educated in class-consciousness was preferable to a whole union under "bureaucratic, sectarian, red-baiting" leadership, he girded on his armor, summoned up his allies, and prepared for battle. For the STFU, it was the eve of Armageddon.

Papers; *Arkansas Gazette*, September 18, 1938; Memphis *Press-Scimitar*, September 18, 1938.

31. *Ibid.* (all sources).

32. C. A. Stanfield to J. R. Butler, August 25, 1938, STFU Papers. For unfavorable responses to Williams's expulsion, see Williams, "Report," February 25–26, 1939, CCP, Reel 2; *The* (Commonwealth) *Commoner*, September, 1938, CCP, Reel 3; Willard Uphaus to Claude Williams, August 27, 1938; Williams to Uphaus, n.d. [August, 1938?], and October 10, 1938; Williams to Roger Baldwin, September 12, 1938, all in Claude Williams Papers; Donald G. Kobler, "To the Friends of Commonwealth College," n.d. [August 31, 1938], STFU Papers.

33. Jay Lovestone to J. R. Butler, August 31, 1938, STFU Papers; Oral History MS, pp. 108–9. For other messages of support, see Norman Thomas to Butler, August 26, 1938; Mary Fox to Butler, August 29, 1938; Ernest Morgan to Butler, August 29, 1938; H. L. Mitchell to Butler, August 31, 1938; Harold E. Fey to Butler, October 7, 1938; with many others, STFU Papers.

Williams drew up a ten-point program based on accusations that he would have known, at a saner time, to be false,[34] and he sought not merely principled supporters who agreed with him, but opportunistic supporters with any grievance whatever. For example, he now discovered his kinship with E. B. McKinney, the black former vice-president of the STFU, who had also been expelled at the September executive council meeting on a variety of charges centering around his attempt to build a separate Negro organization within the union. McKinney's long-time Garveyism had grown stronger as he observed black people getting beaten, year after year, to produce rewards for poor whites. If Negroes could not even take the reins of an organization in which they were the majority, what hope was there for them? "We do not know our power," he cried to a friend; "we are like a mule, which looks into a mans eyes and sees a whole world too big for him to handle, and he submits to him and lets him work him to death."[35] Williams the preacher of unity had always opposed McKinney's separatism, but now the two clergymen persuaded each other that the STFU was racist and hurried off to recruit another outcast, W. L. Blackstone. Ever since being named—as a name—to the President's Commission on Farm Tenancy, Blackstone had held a much higher opinion of his capacities than that commonly held by others, and he resented not controlling an autonomous Arkansas state organization such as

34. The program accused the STFU leaders of not recruiting members, laziness in seeking collective bargaining contracts, Jew-baiting, red-baiting, Negro-baiting, and theft (by innuendo). "One of the most viciously false articles that it has ever been my misfortune to see or yours to produce," J. R. Butler said of it. Butler to Williams, November 2, 1938, Claude Williams Papers. See also the document itself, "A Program for a United, Democratic, and Effective Southern Tenant Farmers' Union." As mailed to all locals, November 12, 1938, STFU Papers.
35. E. B. McKinney to Bob Miller, February 10, 1937; see also McKinney to H. L. Mitchell, April 28, 1937; McKinney to all STFU members, January 28, 1938; J. R. Butler to all members of the STFU Executive Council, July 18, 1938; McKinney to Wiley Harris, July 29, 1938, August 11, 1938; McKinney to Butler, August 3, 1938; Butler to Norman Thomas, August 23, 1938; Butler to McKinney, August 27, 1938, all in STFU Papers. Also, interview with Howard Kester, July 18, 1961; H. L. Mitchell to the author, July 17, 1961; [Mitchell? Butler?] to Leon Turner, n.d. [1938], Claude Williams Papers; Wilson Record, *The Negro and the Communist Party* (Chapel Hill: University of North Carolina Press, 1951), pp. 39–41, 135–36.

Odis Sweeden's in Oklahoma. Unable to understand why the union couldn't support him financially, he gradually became inactive and moved out of Arkansas.[36]

Whether or not Sweeden's autonomy helped cause the Williams-McKinney-Blackstone problems, it certainly caused the Sweeden problems: the irascible Oklahoma Cherokee, after each new extension of independence, simply demanded more. He was, at one moment, convinced that other STFU officials were not sufficiently devoted to labor unionism, and then, at the next moment, equally convinced that nobody else recognized union methods were inapplicable to tenant farmers. Sweeden's only significant achievement was to secure the establishment of a state-aided landlord-tenant bureau at Oklahoma A & M College. Otherwise, his locals apparently served as social clubs with considerable membership figures but much poorer dues-payment records than could be expected from their members' income. Despite this, Sweeden constantly sent expensive telegrams and collect telephone calls to Memphis to complain about inadequate financial support.[37] Unfortunately, after Howard Kester faded out of union activity because of his opposition to UCAPAWA, and Mitchell began working part-time for the

36. Since the Arkansas locals *were* the STFU, for all practical purposes, "Arkansas autonomy" would simply have substituted the inept nonentity, Blackstone, for Mitchell and his associates as heads of the union. There is no evidence the STFU's membership desired this change. On Blackstone's imagined grievances, see J. R. Butler to Howard Kester, November 17, 1937; H. B. Wimmer to Frank Morgan, December 1, 1937; Evelyn Smith to Priscilla Robertson, December 13, 1937; STFU to all locals, January 28, 1938; W. L. Blackstone to H. L. Mitchell, April 6, 1938, and April 25, 1938, all in STFU Papers; Claude Williams to Blackstone, September 9, 1938, and Blackstone to Williams, n.d. [September, 1938], both in Claude Williams Papers.

37. Levenstein report; Odis Sweeden to J. R. Butler, n.d. [February, 1937]; Butler to Sweeden, February 12, 1937; H. L. Mitchell to Gardner Jackson, April 17, 1937; Mitchell report to the Executive Council, n.d. [May, 1937?]; Butler to Sweeden, May 15, 1937; Sweeden to Butler, July 29, 1937; Sweeden to H. L. Mitchell, December 14, 1937; Mitchell, "Southern Tenant Farmers' Union in 1937," p. 5; Mitchell to Sweeden, January 15, 1938, all in STFU Papers; Peter Nelson, "Land Tenure Problems . . . ," Oklahoma *Current Farm Economics* Series, Vol. 10, No. 4 (1937), p. 83. For Sweeden's conflicting conceptions of what the STFU should be, see Sweeden to Butler, February 15, 1937; Sweeden to Mitchell, September 8, 1937; STFU Executive Council, minutes of meeting May 21–22, 1938, all in STFU Papers.

National Youth Authority, only J. R. Butler, meek and mild, was left at STFU headquarters to handle the ill-tempered Sweeden. So, in the fall of 1938, the Oklahoma leader finally bucked his way completely out of the corral, celebrating another sweeping grant of autonomy by moving to Arizona and leaving his locals to subordinates sympathetic to Henderson, UCAPAWA, and the Communists—whom he had previously detested. In addition, he quietly extended feelers about a *sub rosa* alliance with Williams, McKinney, and Blackstone.[38]

As the final week of 1938 approached, the date of the STFU's fifth annual convention—which, in view of the centrifugal forces at work, threatened to resemble a funeral rather than a conference—Claude Williams redoubled his efforts to save the union from Socialist bureaucrats. Meeting with his Commonwealth associates and sympathetic STFU members, Williams hammered the ten-point program into final shape and made plans to appear with McKinney at a series of rallies throughout northeastern Arkansas.[39] These would lead up to the grand finale, the convention itself; under the STFU Constitution all executive council actions could be appealed there, and the spellbinding Williams intended to do so. He, McKinney, and Blackstone, by sending in identically worded letters of appeal, hoped to underline their claim that they were all dismissed be-

38. On Sweeden's hostility to UCAPAWA and the Communists: H. L. Mitchell to Howard Kester, August 31, 1937; Don Henderson to Sweeden, December 21, 1937; Sweeden to Mitchell, December 24, 1937, January 11, 1938; Oklahoma STFU resolutions, January 13, 1938, and "Resolution passed at the Oklahoma state convention of the STFU," April 23, 1938; STFU Executive Council, minutes of special meeting, April 25, 1938; Sweeden to Mitchell, July 22, 1938, all in STFU Papers; *The S.T.F.U. News*, May, 1938. On Sweeden's change of heart, see Sweeden to J. R. Butler, August 1, 1938; Butler to Sweeden, August 5, 1938; Sweeden to Butler, August 9, 1938; Mitchell to Butler, August 10, 1938; STFU Executive Council, minutes of meeting, September 16–17, 1938; Butler to Mitchell, October 17, 1938; "An Open Letter to Friends of the Southern Tenant Farmers' Union," October 1, 1939, all in STFU Papers; Sweeden, postcard to Claude Williams, November 12, 1938, Claude Williams Papers; Williams, "Report," February 25–26, 1939, CCP, Reel 2.

39. Claude Williams to the author, n.d. [February, 1963]; *The* (Commonwealth) *Commoner*, November, 1938; December, 1938, both in CCP, Reel 3; minutes of meeting at home of E. B. McKinney, October 29, 1938, Claude Williams Papers; J. R. Butler to O. H. Whitfield, December 24, 1938, STFU Papers.

cause they had fought for democracy within the union. On the other side, H. L. Mitchell and J. R. Butler, determined to show that the three cases were entirely different, were still more determined to hold the allegiance of the STFU's black members, to whom a McKinney-Williams movement would have powerful appeal. First, forgetting Little Rock and Memphis, Mitchell and Butler scheduled the convention for the Negro school, Baptist, and A.M.E. churches of the tiny town of Cotton Plant, Arkansas, headquarters of two able new black leaders, George Stith and F. R. Betton. Then Mitchell and Butler proceeded to woo McKinney himself, before and during the convention, with sufficient success: his repudiation of black separatism was enough to obtain his re-admission to the union, though not to the vice-presidency.[40]

The expulsions of Williams and Blackstone, on the other hand, were upheld. Williams had planned to continue the fight anyway, but changed his mind when many of his associates, including Don Henderson and the Communist party district organizer, Alfred Wageknecht, insisted this would do more harm than good. They still hoped that a unified STFU, even under antagonistic leadership, could remain a strong segment of UCAPAWA.[41]

Unfortunately for all concerned, such hopes might still linger as ghosts, but in substance they were dead. The dues problem was the coffin; the Williams case had made "Communist subversion" the lid. All that remained was to nail it on, and the first nails were driven at UCAPAWA's San Francisco convention in December, 1938. The STFU was so far behind on per capita payments that its leaders had despaired of sending any-

40. Proceedings of the Fifth Annual Convention, p. 7; transcript of the Convention at Cotton Plant, pp. 3–4, 13–18; interviews with Howard Kester, July 18, 1961, and with H. L. Mitchell, December 3, 1961; E. B. McKinney, statement of allegiance, December 5, 1938, and J. R. Butler to O. H. Whitfield, January 9, 1939, both in STFU Papers. McKinney's decision to rejoin the STFU lasted no more than a week; see McKinney to Don Henderson, January, 1939; McKinney to Claude Williams, January 6, 1939, January 13, 1939, all in Claude Williams Papers.
41. Don Henderson to J. R. Butler, November 8, 1938; Butler to Henderson, November 28, 1938, both in STFU Papers; The (Commonwealth) Commoner, January, 1939, CCP, Reel 3; interview with Claude Williams, August 18, 1962.

thing but a token delegation to the convention; however, Don Henderson arranged for an exchange of bank checks whereby the STFU paid the full amount of its debt and received exactly the same sum back again for "organizing work" along with a bonus of $150 to send a full delegation to San Francisco. Once there, however, they found themselves spectators at their own wake. Dues payment, it was decided, was to be strictly enforced, and all payments were to be made directly to Washington. STFU autonomy was specifically voted down, with only the nine STFU delegates casting contrary ballots.[42] The tenant leaders flatly refused to accept the convention's verdict: all locals were instructed to continue sending their dues to Memphis. Henderson, faced with insubordination, was equally intransigent, especially since he was on record that all dues received would promptly be returned.

And, from the man who had used the STFU to alter the course of the New Deal, he received the most powerful support possible: "You and your associates have not a leg to stand on," Pat Jackson told Mitchell. "On this matter I can see absolutely no basis for possible argument. Having become a part of UCAPAWA, it is obvious that you must abide by its rules."[43]

At this point, as the principals of the duel stood facing each other ready to fire, the most spectacular protest demonstration in the union's history suddenly erupted on the cold, rainy roadsides of southeast Missouri. Predictably, the Missouri Highway Demonstration immediately became a tri-cornered circus featuring UCAPAWA, the STFU, and the planters. The ringmaster

42. Don Henderson to J. R. Butler, July 29, 1938; Henderson to H. L. Mitchell, August 2, 1938; STFU Executive Council, minutes of meeting, September 16–17, 1938; Mitchell to Henderson, September 23, 1938; Henderson to all STFU locals, October 5, 1938; Henderson to Mitchell, November 1, 1938; C. C. House to Mitchell, November 30, 1938; House to Butler, December 5, 1938; Mitchell to Evelyn Smith, December 13, December 15, 1938; STFU, "Report of Delegation to San Francisco . . . ," n.d. [December, 1938]; Henderson, report to the second annual convention of UCAPAWA, December 12–16, 1938, pp. 5, 10–11, all in STFU Papers.

43. Gardner Jackson to H. L. Mitchell, February 21, 1939; see also proceedings of the Fifth Annual Convention, pp. 9–10; J. R. Butler to all locals, n.d. [January, 1939]; STFU Executive Council, minutes of meetings, January 21, 1939, February 11, 1939; Don Henderson to Butler, February 13, 1939, all in STFU Papers.

was Owen H. Whitfield, a shrewd black man who, while draw-
ing a relatively handsome $100 monthly salary from the STFU,
had secretly been cooperating with UCAPAWA ever since San
Francisco had shown him which white men were in the saddle.[44]
Angered by the continual demotion of sharecroppers to seasonal
laborers—by planters heavily subsidized by a government that
no longer even attempted to minimize labor displacement—
Whitfield decided, as Mitchell had three years before, to force
the public to look at the situation. Not by setting up a tent
colony; better than that, let highway travelers see the real
Missouri. Let the shoulders of Highways 60 and 61 become
long, long showcases of human devastation.[45] The people appeared, and the authorities were horrified. Governor Lloyd
Stark ordered relief to be given. Senator Harry S. Truman promised to put ironclad anti-eviction provisions into Federal farm
subsidy laws. Law officers said the evictees were committing no
crime. Secretary of Agriculture Wallace promised to withhold
payments from tenant-evicting landlords, while his whole Department chorused *mea culpas* over the AAA's responsiblity for
the situation.[46]

44. H. L. Mitchell to Owen H. Whitfield, March 23, 1938; Whitfield to
J. R Butler, September 6, 1938; Whitfield to Mitchell, November 8, 1938;
"An Open Letter to Friends of the Southern Tenant Farmers' Union,"
October 1, 1939, p. 5, all in STFU Papers; Louis Cantor, *A Prologue to the
Protest Movement: The Missouri Sharecropper Roadside Demonstrations
of 1939* (Durham, N.C.: Duke University Press, 1969), pp. 30–37, 49–55.
45. On Whitfield's decision: Ben Morris Ridpath, "The Case of the
Missouri Sharecroppers," *Christian Century*, February 1, 1939, pp. 147–
48; Cantor, *Prologue to Protest*, pp. 55–58; *Socialist Call*, January 21,
1939; (New York) *Daily Worker*, January 11, 1939; Owen H. Whitfield
to H. L. Mitchell, December 1, 1938, STFU Papers. On the AAA's role in
demoting sharecroppers to seasonal labor: interviews with R. W. (Pete)
Hudgens, June 24, 1961, and Sam Bledsoe, July 10, 1962; Cantor, *Prologue to Protest*, pp. 41–45; J. D. LeCron to Clarence Hughes, January 6,
1939, Harry L. Brown to Representative J. E. Rankin, January 7, 1939,
and Henry A. Wallace to Senator Morris Sheppard, August 17, 1939, all
in "Tenancy (1939)" folder, RG 16, N Arch; Henry Irving Richards,
*Cotton and the AAA* (Washington: The Brookings Institution, 1936), p.
136; J. G. McNeely and Glen Barton, "Land Tenure in Arkansas: II.
Change in Labor Organization," Arkansas Agricultural Experiment Station Bulletin No. 397 (Fayetteville, 1940), pp. 7, 17, 25–26; E. J. Holcomb, "Wage Laborers vs. Sharecroppers," *Agricultural Situation*, XXIII
(October, 1939), 13–15; St. Louis *Post-Dispatch*, January 7–12, 1939;
Memphis *Press-Scimitar*, January 7–12, 1939.
46. *New York Times*, January 12, 1939; St. Louis *Post-Dispatch*, Janu-

Then the landlords struck back, claiming that the demonstrators were not really evicted tenants; rather, they were impressionable dupes trying to obtain Federal money at the behest of a "nigger preacher" on government pay—for was not Whitfield living on the Farm Security Administration cooperative at LaForge? Touché. Governor Stark now said that the FBI should investigate "certain un-American and communistic practices, which I am reliably informed can be traced directly to certain employees of the Farm Security Administration." Senator Truman announced that the demonstration was "at the instigation of agitators who claim to be representatives of the United States Government. . . . I don't feel as badly about this as I did."[47] And the law officers, alleging a "health hazard" and forgetting the Bill of Rights, forced all the evictees off the high, well-drained, spacious roadside into small, swampy, malarial areas that amounted to concentration camps. When newspapers like the St. Louis *Post-Dispatch* protested police methods, they were assured that such actions were necessary in "handling niggers."[48]

Politicians and the public rapidly forgot the unfortunate evictees. The outcome might have been different if Gardner Jackson, UCAPAWA, and the STFU had been more concerned with the fight against the planters than the fight against each other. As it was, the Highway Demonstration only showed Mitchell and Butler that another of their best leaders had been seduced by UCAPAWA. Whitfield had even ordered the two

ary 9, 1939; Memphis *Press-Scimitar*, January 11, 1939; Gov. Lloyd Stark, telegram to J. R. Butler, January 11, 1939, STFU Papers; Paul Appleby to Marvin McIntyre, January 14, 1939; Appleby, telegram to Butler, January 16, 1939; Henry A. Wallace to Franklin D. Roosevelt, January 21, 1939; Wallace to Attorney General Frank Murphy, January 24, 1939, with attached memo, "Missouri Share-croppers," all in "Tenancy (1939)" folder, RG 16, N Arch.

47. *Sikeston (Mo.) Herald*, January 12, 1939; *Memphis Commercial Appeal*, January 15, 1939; Caruthersville *Democrat* reprint and "The P. C. Editor Says," *Sikeston Standard*, January 17, 1939, clippings in STFU scrapbook, STFU Papers; St. Louis *Post-Dispatch*, January 18–20, 1939; Gov. Lloyd Stark to Henry A. Wallace, January 16, 1939, "Tenancy (1939)" folder, RG 16, N Arch; Oral History MS, pp. 111–13.

48. St. Louis *Post-Dispatch*, January 16–18, 1939; Memphis *Press-Scimitar*, January 17, 1939; Oral History MS, pp. 111–12; "Washington Notes," *The New Republic*, February 8, 1939.

men to stay out of his show entirely.[49] This, added to UCA-PAWA's new determination to collect all dues directly from each STFU local, confirmed the Memphis leaders' decision to regain full control over their union—whatever the price.

On February 11, 1939, the STFU's executive council declared officially that it "positively will not permit any dues payments to be sent directly to the International [UCAPAWA] Office," and Henderson, in reply, circularized all STFU locals with a claim that payment to Memphis *"did not work."* He failed to explain how penniless people could find any more money for Washington than for Memphis, but in the next few weeks he sidestepped the problem by hinting that Mitchell and Butler had been receiving money and misappropriating it. As soon as Pat Jackson lined up on his side, Henderson began trying to recruit as many top STFU organizers and local leaders as possible, suspended Mitchell and Butler from UCAPAWA, and called a special STFU convention for "reorganization."[50] The two STFU leaders desperately sought help from Jackson and John L. Lewis, who appointed John Brophy, one of his closest aides, to confer with STFU and UCAPAWA representatives in Washington on March 8. After the day-long negotiations proved fruitless, Brophy agreed to formulate possible terms of peace, but the best he could produce were slogans: "compliance with the UCAPAWA Constitution" in exchange for "maintenance of autonomy" would reinstate Butler and Mitchell. Backed by their executive council and a hasty membership referendum,

49. O. H. Whitfield, telegram to H. L. Mitchell, January 10, 1939; see also J. R. Butler, telegram to Mitchell, January 9, 1939, and Mitchell, telegram to Butler, January 11, 1939, all in STFU Papers. On Whitfield's alignment with UCAPAWA: Mitchell, "The Southern Tenant Farmers' Union in 1939," pp. 3–4; Gardner Jackson to Mitchell, February 1, 1939; Whitfield to Mitchell, February 28, 1939; STFU Executive Council, memorandum to John L. Lewis, n.d. [February, 1939?], all in STFU Papers; *The UCAPAWA News*, September, 1939; Cantor, *Prologue to Protest*, pp. 74, 109–122.

50. "Chronology of Events in STFU-UCAPAWA Dispute," March 11, 1939; H. L. Mitchell to the UCAPAWA International Executive Board, February 14, 1939; Don Henderson to all STFU locals, February 15, 1939; J. R. Butler and Mitchell to all STFU locals, February 18, 1939; Henderson to Mitchell, January 28, 1939; Gardner Jackson to Mitchell, February 21, 1939; Henderson to D. A. Griffin, February 23, 1939; Mitchell, "The Southern Tenant Farmers' Union in 1939," p. 5, all in STFU Papers.

the two men telephoned Brophy's office to leave the message that "we are willing to accept your proposals if it is clearly understood that maintenance of autonomy . . . means full organizational and administrative self-government with the payment of per capita dues . . . on the basis of which we entered the UCAPAWA."

At ten minutes before two in the afternoon of March 11, 1939, Brophy telephoned STFU headquarters with the CIO's official response, one which proved to be his epitaph for the farm labor organizing efforts of the 1930's: Take it or leave it. "Details to be ironed out afterwards. You will either accept it or you don't."[51] Present as Brophy's call came through was a quorum of the executive council, which promptly voted to secede from UCAPAWA. A week later, a special STFU convention ratified the decision; two weeks after that, when Henderson called a convention of his own, Mitchell invaded it and succeeded in leading most of the delegates out of the hall with him. But there was no doubt that catastrophe had occurred: Williams, McKinney, Leon Turner, and a great many of the STFU's Negro members stayed with the CIO, "the Joe Louis of the labor movement." So did Owen Whitfield and his Missouri locals. So did Oklahoma. Most disastrous of all, Gardner Jackson was bitterly, emphatically, and finally through with Mitchell and Butler, even sending Henderson a message to that effect to be read at his convention.[52]

51. Brophy's refusal to accept Mitchell's interpretation of his slogans left them slanted in Henderson's direction, for the UCAPAWA Constitution provided for direct payment of dues, and the "autonomy" item was defined by Henderson as direction by each *local* of its internal affairs, *e.g.*, which clergyman gives the invocation at meetings, etc. See "Chronology of Events in STFU-UCAPAWA Dispute," March 11, 1939; Mitchell, "The Southern Tenant Farmers' Union in 1939," pp. 5–7; Mitchell to John L. Lewis, March 6, 1939; John Brophy to Mitchell and J. R. Butler, March 9, 1939; Mitchell to Brophy, March 11, 1939, all in STFU Papers. Also in the STFU Papers is Brophy's March 11 telegram to Butler, directing him in impressive Western Union capitals to "ACCEPT WITHOUT DELAY OR QUALIFICATION MY RECOMMENDATIONS AND TRUST TO THE GOOD FAITH OF THE CIO TO PROTECT THE INTERESTS OF THE SOUTHERN TENANT FARMERS."

52. Gardner Jackson to H. L. Mitchell, March 13, 1939; Jackson to Don Henderson, March 31, 1939; Mitchell to Jackson, February 27, 1940, all in STFU Papers. Over twenty years later, having been blinded in one eye by Communist labor goons, Jackson was surprised to rediscover how com-

"THE PROBLEMS OF THE SHARECROPPERS AND TENANTS CAN ONLY
BE SOLVED WITH THE SUPPORT AND AID OF THE ENTIRE LABOR
MOVEMENT THROUGHOUT THE COUNTRY"

IN UNITY THERE IS STRENGTH.
STICK WITH THE C.I.O.!        STICK WITH UCAPAWA!

SEND YOUR DELEGATES TO YOUR CONVENTION, SUNDAY, APRIL 2ND,
200 SOUTH FOURTH STREET, MEMPHIS, TENN.
WRITE TO OUR OFFICE: Leif Dahl
P. O. Box 931, Memphis, Tenn.

*UCAPAWA weapons against the STFU: "CIO," "John L. Lewis"*

Jackson's withdrawal of moral and financial support was the signal for others to act likewise, despite—or perhaps because of —Mitchell's sudden public attacks on UCAPAWA's "Communist rule-or-ruin tactics." The Washington Committee to Aid Agricultural Workers dropped its support. Leading contributors to National Sharecroppers' Week fell away. Increasing the damage done to both unions by the split, many declared a pox on both houses. "I do not care to endorse either organization after the split," declared Roger Baldwin of the American Civil Liberties Union.[53] The labor press was not even neutral; *The CIO News* might have given only UCAPAWA's side even if Editor Len De Caux had not been ideologically sympathetic to Henderson. Following his lead, the labor news service, Federated Press, fed UCAPAWA-slanted accounts to labor journals across the country.[54]

---

pletely he had supported Henderson. Recalling that he did so only over the strong objections of Eleanor Roosevelt, he maintained that he and John Brophy only wanted to keep the STFU in the CIO while they moved to ease Henderson out of power. (Interviews with Jackson, August 14, 1961, June 30, 1962.) There is no contemporary evidence, however, that either Jackson or Brophy ever told anyone he wanted to do this. Mitchell was convinced that Jackson had been persuaded to disown the STFU by his Communist friend Lee Pressman. Mitchell to the author, August 21, 1961. On the final STFU-UCAPAWA break, see *Arkansas Gazette*, March 19, 1939, April 3, 1939; Memphis *Press-Scimitar*, April 3, 1939; Oral History MS, pp. 115–18; "Arkansas-Mississippi-Tennessee State Convention . . . called by Mr. Donald Henderson," April 2, 1939; and Claude Williams to Henderson, March 6, 1939, both in Claude Williams Papers; *The UCAPAWA News*, July, 1939; *The STFU News*, March 21, 1939; J. R. Butler and H. L. Mitchell, bill for injunction, n.d. [March, 1939], STFU Papers; Mitchell to the author, August 7, 1961.

53. Jackson later said of his attempt to minimize STFU support, "That's really shocking. I never thought I had gone that far." (Interview with Jackson, August 14, 1961.) See Roger Baldwin to J. R. Butler, November 22, 1939; James Myers to Butler, December 26, 1939; Lucy Randolph Mason to H. L. Mitchell, April 4, 1939; Lincoln Fairley to Mitchell, April 8, 1939. A few STFU supporters, like Walter White of the NAACP and Mrs. Ethel Clyde, the steamship heiress, were unshaken by the schism and reaffirmed their alliance. Mrs. Clyde to Don Henderson, March 31, 1939, and to Mitchell, May 9, 1939; Walter White to Butler, November 20, 1939. All documents in STFU Papers.

54. Kampelman, *Communist Party vs. C.I.O.*, pp. 19, 60n.; Len De Caux to Evelyn Smith, April 11, 1939; CIO Publicity Department, "Memorandum on Stolberg Article in September 2 [1939] issue Saturday Evening Post," n.d.; Frank McCallister to Smith, October 12, 1939; De Caux

Few STFU members may have known of Roger Baldwin, but his attitude was theirs: have nothing to do with either side. "The situation has been so confusing to the people that they have just shut down and quit for the time being, many of them disgusted with all unions," Mitchell found. Only forty locals were left in the entire STFU. But for UCAPAWA matters were worse. Sweeden, of course, refused to cooperate and tried to return to the STFU. Whitfield found that his office in St. Louis only took him away from his constituency in the Missouri bootheel. By the end of the year, though UCAPAWA made a brave attempt at a "Cotton States" convention, few leaders or officers were mentioned and no membership claims were made. Henderson and his colleagues were finally discovering that farm workers are penniless—and so, in the American tradition, UCAPAWA increasingly abandoned them for cannery workers.[55] Cannery workers can pay dues.

A more fundamental observation—and a fairer one, perhaps: In the year that Hitler invaded Poland, the New Deal Thirties were giving way to the Wartime Forties without ever having produced legal protection for the farm worker's right to bargain collectively. Thanks to congressional committee systems, seniority systems, and over-representation of rural areas, the opportunity to protect farm labor—if there ever was one—had been missed. It would not come again for generations.

And the Southern Tenant Farmers' Union? It limped onward, limited largely to Woodruff and St. Francis counties in Arkansas and the area around the STFU's Hillhouse Cooperative in northern Mississippi. There were a few locals elsewhere, but no organizers could be found in Oklahoma or the Missouri bootheel whose abilities were remotely comparable to those of the

to McCallister, October 30, 1939, all in STFU Papers; Federated Press dispatches, March 13, March 15, 1939, and Federated Press Washington Weekly Letter, March 21, 1939, all in Claude Williams Papers.

55. *The* (Commonwealth) *Commoner*, January, 1940, CCP, Reel 3; The *UCAPAWA News*, October, 1939; February, 1940; May–June, 1940; H. L. Mitchell to Norman Thomas, May 5, 1939; Odis Sweeden, postcard to Mitchell, June 8, 1939; Mitchell to Sweeden, June 16, 1939; Don Henderson to Sweeden, July 25, 1939; Waddie Hudson to J. R. Butler, September 8, 1939; Blaine Treadway to Hudson, September 26, 1939; all correspondence in STFU Papers; Mitchell, "The Southern Tenant Farmers' Union in 1939," pp. 19–20; Oral History MS, pp. 114, 118.

cantankerous Sweeden, whom the STFU dropped, or the absent
Whitfield, who had dropped the STFU. And presiding over it
all was amiable J. R. Butler, whose influence was too weak to
pull in money and whose union was too weak for even its annual
cotton-picking-strike threat.[56]

Stung by such impotence, the STFU's old adviser William
Amberson urged the union's leaders to collect more dues:
"when, after five and a half years you have not succeeded in
getting such support the conviction must grow in the minds of
your friends that you have not yet discovered how to organize
properly," said he. So, throughout 1940, the STFU tried to
"organize properly," and one month they received from their
seventy-two locals almost eighty dollars in dues. Orderly collection of dues, strikes for higher wages, and other trade union
desiderata still obsessed STFU leaders so greatly that, of all the
flaws in a rather inaccurate *Harper's* article about the STFU's
decline, the one that bothered them most was the suggestion
that the STFU had been more a pressure group than a union.[57]

The best way to combine the reality of existence as a meliora-
tive and lobbying body with the ideal of existence as a "real
union" was, of course, to affiliate with a larger union which
could subsidize sharecropper organizing. STFU leaders began
extending feelers to the AFL within a month after their break
with UCAPAWA and the CIO. Finally, at the urging of David
Dubinsky, whose International Ladies' Garment Workers Union
had also left the CIO, the Federation's executive council took up
the STFU request just long enough to decide that an agricultural workers' "international union could not function on a self-
sustaining basis. If chartered it could only function in the event

56. *The STFU News*, November, 1939; Permanent Charters notebook
(charters issued after April 24, 1939); STFU Executive Council, minutes
of meetings, April 12, June 28, 1939; A. R. Roberts to J. R. Butler, July
28, 1939; Butler to Roberts, August 5, 1939; Butler to all locals, August
14, 1939; Butler to all members of the executive council, August 26, 1939;
Blaine Treadway to all locals, September 13, 1939; Butler to Lawrence
Doe, September 27, 1939, all in STFU Papers.
57. William R. Amberson to the officers and executive committee of the
STFU, December 29, 1939; STFU Executive Committee, minutes of
meeting, June 22–23, 1940; H. L. Mitchell to William Green, n.d. [June,
1940]; STFU press release, February 10, 1941; Mitchell to the editor of
*Harper's*, October 30, 1941, all in STFU Papers.

the American Federation of Labor financed it and supported it." Continued AFL President William Green: "The Executive Council was of the opinion that the interests of those you represent would be advanced and promoted more through legislative action than through the use of economic means."[58] The disappointed tenant leaders then approached James Patton, head of the National Farmers' Union, only to find that the AFL's quick rejection was kinder than the NFU's tantalizing procrastination, which consumed a year before the same decision was reached.[59]

As the STFU faded away, most of its leaders found business elsewhere. Mitchell, employed by the National Youth Administration since 1938, returned to Memphis only sporadically, while Howard Kester decided that modernizing Southern Protestantism was now more auspicious than organizing Southern sharecroppers. Then, in 1941, when a Holiness preacher named W. M. Tanner and a Hod Carriers Union official named Roy Raley were able to organize hundreds of white tenants around Sheffield, Alabama, the STFU shifted its theater of operations from depleted Arkansas to the new locale, where Tanner and Raley could ease Butler out of office and begin segregating STFU meetings racially.[60] Mitchell had to accept this for a short time, knowing that even a Raley-Tanner STFU could serve as a base for farm worker participation in Federal wartime programs. There was little that he could do to smooth the country-city transition as defense employment attracted his former followers, but through the Farm Security Administration and the

58. Oral History MS, pp. 129–30; J. R. Butler to Matthew Woll, April 15, 1939; W. R. Purcells to Butler, August 21, 1940; Butler to all locals, September 12, 1940; Butler to members of the executive committee, August 17, 1940, October 9, 1940; William Green to H. L. Mitchell, October 23, 1940, all in STFU Papers.

59. H. L. Mitchell, memo on the NFU, n.d. [August, 1941]; James Patton to Mitchell, September 9, 1941; Mitchell to Patton, October 30, 1941; Patton to Mitchell, October 5, 1942, all in STFU Papers.

60. H. L. Mitchell to J. R. Butler, August 14, 1939; Butler to Mitchell, August 16, 1939; Howard Kester to Mitchell, November 7, 1941, all in STFU Papers; Mitchell to Jonathan Daniels, January 12, 1942, Daniels Papers, Southern Historical Collection, University of North Carolina at Chapel Hill; Mitchell, "The Southern Tenant Farmers' Union in 1941," p. 2; Oral History MS, pp. 122–28, 131–33; interview with Howard Kester, July 18, 1961; Mitchell to the author, August 7, 1961.

Amalgamated Meat Cutters and Butcher Workmen in New Jersey, he arranged labor exchange programs which provided underemployed STFU members with higher paying farm jobs elsewhere—at least, until 1943, when Southern Congressmen succeeded in getting a law passed against it. Those the planters did not need could leave, however, and thousands of displaced sharecroppers, like the Joads of John Steinbeck's *Grapes of Wrath*, became migrant farm laborers, a permanent feature of the rural scene. In testimony before congressional committees, Mitchell was among those who tried fruitlessly to secure laws protecting them. His attempts to regularize and improve the employment of former sharecroppers won him the respect of progressive AFL leaders like Leon Schachter of the Meat Cutters, and in 1946, William Green finally gave Mitchell a charter for formation of a new National Farm Labor Union.[61]

Once more, as part of the AFL's ambitious postwar drive to "organize the unorganized" in competition with the CIO, Mitchell found himself contending against Don Henderson, whose UCAPAWA had become the Food, Tobacco, Agricultural, and Allied Workers—FTA—symbolizing its decreased efforts among field workers in favor of processors. But the final chapter of the Mitchell vs. Henderson story was anti-climactic: the two unions never competed directly and, facing the postwar flooding of the farm labor market, were seldom successful among field workers. The advent of the Cold War made the outcome of the "communism" issue a foregone conclusion: the Taft-Hartley Act and Philip Murray closed in relentlessly, and on March 1, 1950, FTA was kicked out of the CIO. There was no place for Henderson in the labor movement; he faded into obscurity.[62]

Nevertheless, Henderson's work among farm laborers had

61. Mitchell had again become titular as well as actual head of the STFU when Raley resigned in his favor during the war, enabling him to use the remnants of the old union as his administrative nucleus for the new NFLU. Mitchell, "The Southern Tenant Farmers' Union in 1939," pp. 17–18; J. R. Butler and Howard Kester, "The Southern Tenant Farmers' Union in 1940," p. 8; Mitchell to Jonathan Daniels, December 26, 1941, and January 12, 1942, both in Daniels Papers; interview with Kester, July 18, 1961; Oral History MS, pp. 135–49.

62. William Amberson to J. R. Butler, March 19, 1940; H. L. Mitchell to Joe Jacobs, December 21, 1944, both in STFU Papers; Kampelman, *Communist Party vs. C.I.O.*, pp. 173–75.

lasted longer than that of his old comrades at Commonwealth College. Communist party members at Commonwealth became so blatant about their affiliations in 1939 and 1940 that Claude Williams, fearing legal reprisals and resenting Communist as well as Socialist "sectarianism," resigned as director in order to move to Detroit and work among immigrants from the South, black and white, with his People's Institute of Applied Religion. The move saved neither Commonwealth nor Williams. Labeled "subversive" by the Truman administration, Williams was driven into an early retirement on an Alabama farm, while Commonwealth was closed forever in the fall of 1940 by a fundamentalist preacher and a justice of the peace, its assets attached for allowing one of its staff to speak in a park without a permit. The small-town prosecuting attorney who closed the college, J. F. Quillin, seemed to regard Commonwealth students' racial beliefs and coeducational swimming habits as being the major evidence of their un-Americanism, but Quillin was nevertheless eagerly patronized by President Truman's subordinates as they weeded "Communist sympathizers" out of government service.[63]

Mitchell was not "subversive" enough to be governmentally excommunicated, but, lacking Federal legal protection, the members of his NFLU were no more able to benefit from collective bargaining than if Williams or Henderson had led them. From 1947 to 1949, more than a thousand workers at the huge DiGiorgio Farms near Bakersfield, California went on strike, but the corporation brought in strikebreakers, sued the union, and eventually won. In 1951 the union organized several thousand strawberry farmers in Louisiana, but, two years later, President Eisenhower's Justice Department discovered collusion between the NFLU and the strawberry processors and broke up the local with an anti-trust suit. After other bitter

63. Interview with Claude Williams, August 18, 1962; Williams to the author, n.d. [February, 1963]; David Beardsley to the members of the Commonwealth College Association, n.d. [1940], Claude Williams Papers; Willard Uphaus to J. R. Butler, July 1, 1941, STFU Papers; on Commonwealth, see clippings from *Kansas City Star*, December 1, 1940, and other newspapers, 1940, with A. L. Oram to J. F. Quillin, August 6, 1943; *Washington Post* clipping, April 28, 1949, and Joseph McElvain to Quillin, October 28, 1949, all in CCP, Reel 2.

failures, often beaten by blanket injunctions that employers of the 1920's would have envied, Mitchell's union disbanded in August, 1960.[64]

Throughout the 1960's, Mitchell continued to work as the agricultural specialist of the AFL-CIO's Amalgamated Meat Cutters, organizing skilled fishermen and tractor drivers on sugar plantations, attempting through litigation to stretch the bounds of the National Labor Relations Act. But there was no work for Mitchell on Southern plantations, which remained individual empires, not STFU-style cooperatives. And, across their acres, diversified crops were raised by the few rather than the many. The people had gone by the millions to the ghettos of the cities.

Today you can hardly find anyone in the Arkansas Delta who once belonged to the Southern Tenant Farmers' Union. But, on a warm and silent night, if you stop your car on the shoulder of Highway 63 near Marked Tree, if you can hear with your whole being, listen:

From that clump of oaks and sycamores where a ramshackle old Negro church used to stand, could you hear the rich rhythmic voices distantly singing—

The Union is a-marching,
We shall not be moved . . .

64. This brief summary is based on continued correspondence and friendship with H. L. Mitchell, 1961–70; Oral History MS, pp. 149–60; National Agricultural Workers Union [successor to the STFU and NFLU], *Workers in Our Fields*, 25th anniversary brochure (Washington: Privately printed, 1959), copy in STFU Papers.

# Bibliography

*Books*

AGEE, JAMES and WALKER EVANS. *Let Us Now Praise Famous Men.* Boston: Houghton Mifflin, 1941.

ALEXANDER, DONALD CRICHTON. *The Arkansas Plantation, 1920–1942.* New Haven: Yale University Press, 1943.

AUERBACH, JEROLD. *Labor and Liberty: The LaFollette Committee and the New Deal.* Indianapolis: Bobbs-Merrill, 1966.

BALDWIN, SIDNEY. *Poverty and Politics: The Rise and Decline of the Farm Security Administration.* Chapel Hill: The University of North Carolina Press, 1968.

BELFRAGE, CEDRIC. *South of God* [Claude Williams]. New York: Modern Age Books, 1941.

BENTON, THOMAS HART. *An Artist in America.* New York: Halcyon House, 1939.

BURNS, JAMES MACGREGOR. *Roosevelt: The Lion and the Fox.* New York: Harcourt, Brace, and Company, 1956.

CALDWELL, ERSKINE. *God's Little Acre.* New York: Grosset and Dunlap, 1933.

———. *Tenant Farmer.* New York: Phalanx Press, 1935.

———. *Tobacco Road.* New York: Grosset and Dunlap, 1936.

CALDWELL, ERSKINE and MARGARET BOURKE-WHITE. *You Have Seen Their Faces.* New York: The Viking Press, 1937.

CANTOR, LOUIS. *A Prologue to the Protest Movement: The Mis-*

*souri Sharecropper Roadside Demonstration of 1939.* Durham, N.C.: Duke University Press, 1969.

CASH, WILBUR JOSEPH. *The Mind of the South.* New York: A. A. Knopf, 1941.

CONRAD, DAVID EUGENE. *The Forgotten Farmers: The Story of Sharecroppers in the New Deal.* Urbana: University of Illinois Press, 1965.

COOK, JAMES GRAHAM. *The Segregationists.* New York: Appleton-Century-Crofts, 1962.

DABNEY, VIRGINIUS. *Below the Potomac.* New York: D. Appleton-Century Company, 1942.

DANIELS, JONATHAN. *A Southerner Discovers the South.* New York, Macmillan, 1938.

DYKEMAN, WILMA and JAMES STOKELY. *Seeds of Southern Change: The Life of Will Alexander.* Chicago: University of Chicago Press, 1962.

FULMER, JOHN LEONARD. *Agricultural Progress in the Cotton Belt Since 1920.* Chapel Hill: The University of North Carolina Press, 1950.

GREENWAY, JOHN. *American Folksongs of Protest.* Philadelphia: University of Pennsylvania Press, 1953.

HOLLEY, WILLIAM C., ELLEN WINSTON, and T. J. WOOFTER. *The Plantation South, 1934–1937.* Works Progress Administration Research Monograph 22. Washington: Government Printing Office, 1940.

ICKES, HAROLD L. *The Secret Diary of Harold L. Ickes: The First Thousand Days, 1933–1936.* New York: Simon and Schuster, 1953.

JAMIESON, STUART (ed.). *Labor Unionism in American Agriculture.* Bureau of Labor Statistics Bulletin 836. Washington: Government Printing Office, 1945.

JOHNSON, CHARLES SPURGEON, EDWIN R. EMBREE, and W. W. ALEXANDER. *The Collapse of Cotton Tenancy.* Chapel Hill: The University of North Carolina Press, 1935.

KAMPELMAN, MAX M. *The Communist Party vs. the C.I.O.* New York: Frederick A. Praeger, 1957.

KEMPTON, MURRAY. *Part of Our Time.* New York: Simon and Schuster, 1955.

KESTER, HOWARD. *Revolt Among the Sharecroppers.* New York: Covici-Friede, 1936.

KIRKENDALL, RICHARD S. *Social Scientists and Farm Politics in the*

*Age of Roosevelt.* Columbia: University of Missouri Press, 1966.

KROLL, HARRY HARRISON. *I Was a Share-Cropper.* Indianapolis: Bobbs-Merrill, 1937.

KRUEGER, THOMAS A. *And Promises to Keep: The Southern Conference for Human Welfare, 1938–1948.* Nashville: Vanderbilt University Press, 1967.

LANDIS, BENSON Y. *and* G. E. HAYNES. *Cotton-growing Communities: Case Studies of 10 Rural Communities and 10 Plantations in Arkansas.* Study No. 2. New York: Federal Council Churches of Christ in America, 1935.

LORD, RUSSELL. *The Wallaces of Iowa.* Boston: Houghton Mifflin, 1947.

MCCONNELL, GRANT. The Decline of Agrarian Democracy. Berkeley: University of California Press, 1953.

MITCHELL, BROADUS. *Depression Decade: From New Era through New Deal, 1929–1941.* Vol. IX. The Economic History of the United States. New York: Holt, Rinehart, and Winston, 1947.

NOURSE, EDWIN GRISWOLD, JOSEPH S. DAVIS, *and* JOHN D. BLACK. *Three Years of the Agricultural Adjustment Administration.* Washington: The Brookings Institution, 1937.

PERKINS, FRANCES. *The Roosevelt I Knew.* New York: The Viking Press, 1946.

RAPER, ARTHUR FRANKLIN. *Preface to Peasantry.* Chapel Hill: The University of North Carolina Press, 1936.

RAPER, ARTHUR FRANKLIN *and* IRA DEA. REID. *Sharecroppers All.* Chapel Hill: The University of North Carolina Press, 1941.

RAUCH, BASIL. *The History of the New Deal, 1933–1938.* New York: Creative Age Press, 1944.

RECORD, WILSON. *The Negro and the Communist Party.* Chapel Hill: The University of North Carolina Press, 1951.

RICHARDS, HENRY IRVING. *Cotton and the AAA.* Washington: The Brookings Institution, 1936.

ROOSEVELT, FRANKLIN DELANO. *F.D.R.: His Personal Letters, 1928–1945,* ed. Elliott Roosevelt. 2 vols. New York: Duell, Sloan, and Pearce, 1950.

SCHLESINGER, ARTHUR MEIER, JR. *The Coming of the New Deal.* Vol. II of *The Age of Roosevelt.* Boston: Houghton Mifflin, 1959.

SIMON, MRS. CHARLIE MAY. *The Share-Cropper.* New York: E. P. Dutton and Company, 1937.

STERNSHER, BERNARD. *Rexford Tugwell and the New Deal.* New Brunswick, N. J.: Rutgers University Press, 1964.

STREET, JAMES HARRY. *The New Revolution in the Cotton Economy.* Chapel Hill: The University of North Carolina Press, 1957.

THOMAS, NORMAN. *The Plight of the Share-Cropper.* New York: League for Industrial Democracy, 1934.

TUGWELL, REXFORD GUY. *The Democratic Roosevelt.* Garden City, New York: Doubleday, 1957.

"Unofficial Observer" [Literary Guild of New York]. *The New Dealers.* New York: Simon and Schuster, 1934.

VANCE, RUPERT BAYLESS. *Human Factors in Cotton Culture.* Chapel Hill: The University of North Carolina Press, 1929.

————. *Human Geography of the South.* Chapel Hill: The University of North Carolina Press, 1932.

WOOFTER, THOMAS JACKSON *et al. Landlord and Tenant on the Cotton Plantation.* Washington: Works Progress Administration Social Research Division, 1936.

## Interviews and Correspondence

BLEDSOE, SAM. Former member, Agricultural Adjustment Administration Information staff. Washington, D. C.

BUTLER, J[OHN] R[USSELL]. Former president, Southern Tenant Farmers' Union. Bald Knob, Arkansas.

DAHL, LEIF. Former organizer, United Cannery, Agricultural, Packing, and Allied Workers of America. Philadelphia.

*DAVIS, CHESTER. Former Agricultural Adjustment Administrator. San Marino, California.

*EAST, CLAY. Co-founder, Southern Tenant Farmers' Union. Oracle, Arizona.

*HAYS, LEE. Folk song authority, former associate of Southern Tenant Farmers' Union leaders. New York City.

HUDGENS, R[OBERT] W[ATTS] (PETE). Former Southern Administrator, Farm Security Administration. Chapel Hill, North Carolina.

†JACKSON, GARDNER. Former Washington representative, Southern Tenant Farmers' Union and other agricultural labor organizations. Washington, D. C.

* Denotes correspondence only.     † Deceased.

KESTER, HOWARD. Former official, Southern Tenant Farmers' Union. Black Mountain, North Carolina.

*MITCHELL, EDWIN. Labor organizer, brother of H. L. Mitchell, Southern Tenant Farmers' Union leader. New York City.

MITCHELL, H[ARRY] L[ELAND]. Co-founder and former executive secretary, Southern Tenant Farmers' Union. Metairie, Louisiana.

*NIEBUHR, REINHOLD. Theologian formerly associated with Howard Kester and interested in the Southern Tenant Farmers' Union. New York City.

PERKINS, MILO. Associate of Gardner Jackson; former official of the Department of Agriculture. Washington, D. C.

*SEEGER, PETE. Folk singer, authority on songs of the Southern Tenant Farmers' Union. Beacon, New York.

†THOMAS, NORMAN. Socialist party leader, "godfather" of the Southern Tenant Farmers' Union. New York City.

WILLIAMS, CLAUDE. Former official, Southern Tenant Farmers' Union, Helena, Alabama.

*Manuscript Collections*

Commonwealth College. Papers, including student newspaper file, press releases, announcements, correspondence, and other papers collected by E. W. St. John, publisher of the Mena (Arkansas) *Star.* Microfilm No. 356, 3 Reels. University of Arkansas Library, Fayetteville.

COX, A. E[UGENE]. Papers relating to the Southern Tenant Farmers' Union and Delta Co-operative Farms. In Mr. Cox's possession, Memphis, Tennessee.

EAST, CLAY. Personal letters. In Mr. East's possession, Oracle, Arizona.

ROOSEVELT, FRANKLIN DELANO. Papers relating to tenancy. Official Files 407–B and 1650, Franklin Delano Roosevelt Library, Hyde Park, New York.

Socialist Party. Archives, including correspondence, press releases, etc. Manuscripts Division, Duke University Library, Durham, North Carolina.

Southern Tenant Farmers' Union. Papers, including scrapbook, account books, correspondence, press releases, affidavits, etc.

* Denotes correspondence only.     † Deceased.

Southern Historical Collection, University of North Carolina, Chapel Hill.
U. S. Department of Agriculture. Correspondence, including press releases, clippings, interoffice memoranda, copies of speeches, etc. Record Group 16, Agricultural Records Section, Social and Economic Branch, National Archives, Washington, D. C.
U. S. Department of Agriculture, Agricultural Adjustment Administration. General correspondence. Record Group 145, Agricultural Records Section, Social and Economic Branch, National Archives, Washington, D. C.
WILLIAMS, CLAUDE. Personal papers. In the Rev. Williams's possession, Helena, Alabama.

*Newspapers*

*Arkansas Democrat* (Little Rock), 1934–1937.
*Arkansas Gazette* (Little Rock), 1934–1937.
*Chicago Daily Tribune*, May–June, 1936, February, 1937.
*Chicago Daily News*, April, 1934.
*The Daily Worker* (New York), January–June, 1936, May, 1937.
*Jonesboro* (Arkansas) *Daily Tribune*, 1934–1937.
Hot Springs (Arkansas) *New Era*, August–September, 1936.
*Lepanto* (Arkansas) *Press*, 1934.
*Marked Tree* (Arkansas) *Tribune*, 1934–1939.
*Memphis Commercial Appeal*, 1934–1939.
Memphis *Press-Scimitar*, 1934–1939.
*Modern Times* (Harrisburg, Arkansas), 1934–1937.
*New York Post*, 1936.
*New York Times*, 1934–1937.
New York *World-Telegram*, January–May, 1935, September, 1936.
The *Osceola* (Arkansas) *Times*, 1934–1937.
St. Louis *Post-Dispatch*, 1936–1939.
*The* (Southern Tenant Farmers' Union) *Sharecroppers Voice*, 1935–1939.
*Southwest American* (Fort Smith, Arkansas), August–October, 1936.
(United Cannery, Agricultural, Packing, and Allied Workers of America) *UCAPAWA News*, 1939–1940.
*Washington Post*, 1936.

*Periodicals*

ALEXANDER, WILL W. "Rehabilitation for the Dispossessed Farmer," *Extension Service Review*, X (April, 1939), 50.
————. "Rural Resettlement," *Southern Review*, I (1936), 528.
AMBERSON, WILLIAM R. "Forty Acres and a Mule," *Nation*, March 6, 1937, p. 264.
————. "The New Deal for Share-Croppers," *Nation*, February 13, 1935, p. 174.
ASCH, NATHAN. "Marked Tree, Arkansas," *New Republic*, June 10, 1936, p. 119.
ASHBURN, K. E. "Economic and Social Aspects of Farm Tenancy in Texas," *Southwestern Social Science Quarterly*, XV (March, 1935), 298.
AUERBACH, JEROLD. "The LaFollette Committee: Labor and Civil Liberties in the New Deal," *Journal of American History*, LI (December, 1964), 435.
————. "Southern Tenant Farmers: Socialist Critics of the New Deal," *Labor History*, VII (Winter, 1966), 3.
BABCOCK, H. E. "Cooperatives the Pace-Setters in Agriculture," *Journal of Farm Economics*, XVII (February, 1935), 153.
BAKER, J. A. "Farm Tenancy: Report of the Arkansas State Policy Committee," *Journal of Land and Public Utility Economics*, XIII (February, 1937), 90.
BAKER, J. A. *and* J. G. MCNEELY. "Land Tenure in Arkansas: 1: The Farm Tenancy Situation," Arkansas Agricultural Experiment Station Bulletin No. 384 (Fayetteville, 1940).
BALDWIN, C. B. "Helping Tenants Become Owners," *Agricultural Situation*. XXII (September, 1938), 11.
BALLINGER, R. A. "Important Provisions in the 1934–1935 Cotton Acreage Reduction Contract," Oklahoma *Current Farm Economics* Series, Vol. 6, No. 6 (December, 1933), inside front cover.
BARRY, DONALD L. "Share-Croppers, the Real Issue," *Commonweal*, October 2, 1936, p. 533.
BEECHER, JOHN. "The Sharecroppers' Union in Alabama," *Social Forces*, XIII (October, 1934), 124.
BLACK, ARTHUR G. "Discussion [on Farm Tenancy]," *Journal of Farm Economics*, XX (February, 1938), 158.
BLACKMAN, M. C. "Arkansas's Largest Landlord [Resettlement

Administration]," *Arkansas Gazette Magazine,* October 13, 1935, p. 5.

―――. "Tenancy in Arkansas," *Arkansas Gazette Magazine,* April 4, 11, 18, 25, 1937.

BLAGDEN, WILLIE SUE. "Arkansas Flogging," *New Republic,* July 1, 1936, p. 236.

BLALOCK, HENRY WILLIAM. "Plantation Operations of Landlords and Tenants in Arkansas," Arkansas Agricultural Experiment Station Bulletin No. 339 (Fayetteville, 1937).

BRANDT, KARL. "Farm Tenancy in the United States," *Social Research,* IV (May, 1937), 142.

―――. "Potentialities of Agricultural Reform in the South," *Social Research,* III (November, 1936), 434.

BRANNEN, C. O. "Problems of Croppers on Cotton Farms," *Journal of Farm Economics,* XX (February, 1938), 153.

―――. "Tax Delinquent Rural Lands in Arkansas," Arkansas Agricultural Experiment Station Bulletin No. 311 (Fayetteville, November, 1934).

CARLSON, OLIVER. "The Revolution in Cotton," *American Mercury,* XXXIV (February, 1935), 129.

CARPENTER, C. T. "King Cotton's Slaves," *Scribner's,* XCVIII (October, 1935), 193; XCVIII (December, 1935), 384; XCIX (January, March, 1936), 64, 191.

CARR, WILLIAM G. "The Return of the Carpetbagger!" *Nation's Agriculture,* XVII (April, 1942), 7.

CATE, HORACE. "Rehabilitation in Arkansas," *Nation's Agriculture,* XVII (June, 1942), 7.

COBB, WILLIAM H., *and* DONALD H. GRUBBS. "Arkansas' Commonwealth College and the Southern Tenant Farmers' Union," *Arkansas Historical Quarterly,* XXV (Winter, 1966), 293.

COLLINS, J. M. "End of His Row," *New York Times Magazine,* June 4, 1939, p. 11.

COOPER, M. R. *et al.* "The Causes: Defects in Farming Systems and Farm Tenancy," *U. S. Yearbook of Agriculture, 1938* (Washington: Government Printing Office, 1938), pp. 137–157.

"Cotton and the South," *Nation,* May 8, 1935, 525.

DAHL, LEIF. "Agricultural Labor and Social Legislation," *American Federationist,* XLIV (February, 1937), 137.

DAVIS, JOHN P. "A Survey of the Problems of the Negro Under the New Deal," *Journal of Negro Education,* V (January, 1936), 6.

Bibliography / 201

DEVYVER, FRANK TREAVER. "The Present Status of Labor Unions in the South," *Southern Economics Journal*, V (April, 1939), 485.

DICKERSON, JOHN H. "Proposed Adjustments in the Farm Tenancy System in Missouri," Missouri Agricultural Experiment Station Research Bulletin 270 (Columbia, December, 1937).

DUNCAN, O. D. "Some Sociological Implications of the Agricultural Adjustment Program," *Journal of Farm Economics*, XVI (July, 1934), 504.

DUNCAN, ROBERT B. "Notes from Arkansas," *New Masses*, December 21, 1937, p. 17.

EMBREE, EDWIN R. "Southern Farm Tenancy, The Way Out of its Evils," *Survey Graphic*, XXV (March, 1936), 149.

"Farm Tenancy," *Congressional Digest*, XVI (August–September, 1937), 194.

"Farm Tenancy Projects of the Resettlement Administration," *Congressional Digest*, XVI (February, 1937), 44.

"Farm Wage and Labor Situation," *Monthly Labor Review*, XLIII (September, 1936), 694; XLV (October, 1937), 955.

FORSTER, G. W. "Progress and Problems . . . ," *Journal of Farm Economics*, XVIII (February, 1936), 91.

FREY, FRED C. *and* T. LYNN SMITH. "The Influence of the AAA Cotton Program upon the Tenant, Cropper and Laborer," *Rural Sociology*, I (December, 1936), 483.

"From Share-Croppers Into Farmers [LaForge]," *Wallace's Farmer*, January 28, 1939, p. 41.

GARD, WAYNE. "The American Peasant," *Current History*, XLVI (April, 1937), 47.

GARD, WAYNE *and* NORMAN THOMAS. "Decline in the Cotton Kingdom," *Current History*, XLII (April, 1935), 31.

GEE, WILSON. "Acreage Reduction and the Displacement of Farm Labor," *Journal of Farm Economics*, XVII (August, 1935), 522.

———. "Reversing the Tide Toward Tenancy," *Southern Economics Journal*, II (April, 1936), 1.

"Getting at the Bottom of Oklahoma's Landlord-Tenant Problem," *Extension Service Review*, IX (November, 1938), 162.

GILE, BUEFORD MONROE *and* A. N. MOORE. "Farm Credit in a Plantation and an Upland Cotton District in Arkansas," Arkansas Agricultural Experiment Station Bulletin No. 228 (Fayetteville, 1928).

GRAY, LOUIS C. "Disadvantaged Rural Classes," *Journal of Farm Economics*, XX (February, 1938), 71.

———. "The Social and Economic Implications of the National Land Program," *Journal of Farm Economics*, XVIII (May, 1936), 257.

GRUBBS, DONALD H. "Gardner Jackson, That 'Socialist' Tenant Farmers' Union, and the New Deal," *Agricultural History*, XLII (April, 1968), 125.

HARRIS, MARSHALL D. "A Suggested Adjustment in the Farm Tenancy System," *Journal of Farm Economics*, XIX (November, 1937), 892.

HENDERSON, DON. "Agricultural Workers," *American Federationist*, XLIII (May, 1936), 482.

HERLING, JOHN (JACK). "Field Notes from Arkansas," *Nation*, April 10, 1935, p. 419.

———. "Sharecroppers Fight for Life," *New Republic*, January 29, 1936, p. 336.

HILL, J. GILBERT. "Land Ownership Won't Make Smart Farmers," *Nation's Business*, XXVI (March, 1938), 28.

HOFFSOMMER, HAROLD. "The AAA and the Cropper," *Social Forces*, XIII (May, 1935), 494.

———. "Some Tenant Problems of the South," *Rural America*, XV (February, 1937), 8.

HOLCOMB, E. J. "Wage Laborers vs. Sharecroppers," *Agricultural Situation*. XXIII (October, 1939), 13.

HOOVER, CALVIN B. "Agrarian Reorganization in the South," *Journal of Farm Economics*, XX (May, 1938), 474.

HUTCHINSON, PAUL. "The J. B. Matthews Story," *Christian Century*, July 29, 1953, p. 864.

JACKSON, AL. "On the Alabama Front," *Nation*, September 18, 1935, p. 329.

JOHNSON, JOSEPHINE. "The Arkansas Terror," *New Masses*, June 30, 1936.

KOCH, LUCIEN. "War in Arkansas," *New Republic*, March 27, 1935, p. 182.

LIGUTTI, L. G. "The Man With a Plow," *Commonweal*, March 5, 1937, p. 513.

MCCORMICK, T. C. "Recent Increases of Farm Tenancy in Arkansas," *Southwestern Social Science Quarterly*, XV (June, 1934), 64.

MACLACHLAN, J. M. *and* E. W. S. MACLACHLAN. "Don't Rescue Tenancy: Abolish It," *New Republic*, June 13, 1934, p. 117.

MCNEELY, J. G. *and* GLEN BARTON. "Land Tenure in Arkansas: II. Change in Labor Organization," Arkansas Agricultural Experiment Station Bulletin No. 397 (Fayetteville, 1940).

MADDOX, JAMES G. "Suggestions for a National Program of Rural Rehabilitation and Relief," *Journal of Farm Economics,* XXI (November, 1939), 881.

MARIS, PAUL V. "Farm Tenancy," *U. S. Yearbook of Agriculture, 1940* (Washington: Government Printing Office, 1940), p. 887.

————. "From Tenant to Owner [1st year results Bankhead Act]," *Extension Service Review,* IX (October, 1938), 154.

"Medical Care for Low Income Farm Families," *Monthly Labor Review,* XLVIII (March, 1939), 592.

MENCKEN, H. L. "Semper Fidelis [Joseph T. Robinson]," *American Mercury,* XLII (December, 1937), 436.

METZLER, WILLIAM H. "Population Trends and Adjustments in Arkansas," Arkansas Agricultural Experiment Station Bulletin No. 388 (Fayetteville, May, 1940).

"Misery in Arkansas," *Nation,* March 13, 1935, p. 294.

MITCHELL, BROADUS. "Southern Quackery," *Southern Economics Journal,* III (October, 1936), 143.

MITCHELL, GEORGE SINCLAIR. "The Negro in Southern Trade Unionism," *Southern Economics Journal,* II (January, 1936), 26.

MITCHELL, H. L. *and* J. R. BUTLER. "The Cropper Learns His Fate," *Nation,* September 18, 1935, p. 328.

MITCHELL, H. L. *and* HOWARD KESTER. "Sharecropper Misery and Hope," *Nation,* February 12, 1936, p. 184.

MITCHISON, NAOMI. "Arkansas Through British Eyes," *Living Age,* CCCXLVIII (May, 1935), 278.

————. "The White House and Marked Tree," *New Statesman and Nation,* April 27, 1935, p. 585.

MONTROSS, W. C. "Stepchildren of the New Deal," *Nation,* September 12, 1934, p. 301.

MUNRO, W. CARROLL. "King Cotton's Stepchildren," *Current History,* XLIV (June, 1936), 66.

"The Nation-wide Problem of Farm Tenancy," *Congressional Digest,* XVI (February, 1937), 37.

"Nearly Three Million Tenants," *Saturday Evening Post,* January 1, 1938, p. 24.

NELSON, PETER. "Is Farm Tenancy Inherently an Evil?" Oklahoma *Current Farm Economics* Series, Vol. 10, No. 2 (April, 1937), 29.

————. "Land Tenure Problems in Oklahoma," Oklahoma *Current Farm Economics* Series, Vol. 10, No. 4 (August, 1937), 74.

NIEBUHR, REINHOLD. "Meditations from Mississippi," *Christian Century*, February 10, 1937, p. 183.

"No Peonage," *Nation*, June 24, 1936, p. 794.

NORFJOR, HELEN. "A Southern Tenant Farmer and a Birthday Dinner," *Farmers' National Weekly*, August 7, 1936.

PETRIE, JOHN CLARENCE. "Flogging Arouses Varied Opinions," *Christian Century*, July 22, 1936, p. 1021.

POWELL, W. *and* CUTLER, A. T. "Tightening the Cotton Belt," *Harper's*, CLXVIII (February, 1934), 308.

"The President's Committee at Work," *Congressional Digest*, XVI (February, 1937), 41.

"A Program for Farm Tenancy," *Nation*, March 6, 1937, p. 257.

"Purging the Relief-Rolls to Save the Nation's Crops," *Literary Digest*, August 3, 1935, p. 8.

RANDALL, C. C. "Landlord Tenant Problem in Arkansas," *Nation's Agriculture*, XIII (June, 1938), 3.

REID, J. W. "Geographic Distribution of Arkansas Crops and Livestock," Arkansas Agricultural Experiment Station Bulletin No. 367 (Fayetteville, November, 1938).

REID, T. ROY. "Public Assistance to Low-Income Farmers of the South," *Journal of Farm Economics*, XXI (February, 1939), 188.

ROBERTSON, PRISCILLA. "Split and Ruin," *Harper's*, CXCVIII (January, 1949), 19.

"Robinson Will Not Do!" *Nation*, May 29, 1937, p. 607.

SANDERS, J. T. "The Battle Against Farm Tenancy in Oklahoma Has Started," Oklahoma *Current Farm Economics* Series, Vol. 8, No. 6 (December, 1935), p. 122.

————. "Lessons from the Old Cotton Program for the New Program," Oklahoma *Current Farm Economics* Series, Vol. 9, No. 1 (February, 1936), p. 29.

"The Senator from Arkansas," *Fortune*, XV (January, 1937), 88.

"Share-Cropper Hope:" *Literary Digest*, October 3, 1936, p. 9.

"Share-Croppers: Whites and Negroes," *Newsweek*, June 13, 1936, p. 7.

"Sharing Poverty," *Today*, March 30, 1935, p. 20.

"Slavery," *Commonweal*, December 11, 1936, p. 188.

"Slavery In Arkansas," *Time*, December 7, 1936, p. 17.

"Slavery Seventy Years After," *Christian Century*, December 9, 1936, p. 1645.

"'Slaves':" *Newsweek*, December 5, 1936, p. 18.

SMITH, ALSON JESSE. "Is It True What They Say About Dixie?" *Christian Century*, September 9, 1936, p. 1188.

SMITH, T. LYNN. "Discussion [on tenancy]," *Journal of Farm Economics*, XX (February, 1938), 161.

SOUTHERN, JOHN H. "Farm Tenancy in Oklahoma," Oklahoma Agricultural Experiment Station Bulletin No. 239 (Stillwater, December, 1939).

SPARKES, B. "Reducing the Human Crop," *Saturday Evening Post*, July 13, 1935, p. 16.

SPARLIN, ESTAL E. "Inequalities in the Arkansas Property Tax Assessment System," Arkansas Agricultural Experiment Station Bulletin No. 369 (Fayetteville, January, 1939).

"Starvation in Arkansas: Evicted Sharecroppers," *New Republic*, April 1, 1936, p. 209.

STEPHENS, OREN. "Revolt on the Delta, *Harper's*, CLXXXIII (November, 1941), 656.

"Storm Over Bankhead Bill," *Literary Digest*, July 6, 1935, p. 9.

STRAUS, ROBERT KENNETH. "Enter the Cotton Picker," *Harper's*, CLXXIII (September, 1936), 386.

"Striking 'Croppers,' " *Literary Digest*, June 13, 1936, p. 7.

SWING, R[AYMOND] G[RAM]. "The Purge at the AAA," *Nation*, February 20, 1935, p. 216.

TALLEY, ROBERT. "Exit the Share-Cropper," *Nation's Business*, XXV (September, 1937), 17.

TAYLOR, ALVA W. "Cotton Tenants Held in Peonage," *Christian Century*, October 7, 1936, p. 1341.

————. "Plight of the Southern Tenant," *Christian Century*, April 3, 1955, p. 427.

————. "Tenancy Report Scores System," *Christian Century*, December 23, 1936, p. 1730.

TAYLOR, CARL W. *and* HELEN W. WHEELER. "Disadvantaged Classes in American Agriculture," *Agricultural Situation*, XXII (November, 1938), 17.

TAYLOR, HENRY C. "What Should Be Done About Farm Tenancy," *Journal of Farm Economics*, XX (February, 1938), 145.

"Tenancy—A Way Out?" *New Republic*, February 24, 1937, p. 61.

"Tenant Farmers:" *Literary Digest*, August 29, 1936, p. 9.

"They'd Rather Live on Relief," *Nation*, August 7, 1935, p. 144.
THOMAS, NORMAN. "At the Front," *Socialist Call*, February 11, 1936.
TINLEY, J. M. "Agricultural Adjustment Policies in America," *South African Journal of Economics*, VII (December, 1939), 389.
TOLLEY, H. R. "Objectives in National Agricultural Policy," *Journal of Farm Economics*, XX (February, 1938), 24.
TUGWELL, REXFORD G. "Behind the Farm Problem: Rural Poverty; Not the Tenancy System But a Low Scale of Life . . . ," *New York Times Magazine*, January 10, 1937, p. 4.
"Unions of Agricultural Workers," *American Federationist*, XLIII (June, 1936), 632.
VENKATARAMANI, M. S. "Norman Thomas, Arkansas Sharecroppers, and the Roosevelt Agricultural Policies, 1933–1937," *Mississippi Valley Historical Review*, XLVII (September, 1960), 225.
WALLACE, HENRY A. "Farm Tenancy," speech over CBS radio network, January 22, 1937, in *Vital Speeches*, February 1, 1937, p. 243.
————. "In Quest of Farm Security," *Extension Service Review*, VIII (March, 1937), 34.
————. "The South Faces Changing Demands," *Southern Economics Journal*, V (April, 1939), 423.
WARD, P. W. "Wallace the Great Hesitater," Nation, May 8, 1935, p. 535.
"Washington Notes," *New Republic*, January 13, 1937, p. 326; March 3, 1937, p. 109.
WATKINS, D. W. "Agricultural Adjustment and Farm Tenure," *Journal of Farm Economics*, XVIII (August, 1936), 469.
WEHRWEIN, GEORGE S. "An Appraisal of Resettlement," *Journal of Farm Economics*, XIX (February, 1937), 190.
————. "Changes in Farms and Farm Tenure, 1935–1940," *Journal of Land and Public Utility Economics*, XVII (August, 1941), 372.
————. "Goals in Land Use Policy," *Journal of Farm Economics*, XX (February, 1938), 237.
WESTBROOK, LAWRENCE. "Farm Tenancy: A Program," *Nation*, January 9, 1937, p. 39.
"What Has Happened to the AAA?" *Christian Century*, March 6, 1935, p. 293.

WHERRY, ELIZABETH C. "A Chance for the Share-Cropper [The Dyess Colony]," *Wallace's Farmer*, May 7, 1938, p. 333.

WHITE, OWEN P. "Devil in de Cotton," *Collier's*, January 1, 1938, p. 9.

WILEY, B[ELL] I[RVIN]. "Salient Changes in Southern Agriculture Since the Civil War," *Agricultural History*, XIII (April, 1939), 65.

WILEY, C. A. "Tenure Problems and Research Needs in the South," *Journal of Farm Economics*, XIX (February, 1937), 128.

WILSON, ISABELLA C. "Sickness and Medical Care Among the Negro Population in a Delta Area of Arkansas," Arkansas Agricultural Experiment Station Bulletin No. 372 (Fayetteville, March, 1939).

WILSON, W. T. *and* WM. H. METZLER. "Characteristics of Arkansas Rehabilitation Clients," Arkansas Agricultural Experiment Station Bulletin No. 348 (Fayetteville, June, 1937).

"Woman Flogged," *Literary Digest*, June 27, 1936, p. 29.

ZEICHNER, OSCAR. "The Transition from Slave to Free Agricultural Labor in the Southern States," *Agricultural History*, XIII (1939), 23.

*Phonograph Records*

SEEGER, PETE. "American Industrial Ballads," Folkways Album No. FH-5251. New York: Folkways Records, n.d.
———. "Gazette," Folkways Album No. FN-2501. New York: Folkways Records, n.d.

SEEGER, PETE *and* THE ALMANAC SINGERS. "The Original Talking Union and Other Union Songs," Folkways Album No. FH-5285. New York: Folkways Records, n.d.

THOMAS, NORMAN. "Norman Thomas Reminisces," Spoken Arts Recording No. 759, directed by Arthur Luce Klein. New Rochelle, New York: Spoken Arts, Incorporated [1959].

*Reports, Pamphlets, and Government Documents*

Arkansas Farm Tenancy Commission. "Findings and Recommendations." Hot Springs, November 24, 1936.

Arkansas State Policy Committee. *Agricultural Labor Problems in Arkansas*. [Little Rock?], October 31, 1936.

BROPHY, JOHN et al. *The C.I.O. and the Farmers.* Denver, July 10, 1937.

Commonwealth College. "Commonwealth Labor Songs." Mena, Arkansas, 1938.

HOOVER, CALVIN B. "Human Problems in Acreage Reduction in the South." Personal report to Henry A. Wallace and Chester C. Davis. Durham, North Carolina, March, 1934.

MITCHELL, H. L. "The Southern Tenant Farmers' Union in 1935." Official report, n.d. [January, 1936].

————. "The Southern Tenant Farmers' Union in 1936." Official report, n.d. [January, 1937].

————. "The Southern Tenant Farmers' Union in 1937." Official report, n.d. [January, 1938].

Southern Tenant Farmers' Union. "Convention Proceedings, Official Report of Second Annual Convention." Little Rock, January 3–5, 1936.

————. "The Disinherited Speak: Letters from Sharecroppers." New York: Workers' Defense League [1938?].

————. "Proceedings Third Annual Convention." Muskogee, Oklahoma, January 14–17, 1937.

U. S. Congress. *Congressional Record.* Vol. 79, 74th Congress, 1st Session, 1935.

————. *Congressional Record.* Vol. 80, 74th Congress, 2nd Session, 1936.

————. *Congressional Record.* Vol. 81, 75th Congress, 1st Session, 1937.

U. S. Congress, House Committee on Agriculture. *Hearings, Farm Tenancy.* 75th Congress, 1st Session, 1937.

————. *Farm Security Act of 1937.* House Reports 586, 1065, 75th Congress, 1st Session, 1937.

U. S. Department of Agriculture, Agricultural Adjustment Administration. "Administrative Rulings . . . 1934 and 1935 Cotton Acreage Adjustment Plan." Washington, February 20, 1935.

————. "Cotton Regulations Pertaining to Option-Benefit, Benefit, and Option Contracts . . . ." Washington, July, 1933.

————. "1935 Instructions Pertaining to the Administration of the Cotton Act of April 21, 1934, for the Use of Extension Agents . . . and Others . . . ." Washington, 1935.

————. "Questions and Answers Covering 1934 and 1935 Cotton Acreage Reduction Plan." Washington, 1933.

U. S. Department of Agriculture, Bureau of Agricultural Economics. *Farm Tenancy in Arkansas.* Washington: Government Printing Office, 1941.

U. S. Department of Agriculture, Farm Security Administration. *Toward Farm Security,* by Joseph Gaer, consultant. Washington: Government Printing Office, 1941.

U. S. Department of Commerce, Bureau of the Census. *United States Census of Agriculture: 1935.* Vol. III. Washington: Government Printing Office, 1937.

U. S. President's Committee on Farm Tenancy. *Farm Tenancy, Report of the President's Committee.* Washington: Government Printing Office, 1937.

Workers' Defense League. "To Establish Justice: Sharecroppers Under Planters' Law." New York [1940].

*Theses and Dissertations*

BLAKE, EARL CLEMENT, JR. "Farm Tenancy in Arkansas." University of Arkansas College of Business Administration Seminar Theses, No. 53 (Fayetteville, 1939).

CARMICHAEL, MAUDE. "The Plantation System in Arkansas, 1850–1876." Ph.D. thesis, Radcliffe College, 1935.

COBB, WILLIAM HENRY. "Commonwealth College: A History." Master's thesis, University of Arkansas, 1962.

GRUBBS, DONALD H. "The Southern Tenant Farmers' Union and the New Deal." Ph.D. dissertation, University of Florida, 1963.

HOFSTADTER, RICHARD. "The Southeastern Cotton Tenants Under the AAA, 1933–1935." Master's thesis, Columbia University, 1938.

JACKSON, HOWARD R. "An Economic and Social Analysis of Three Cotton Plantations in Arkansas in 1934." Master's thesis, University of Arkansas, 1937.

NEAL, NEVIN E. "A Biography of Joseph T. Robinson." Ph.D. dissertation, University of Oklahoma, 1958.

# Index

Bennett, Sam: escapes, 104, 105–6
Benson, Dave, 103–4
Benton, Thomas Hart, 6, 146
Black, Dr. Arthur G., 141, 157
Black, Rep. Hugo, 144
Black, Dr. John D., 59, 141
Blacks: characteristics as share-croppers, 4, 69; higher share-cropper eviction rates, 24; in STFU, 67–69, 77, 189; national-ism, 67, 84n, 176, 179; suffer disproportionate violence, 73, 90–91, 103–6, 109, 113; blame Mitchell for violence, 114; white resistance to farm ownership by, 130, 149, 155; participation in FSA, 158. See also Race rela-tions, Racism, Sharecroppers, Sharecropping
Blackstone, W. L., 121, 122, 142, 176–77, 178–79
Blagden, Willie Sue: beating, 112–14, 113n, 116; compared with anti-black violence, 113
Bourke-White, Margaret, 147
Brandeis, Louis D., 72, 79, 93; changes tenancy opinions, 150
Bridges, Harry, 165–66
Brookins, A. B., 65, 73, 168
Brophy, John: attempts to heal UCAPAWA-STFU split, 183–84, 186n
Bunche, Ralph, 78
Butler, J. R., 63, 120, 121, 122, 124, 174, 183; secures promise of CIO affiliation, 165; becomes UCAP-AWA official, 167; weak leader-ship, 167n, 178, 188; disillusion with Claude Williams, 174, 176n

C
Caldwell, Erskine, 26–27, 145; and Margaret Bourke-White, 147
Cameroon, J. E., 85, 89, 91
Campbell, J. Phil: "investigation" and report, 35–39
Carpenter, C. T., 43, 44, 73, 75, 119
Christgau, Victor, 53, 56
Churches: and STFU, 64–65, 68, 76–77; anti-capitalism, 76
Civil rights violations, 70, 72–73,

77, 85, 91n, 92n, 103–5, 182; protection urged, 96–98, 121, 122n, 134, 137. See also Violence against STFU
Clyde, Mrs. Ethel, 79, 96, 186n
Cobb, Cully A., 33–34, 43, 47, 53, 74
Committee for Industrial Organiza-tion (CIO): appeal to farm workers, 162; attitudes toward STFU, 164, 183–86. See also UCAPAWA
Commons, John, 72
Commonwealth College, 71–72, 81, 114, 163, 172–75; closed, 191
Communist party, 71, 78–79, 81–84, 100, 167n, 174, 179, 191; divide-by-tenure farm worker policy, 82, 163, 166, 171, 173; and black nationalism, 84n
"Communist subversion," 33–34, 70–71, 83–84, 122, 137, 163, 169, 186, 191; home ownership to counteract, 128–29; blamed on FSA, 160, 182; in CIO, 171–73, 190; and Williams case, 173–75; and Left division, 175–76, 179; and mixed swimming, 191
Connally, Sen. Tom, 127, 129, 130
Cooke, Morris L.: and tenancy changes, 140–41
Cotton prices, 15, 17–18, 59. See also Agriculture, commodity pric-es; One-crop system
County agents. See Extension Ser-vice
Cummings, Homer, 115, 117
Curlin, Sheriff Howard, 72, 90, 104, 110, 136

D
Dabney, Virginius, 130
Dahl, Leif, 82, 167n, 185
Davis, Chester, 32–33, 34–37, 40, 42, 51, 52, 53, 60; favors AAA conservatives, 33, 51n, 54–57
Davis, John P., 78, 137
DeCaux, Len, 186
Delta, Arkansas: described, 3–4; health and religion, 6; history, 6–8